This Crazy Thing a Life

Australian Jewish Autobiography

RICHARD FREADMAN

University of Western Australia Press

First published in 2007 by
University of Western Australia Press
Crawley, Western Australia 6009
www.uwapress.uwa.edu.au

This Publication has been supported by La Trobe University.
http://www.latrobe.edu.au

National Library of Australia
Cataloguing-in-Publication entry:

Freadman, Richard, 1951– .
     This crazy thing a life: Australian Jewish autobiography.

     Bibliography.
     Includes index.
     ISBN 978 0 9802964 2 6 (pbk.)

     1. Autobiography—Jewish authors. 2. Jews—Australia—Biography. I. Title.

920.0092924094

Cover photograph: Mendel Glick, founder of Glick's bakery, Carlisle Street, Balaclava, Melbourne, delivering his bagels, early 1990s.
(Photo courtesy of the *Australian Jewish News* and the Glick family)
Author photograph: Wendy Mak, 2007

Consultant editor: Alex Skovron
Text design: Ron Hampton
Cover design: Anna Maley-Fadgyas
Typeset in Minion by Pages in Action
Printed by McPherson's Printing Group

For Robin,
with thanks and
All good wishes,
Richard   2/10

This Crazy Thing a Life

Other books by Richard Freadman

Eliot, James and the Fictional Self: A study in character and narration

On Literary Theory and Philosophy: A cross-disciplinary encounter
(with Lloyd Reinhardt)

*Re-thinking Theory: A critique of contemporary literary theory
and an alternative account*
(with Seamus Miller)

Renegotiating Ethics in Literature, Philosophy, and Theory
(with David Parker and Jane Adamson)

Threads of Life: Autobiography and the will

Shadow of Doubt: My father and myself

To the Australian Jewish community

Every story has a life of its own, and every life
has its own story.

JACOB G. ROSENBERG, *Lives and Embers*

To understand the extent of the human tragedy of the
deportation of the Warsaw Jews during July and August 1942 to
Treblinka, one would have to frame the drama in single images
and study the details; the faces of the victims. One would need
the story behind each picture. For only in the individual stories
could one begin to grasp the depth of the tragedy.

DAVID J. LANDAU, *Caged*

Contents

Acknowledgments

The research and writing of this book have enabled me to share the stories of many Jews, some of them friends, others known to me only through their writing. It has been a privilege. My oldest friend, Rabbi Shimon Cowen, has been warm and unwavering in his support (even though we are very different styles of Jew), and a constant source of scholarly information. Other friends who have read and discussed portions of the book with me include La Trobe University colleagues John Gatt-Rutter, Greg Kratzmann and Sue Thomas, and Holocaust autobiographer Abraham Biderman. Serge Liberman has been there all along, providing precious bibliographical information in the early stages, unstinting encouragement, and detailed manuscript comment towards the end. George Halasz has been a generous and expert reader. I have also been most grateful for his emotional support and understanding as I made my way through many pages of infinitely dismaying Holocaust memoir. Alex Skovron, my copy editor, is quite simply the best I have ever worked with. He has been a good and knowledgeable friend throughout. I have greatly appreciated Arnold Zable's wisdom and enthusiasm. My friends in the International Auto/Biography Association are too numerous to name, but our conferences and the friendships that have sprung from them have been a marvellous source of intellectual exchange and inspiration.

In recent years Diane and I have been blessed by the friendship of Esther and Jacob Rosenberg. I could say that Jacob has been like a father to me, but I won't because he'd say he's not old enough to be my father. I am 56; he is 84.

Leonie Fleiszig and Julie Meadows have graciously reviewed the chapter about the Makor Jewish Community Library's 'Write Your Story' project. Mary Besemeres provided invaluable comment on the entire manuscript.

Other writers with whom I discussed aspects of the book include Ian Grinblat, Kathy Grinblat, Otto Gunsberger and Israel Kipen.

Ian Britain, Craig Howes, Richard McGregor, David Parker, Peter Rose and others made helpful editorial comment when portions of this book were being prepared for journal publication. Hilary McPhee made important editorial suggestions about the book's structure.

My research assistant, Brian Flanagan, has been unfailingly patient, expert and enterprising; he has been superb. Early on, Marisa Mowszowski performed a similar role. Special thanks go to Maureen de la Harpe at University of Western Australia Press for fostering this project, and to her colleague, Janine Drakeford, who provided incisive and encouraging editorial advice throughout. Thanks also to UWAP's Linda Martin and Olivier Breton; and to Diane Carlyle for her meticulous work on the index. To Ron Hampton, my gratitude for a clear and elegant text design.

La Trobe University has been immensely supportive of the project through research grants, study leave, and a publishing subvention. I particularly want to thank Christine Burns, Christine Freeman, Marie Mackenzie and Marilyn Richmond for their patient and precise administrative help. Thanks also to my colleagues in the La Trobe English Program. The book benefited greatly from my period as Visiting Fellow at the Curtin University Life Writing Research Unit, and from a visit to the University of Queensland as the George Watson Fellow.

I have received patient and expert help from the staff at the La Trobe University Borchardt Library, from Sister Marianne Dacy at the Judaica Archive, University of Sydney, and from the staff in the Monash University Rare Books Room. Thanks also to Daniel Bloom and others associated with the Australian Centre for the Study of Jewish Civilization at Monash University, and to Rose Freilich at the Holocaust Centre Library, Melbourne. Susan Faine spent several generous hours taking me through the photographic archives at the Jewish Museum of Australia. Leonie Fleiszig and staff at the Makor Jewish Community Library have been tremendous throughout; Leonie's good cheer makes everyone around her walk taller.

Earlier versions of parts of this book have appeared in: *Meanjin, Australian Journal of Jewish Studies, Biography, Life Writing,* and *Australian Book Review*. My thanks to these excellent publications.

As always, my family—Diane, Ben, Madeleine and Elliot—have been forbearing. Ben has provided encouragement, calm and top-notch IT support; Maddie's penchant for Jewish humour has helped keep my spirits up; as have football and cricket in the park with the ebullient Elli.

My thanks, above all, go to the authors whose courage and eloquence gave us the narratives that occasion this book. These people have achieved great things—for themselves, for their families, for Jewish communities here and abroad, and for a general public that cares, and cares to know about Jewish experience.

This book is for everyone, but I dedicate it to the Australian Jewish community.

Preface

Esther, now in her eighties, is a Polish Australian Jew and a Holocaust survivor. When, as she often does, she declares someone or something 'crazy', she pronounces it with feeling and as if it had a triple 'r'—*crrrazy!* I invite the reader to hear the main title of this book thus: *This Crrrazy Thing a Life*, the syntax and intonation echoing the linguistic and cultural world (the *Yiddishkeit*) of eastern European Yiddish-speaking Jews. *Crrrazy* covers a spectrum: from the gruff *non sequiturs* of Jewish humour to the delusional sadism of a planned, technologically advanced effort to annihilate an entire people.

Of course, not all Australian Jews or Jewish autobiographers hail from the world of *Yiddishkeit*, and this book attempts, so far as possible, to reflect the entire corpus of Australian Jewish autobiographical writing—a large and growing body of work by people from a vast range of cultural backgrounds, including many born in Australia. Jews have been in Australia since the First Fleet and on the whole it has been a blessed place for them. Australian Jewish autobiography narrates many successful and thankful Jewish lives Down Under. Inevitably the Holocaust looms very large in Australian Jewish consciousness, and this book reflects that fact; but it is important to see and to say that the Holocaust does not completely overshadow everything else. Jewish life in Australia has many dimensions and, as I have tried to show, Australian Jewish autobiography bespeaks an enormous range of experience, awareness and disposition.

How large in fact is this body of work? My best guess is that, as of now in early 2007, it comprises some 300 published volumes of autobiography and perhaps 400 shorter autobiographical pieces (a figure that includes shorter narratives published in anthologies). It might seem odd that one can't be more precise than this, but for several reasons certainty simply isn't possible. First, there are degrees of 'publication'. Some of these narratives have been accepted by commercial publishers and have all the trappings of a published book; but many are self-published, often in small print-runs. Most of these have ISBN numbers and other hallmarks of formal publication, but some are typed manuscripts slung together with amateur binding and lodged in Jewish libraries. Second, the less formal the 'publication' the harder it is to trace such volumes. I have relied principally on three bibliographical sources: Serge Liberman's *Bibliography of Australian Judaica*[1] (together with his updated lists, as yet unpublished), the National Library of Australia catalogue, and the Monash University Library Index of Holocaust memoirs. Other—particularly Jewish—library catalogues have also been very helpful.[2] Yet a significant number of titles have come to light through word of mouth: someone knows someone whose grandmother has just written a memoir. Informal networks of this kind can never be exhaustive. Third, autobiographies by Australian Jews continue to appear at a striking rate. Most of these are by survivors who want to bequeath their stories before they die, or by their children, even grand-children. However, Australian society in general is currently so enamoured of autobiographical genres that even Australian Jews not closely touched by the Holocaust continue to publish personal narratives in considerable numbers. In order to finish the present study I had to draw a line. I couldn't trace or look at everything. Many more Australian Jewish autobiographies will have appeared by the time *This Crazy Thing a Life* comes out. In researching it I have consulted about 270 volumes and something like 300 essay-length narratives. The majority of these were written in English; most of the remainder were translated into English by friends or family members.

In an attempt to best reflect this large and impressively diverse literature I have divided the book into three parts. Part One, 'Australian Jewish Autobiography: Scope, Contexts, Approaches', is a wide-ranging introduction to the field. It surveys the existing body of work, including matters of genre and form; it considers demographic trends (for instance, gender and generational patterns), along with cultural and ideological factors; it offers working definitions of key notions such as Jew, Australian Jew, autobiography, memoir, testimony, identity; and it provides historical background on the Australian Jewish diaspora—its development; its inclinations towards self-sufficiency, acculturation, assimilation; evolving attitudes towards Zionism and the state of Israel; and the massive ongoing impact of the Holocaust. Part One also addresses topics that crop up in more academic discussions: humanist and postmodern approaches to Holocaust autobiographical writing; and theories of gender, diaspora, multiculturalism, migrant writing, trauma, and racial/ethnic prejudice.

Part Two, 'Narrative Art, and the Art of Community Narrative', contains essays on texts or bodies of work by particularly significant and accomplished writers: Jacob Rosenberg, David Martin, Andrew Riemer, Susan Varga, Mark Baker, Doris Brett and Lily Brett, and Arnold Zable. It concludes with a discussion of a remarkable community life-writing initiative: the Makor Jewish Community Library 'Write Your Story' project. Many significant writers do not appear in Part Two's single-author essays simply because they did not satisfy the criteria I employed in making my selections. Chief among these criteria were, first, that the writing possesses manifest and sustained aesthetic complexity; and second, that it reflects, even if only incidentally, a significant sense of encounter between Jewish experience and Australian life. I say more about these criteria in Part One.

Part Three, 'Tracings: An Anthology of Short Excerpts', contains a selection of extracts from texts not discussed, or not accorded detailed comment, elsewhere in the book. Given the vast quantity of material available, and the limitations of space, I was able to include in this part only about 40 percent of the material I would have liked to use. Here too I chose according to the quality of the writing (broadly understood to include dramatic power), rather than in terms of the content of what was reported.

Had this book been written by a historian, its structure and principles of selection would no doubt have been different: choices would have been governed more by the contribution that given texts, excerpts or ideas make to historical understanding. I am a literary scholar and autobiographer. The principles that have shaped this book reflect my professional skills and interests and, no doubt, limitations. Since this is already a large project, and because I do not have comprehensive knowledge of other traditions of Jewish autobiography, I have refrained from detailed comparison of (say) Australian and American Jewish autobiography. A considerable body of scholarship now exists for readers who wish to pursue such comparisons.[3]

Inevitably, the book also reflects the sort of Jew I take myself to be. I am a secular Jew who finds conventional religious belief problematic after the Holocaust. I do however feel a powerful cultural identification with Judaism—but always as a component of a larger and tolerant multi-cultural community. Like most Jews, and many others, I am haunted by the enormity of the Jewish fate.

This Crazy Thing a Life is intended for a general audience both within and beyond the Jewish community. I hope that anyone with a serious interest in its subject-matter will find most of the book accessible. Where I feel moved to have my say in intellectual debates, or to frame thoughts in more academic terms, I may risk straining the patience of the general reader. I regret this, but it is inevitable. Given the range of issues that arise in a study such as this, it is impossible to stay 'on song' for all readers all of the time. In places where the going gets too academic, I invite the general reader to skip a few pages and resume reading where I've taken off my academic hat.

Many of the autobiographers who feature in this book have experienced terrible things. It is remarkable that they have been able to build viable and vibrant post-Holocaust lives. It is also remarkable that they have found the composure to commit their memories to print. There are degrees of 'survival'. The capacity to write autobiography is often a sign of survival of a high order. But not all survivors are so lucky. Many have lacked the wellbeing, and most have lacked the inclination, to write. This book remembers them too, as it does those who perished without being able to tell their stories.

Richard Freadman
March 2007

Part One

Australian Jewish Autobiography: Scope,
Contexts, Approaches

Two Books

You could hardly imagine a more humble-looking book. Soft yellow covers secured by two staples whose outline protrudes through the red masking-tape binding. The title, *Difficulties of Remembering*,[4] is in large bold black type. The author's name—Otto Gunsberger—appears above the title in more discreet light capitals. There's a none too accomplished sketch of a scroll-like object below the title and subtitle (*Reflections about an exhibition*). You look in vain for a title-page bearing the name of a publisher, an ISBN number, acknowledgments, or other familiar signs of a book's bona fides. Copyright is recorded on a strip of adhesive paper stuck to the inside of the front cover: 'Copyright Otto Gunsberger, 1997 All rights reserved'. The production quality of the text's 128 pages could be achieved on any personal computer, and indeed this book has clearly been self-published.

Difficulties of Remembering is a work of Holocaust memoir, one of about 160 book-length Holocaust memoirs to have been published in Australia. Gunsberger's first book, *Choice of Profession: Message from a survivor to the succeeding generations*,[5] is a harrowing—but also impressively probing—account of his incarceration in the Monowitz concentration camp near the main camp of Auschwitz. This volume has a slightly more professional-looking cover, publication details and an ISBN number, but its pages replicate the formatting of a manual typewriter. Neither book appears to have passed through the hands of a trained editor. *Difficulties of Remembering* retains the Hungarian inflections of the author's speaking voice: he explains that he knew at the time of Germany's claim to Sudentenland in 1938 'that victory for the German Führer brings no good omens to the Jews. We wished him no luck. On the other hand, I was hopeful that Hungary's claim will be successful.'[6]

We speak of stage presence in acting. Autobiography's equivalent is a sort of page presence: the mysterious way in which some autobiographical personalities radiate off the page, so vital and communicative that we feel we're in a conversation with the author. Gunsberger's voice seems utterly authentic, its Hungarian rhythms a linguistic indicator of the man's personal history and the cultural position from which he speaks. Hence in part the book's remarkable air of authenticity. He seems to write as he speaks, and to speak without art, using an apparently transparent medium to bear witness to the past and to the Jewish present that has been shaped by it.

But in fact the book is far from artless. It has an intricate narrative structure which begins (after a brief preface) on a plane *en route* to Germany where the author has been invited to attend the opening of an exhibition in the town of Bisingen. The exhibition is being staged by the Municipality of Bisingen. Its purpose is to acknowledge and record the dreadful story of the Bisingen concentration camp where Gunsberger was incarcerated after his removal from Monowitz. The narrative now shifts to an interview with a journalist to whom Gunsberger provides a brief autobiographical sketch—an economical means of conveying background for the reader. Next the story loops back to Melbourne and to disagreements within the Holocaust survivor community over a suggestion that the Hungarian Ambassador should be invited to the Melbourne Holocaust Centre to help mark the fiftieth anniversary of the deportation of Hungarian Jews. Gunsberger, a firm believer in reconciliation and dialogue, is in favour of the idea; some strongly oppose it. The book's 'difficulties of remembering' are then twofold: Bisingen's painful but laudable acknowledgment of its Holocaust past, and the disagreement among Melbourne survivors. After a section of detailed historical information the narrative returns to the present—to the exhibition and the events surrounding it. The author then appears at a school in the town. More historical detail follows, in particular about the history of antisemitism. The book ends as Gunsberger and his wife commence their return journey to the Antipodes. The weave of present and past, event and attitude, is richly effective. There is little fanfare about self, much concern for the future. Indeed *Difficulties of Remembering*, like many attempts at recollection, is emphatically motivated by a commitment to the future. Such books insist that the many

difficulties of remembering must be confronted for the sake of the generations who come after the Holocaust.

Now a very different-looking book, also a work of Australian Jewish
autobiography. *In Full View*[7] by Lily Brett is a beautifully produced volume
published by Picador, an arm of Pan Macmillan Australia, a mainstream
commercial publishing house with international affiliates. The exquisite
cover, in muted lilacs and olive-greens, features a lily, its six petals extend-
ing to the boundaries and corners. A pale olive dot at the lily's centre signals
that this decidedly feminine plant is 'open', its openness symbolizing
(among other things) the frankness of autobiographical self-revelation.
Lily's reputation as a raunchy, 'in your face' Jewish novelist and memoirist
precedes the volume. The back cover features a photograph of a command-
ing, smiling author. Reputation and cover alike give us to expect a kind of
autobiographical self-talk which is intimately revealing, introspective—a
mode much more characteristic of 'second-generation' Australian Jewish
autobiographers than of their parents' generation, people like Otto Gunsberger who wrote as migrants. Brett is the child of survivors and the
Holocaust is a massive presence in her books, along with other recurrent
preoccupations: family life, writing, New York where she now resides, the
body—its desires, its inescapable menace as a bearer of illness, pain and
death, its endlessly complex entanglements in female identity. *In Full View*
is a collection of autobiographical essays ('Ageing', 'My Daughter', 'Sex',
'New York', 'My Body', 'Food', 'Death', 'Love', 'The Writing Life'), all of
them addressed by a self-proclaimed earthy bourgeois sophisticate to a
broad international audience which includes Australia but centres on the
vast American market.

Australian Jewish autobiography runs the full gamut from Gunsberger
to Brett; from humble self-publication by amateur chroniclers to the
celebrated and highly publicized offerings of famous professional writers.
Roughly 75 percent of postwar Australian Jewish autobiography comprises
Holocaust memoir, or memoir written by children of survivors, or by 'child
survivors' (people who lived through the Holocaust as children). But there
are many narratives written by Australian Jews in which the genocide does
not figure prominently. Generally this is because their immediate families
had left Europe well before the war. Some not directly touched by the
Holocaust are disinclined to make frequent reference to it, feeling that this

is the prerogative of the survivors and their families. A case in point is Nancy Keesing's *Riding the Elephant*.[8] Keesing, who died in 1993, was a distinguished Australian woman of letters whose family, western European in origin, settled in Australia and New Zealand in the mid-nineteenth century. The book's elegantly engaging pages record a life in which being Jewish was significant—she edited an anthology of Australian Jewish writing[9]—but not, at least on the evidence of this literary memoir, pre-dominant. A reference to 'the genocide of my people'[10] is one of its rela-tively few allusions to the Holocaust.

What is Australian Jewish Autobiography?

The question might sound simple, but it has no simple answer. In part this is because Jewishness itself is hard to define, as indeed is the genre of autobiography. Even the notion of Australianness in the present context requires discussion.

Jewishness

It is impossible in my view to give a categorical definition of Jewishness because it comes in so many kinds and degrees, and because attempts at definition are inevitably made from various and often incompatible points of view. Does Jewishness indicate membership of a religion, a culture, a race, a sort of transnational family, or some combination of these? Even this fundamental question will elicit different answers depending upon who is speaking and in what context.

It will be useful for non-Jewish readers of this book to be aware of certain widely accepted designations of Jewishness, though even some of these are the subject of debate. One designation refers to place of origin: *Ashkenazic* Jews, who form something like 93 percent of the Australian Jew-ish community, have their ancestral roots in Germany, northern France, Poland, Russia and Scandinavia. *Sephardic* Jews, estimated at about 7 per-cent of the community, hail originally from Spain, Portugal and countries of the Mediterranean. Another grouping refers to styles and degrees of religious observance. For our purposes the most helpful distinctions are as follows. *Ultra-Orthodox* or *Hasidic* Judaism: *Hasidism* is a movement founded in eighteenth-century eastern Europe which emphasizes equality before God, purity of heart above dry scriptural hermeneutics, rigorous devotion to prayer and other forms of observance, and an openness to intense and even mystical religious experience. *Orthodox* Judaism: traditional Judaism which believes in the divine origin of written and oral law, places a very high value on scholarship, and generally requires (even if it does not always produce) rigorous religious observance. *Liberal* (or *Reform*) Judaism: a movement established in nineteenth century Europe which sought workable accommodations between Jewish tradition and aspects of the modern world. *Secular* or *cultural* Judaism: comprises people who regard themselves as Jews but do not hold conventional religious beliefs—though many would hold spiritual beliefs of a more personal kind.

If you ask a Hasidic or Orthodox Jew what constitutes Jewishness, the answer will follow *Halacha*, or Jewish religious law: a Jew is someone born of a Jewish mother. On this account Jewishness is a religious but also a 'racial' designation. But there is a major qualification: both of these traditions accept conversion to Judaism, albeit with quite stringent requirements; so the racial—or 'genetic'—aspect of the definition is not absolute.

Ask a Liberal Jew the same question and the answer is likely to be that someone is Jewish if either the mother or the father is Jewish. Ask a secular/cultural Jew—one such as myself—and you can get an even more inclusive view: I would be inclined to say that anyone who sees themselves as Jewish, and whose mode of life shows signs of serious and ongoing identification and/or engagement with Jewishness, is entitled to be regarded as a Jew. In espousing this position I mean no disrespect to more traditional ones, all of which have august histories. However, since this is my view it needs to be stated at the outset because, of course, it has a significant bearing on the shape and content of this book about Australian Jewish autobiography.

I will have more to say about autobiography presently, but it's worth noting now that one way in which someone can demonstrate a serious and ongoing commitment to Judaism (or to anything else) is through the account they give of their life in an autobiography. Moreover, many autobiographies are, among other things, spiritual-quest narratives which record a journey in search of religious belief and identity. Often, indeed, the writing of the narrative is an important part of the journey. Some Jews discover much about what it means to be Jewish through the process of writing. 'Jewish autobiography', whether written in Australia or elsewhere, does not necessarily entail a fixed sense of Jewish authorial identity prior to the act of composition.

Identity is multi-dimensional. What we call 'personal identity' can take a first-person form which refers to the person I take myself to be, but also a third-person form which concerns how others see me. Sophisticated accounts of so-called 'identity formation'[11] generally assume a reciprocal relationship between the first-person and third-person perspectives: my sense of myself is in large part derived from the already existing social scripts of selfhood (cultural notions of what a self is or should be like) and from feedback I receive about myself from others. But others' responses are in turn influenced by the way I present myself to them. Of course the third-person perspective is seldom monolithic: different people will tend to see me in different ways. A Liberal Jew, for instance, might be seen in one way by another Jew, and in a rather different way by a non-Jew who is operating with a necessarily generalized sense of what a Jew is. Then again, different Jews may see him in varying ways. A fellow Liberal Jew is likely to find this person's version of the Jewish life unexceptionable, but a Hasidic Jew may think his form of Judaism a travesty and look upon him with a degree of scepticism or disapproval. Personal identity, then, is constantly entangled in and at the mercy of forces that lie outside of the 'self' whose identity it is, and these forces can change over time. Jewish attitudes to the all-important issue of conversion have been subject to change, not only with the advent of modernizing reform movements, but as a result of sometimes subtle shifts within earlier Orthodox traditions. In times of acute crisis the 'outside', the third-person perspective, can quite brutally overpower the first-person one—as when Jews were compelled to convert to Christianity during the Spanish Inquisition, or forced to pose as (and even in some cases 'become') Christians in order to survive the Holocaust.

Australian Jewishness

The conventional third-person conception of an Australian Jew would simply be: someone who is an Australian citizen and a Jew. Even this is too restrictive, since there are many people—Jews among them—who have not taken out Australian citizenship but nevertheless see themselves as Australian. But 'Australian' will be one of several components of their personal identity, along with such factors as gender, race, class, ethnicity, religious affiliation, family roles and profession. Moreover, there will often be an order of significance among these components. It makes sense, for instance, to ask some individuals whether they see themselves as Australian Jews or as Jewish Australians. Judah Waten, one of the most important Australian Jewish writers, once wrote: 'I do not regard myself as a Jewish writer but as an Australian writer who happens to be Jewish.'[12] Being Jewish mattered a good deal to Waten, but it seems to have mattered less than being Australian—and still less than being a communist. Waten, we might say, considered being Australian as a more decisive, or *determinative*, feature of his personal identity than being Jewish. Many of the autobiographers who appear in this book seem to feel as Waten did, but many do not. It is hard to generalize, and here too external forces can impinge in complex ways. Some Holocaust survivors who came to Australia retained powerful religious commitments, notwithstanding what had happened to them—commitments that might have prompted them to describe themselves as 'Jewish Australians'. But for most, to come here after the horrors they had experienced in Europe was to find a place almost unbelievably free of terror and persecution. This experience frequently engendered an enormous feeling of loyalty to this country; so much so that 'being Australian' came to count for a great deal, perhaps as much as, or more than, 'being Jewish'.

For purposes of this book, any Jew who has resided for a significant period of time (say a year or more) in Australia is deemed to be an 'Australian Jew'—unless of course there is reason to think that the person would reject this characterization. Some very fine Jewish writers, like Janina David, resided here but have spent the bulk of their lives elsewhere. David's superb work is represented in the anthology that comprises the third part of this book. However, I have not accorded such figures detailed discussion: I have reserved such commentary for writers whose autobiographical work features a significant sense of encounter between the worlds of Jewish and Australian culture. These are the writers who are discussed at length in the second part of the study.

Autobiography, memoir, testimony

Many believe that there is a meaningful distinction between autobiography and memoir. The distinction, which is often left implicit, goes something like this: memoir tends not to be deeply introspective but seeks rather to provide an eyewitness report of some phase, place, person or set of events. Such accounts tend to focus on a particular time and place—say, the literary life in Paris in the 1920s. Autobiography, by contrast, tends to narrate the entire sweep of a life, from cradle (or even forebears) to the edge of the grave, and to be heavily introspective, though not to the exclusion of detailed representation of social and historical circumstances. There is something in this distinction, but as is always the case with such definitions, the line between one 'genre' and the other is at best hazy, and sometimes illusory.

In the present book I use 'autobiography' as an umbrella term for certain forms of first-person narrative, my assumption being that 'memoir' is best thought of as a tendency within autobiography rather than as an alternative genre. The distinctive (but not exclusive) tendencies of memoir are towards the narration of particular life-episodes rather than the sweep of a 'whole life', and towards a degree of personal reticence. Because I am not making an absolute distinction between 'autobiography' and 'memoir', I will use the familiar term 'Holocaust memoir' as synonymous with 'Holocaust autobiography'. Where autobiographical narratives notably eschew the inner life—that is, avoid detailed authorial introspection—in favour of bearing witness to historical events, I will sometimes associate that witnessing dimension with the act of testimony. The act of testimony will often—but not necessarily—result in a work in the genre of 'testimony', where the writing or speaking self is subordinated to the witnessing of particular, momentous and often traumatic historical and/or personal events. Here the focus is squarely on the particular events, whether they be an isolated incident like a rape, or a life-phase characterized by traumatic experiences, such as incarceration in a concentration camp. Unlike the Latin American genre of *testimonio*,[13] which tends to be Marxist in orientation, testimony of the kind discussed in this book is seldom associated with any political creed. It is however generally informed by deep humanitarian commitments: most of these authors hope that by bearing witness they can help to promote a better world than the one they have experienced.

Since many autobiographies contain acts of momentous witnessing, but much else as well, even the generic distinction between 'testimony' and 'autobiography' is not absolute. Indeed all of the forms of first-person narrative that I have been discussing have a further and defining feature in common: each operates through what the French theorist of autobiography, Philippe Lejeune, terms a 'pact'[14] whereby the author undertakes to be as truthful as he or she possibly can, and the reader agrees, subject to the apparent reliability of the narrative, to take on trust what the author conveys. Such pacts are complex and variable; so much so that Lejeune has been moved to amend his initial definition in order to better accommodate (for instance) variations in the kinds of narrator/reader relations that actually obtain in various autobiographies, and the aesthetic properties of literary autobiography.[15] The existence of pacts of this kind need not imply that total narrative truthfulness is achievable: most would now concede that one hundred percent truthfulness (whatever that might mean) is beyond human reach. Nor is such truthfulness necessarily restricted to absolutely literal notions of the 'truth'. As Kay Schaffer and Sidonie Smith write in their important study of human rights and life-writing, 'There are different registers of truth beyond the factual: psychological, experiential, historical, cultural; communal, and potentially transformative.'[16] But pacts of this kind do assume that truthfulness is an intrinsically valuable aspiration in first-person non-fictional writing. In a sense, such writers narrate as if under oath, though Leigh Gilmore rightly cautions against rigidly juridical notions of autobiographical 'truth',[17] against predicating our notions of autobiographical 'fact' exclusively on legal models.

The term 'autobiography' has become contentious in some academic circles, and I need to say something about this for academic and other interested readers of this book.

Since the 1960s, a multifaceted intellectual and cultural movement known as postmodernism has had a significant impact on the academic study of literature, and more recently on the study of autobiography. Postmodernism tends to oppose what it sees as an ethos of individualism that has dominated Western society since the eighteenth-century Enlightenment. It argues that the modern genre of autobiography is rooted in, and is an expression of, this culture of Enlightenment individualism. This ethos—the argument goes—grossly overstates the freedom that individuals have to shape their own lives, and grossly understates the limits that class, race, gender and other ideologies set on such freedom. Indeed—the argument continues—such ideologies powerfully shape our very sense of what a human individual is like, and stultify our ability to envision more emancipated and creative forms of personhood. On this view, even the generic term 'autobiography' is suspect because it is steeped in false assumptions, and because it gives the misleading impression that all forms of first-person non-fictional prose are exempt from ideological falsification.

This postmodern view of autobiography informs Sidonie Smith and Julia Watson's *Reading Autobiography: A guide for interpreting life narratives*, a book fired by an exemplary passion for social justice. Interested readers might like to consult a review of this book[18] in which I set out in some detail objections that I will simply touch on here. First, I suggest the book's account of the Enlightenment is too sweeping and rests on a highly debatable disjunction between certain Enlightenment conceptions of selfhood and the massive emancipatory changes that occurred during the period. Smith and Watson arguably understate the extent to which what we now think of as 'autobiography' has deep roots in pre-Enlightenment Western culture, and the powerful presence of certain emancipationist Enlightenment values in ostensibly oppositional movements like postmodern literary theory. Second, Smith and Watson's deterministic position, according to which selves and the life-stories they write are powerfully shaped from without by falsifying ideology, leaves little room for the autobiographical author as an active *agent* in the text. The philosophical term 'agent' ascribes to the human individual, in principle at least, the capacity to ponder and sift incoming messages and pressures, including coercive ideological messages; to factor these into deliberations about how he or she wants to act; and to act accordingly. Were it not so, individuals would be incapable of absorbing and acting upon counter-messages—say, those of feminism or Marxism—which emancipationist doctrines address to the victims of ideological stupefaction and oppression.[19] Simplistic anti-determinist invocations of agency impute almost total freedom of action to such agents; more sophisticated ones admit that, of course, freedom and agency are always constrained by external forces and that no one acts or writes without the impingement of certain kinds of restriction. This applies to a compositional act, such as writing an autobiography, no less than to other acts in which we might be engaged. As I argue in *Threads of*

Life,[20] a study of autobiography and the will, the most plausible conceptions allow both for the individual's so-called 'agential' capacities and for constraints that limit the exercise of such capacities. Central to the present study is the proposition that potentially, if not always in practice, Australian Jewish autobiographers operate as (constrained) agents when writing their texts.

Despite these misgivings, Smith and Watson do not jettison the term 'autobiography' from their title. Their preferred term, 'life narratives', figures only as a subtitle. This underlines the problems involved in discarding generic labels that have wide general currency both in and beyond the academy.

Autobiography and/as Literature

Some great works of autobiography are clearly great works of literature: Saint Augustine's monumental volume, the *Confessions* (AD 397), for example, is a beautifully written and structured narrative, as well as a brilliant theological and religious text. Many lesser autobiographies also possess a measure of literary sophistication; but not all of them do. The notion of Literature is not easy to define and has been much debated in recent decades, but if we take it to mean something like 'sophisticated writing which exhibits substantial technical accomplishment allied to imaginative subtlety', then it's clear that not all autobiography qualifies as Literature. Autobiographers who aren't adept at telling a story risk losing their readers; however, in general they enjoy a greater margin of aesthetic tolerance from readers than do practitioners of more straightforwardly 'literary' genres: a poorly written novel quickly exhausts discerning patience because we expect a novel to be well written; but discerning patience will often 'stay with' a poorly constructed autobiography because the genre does not carry expectations of high literary accomplishment. If the life told or the historical situation in which it unfolds is compelling in some way, or if the author's effort at narrative sincerity commands respect, we will often see the story through. Sometimes we hear autobiographers out just because there is an ethical obligation to acknowledge the lives and life-stories of others. And rightly so.

This sense of ethical obligation plays a fundamental part in shaping the way we read forms of autobiography that set out to bear witness:

testimonies of various sorts, most notably for our purposes Holocaust memoirs. Some Holocaust memoirs—the works of Primo Levi or Elie Wiesel, for instance—are clearly great literature, and at the same time awesome works of testimony. But many Holocaust first-person narratives, though precious as human documents, have little literary aspiration or sophistication. We read these for their testimony and not for their art. Leona Toker has argued that in the case of great Holocaust writers we do a kind of double reading.[21] Our first reading of, say, Primo Levi's *If This Is a Man*[22] is likely to be consumed by the horror and lunacy of that to which he bears witness. It takes little art to impress such things upon any sane reader, but in the case of a great literary craftsman like Levi we may be aware, however subliminally, that remarkable artistry is at work, and we may undertake a second reading which pays particular attention to the narrative's literary dimension. In practice the two readings may not be this distinct: reading Levi often involves criss-crossing between the subject-matter and the art, as each infuses the other. In any case, it seems clear that in great writing of this kind art deepens testimony, revealing more, at least in some respects, than lesser writing can. To this extent the philosopher Theodor Adorno's oft-quoted pronouncement that 'To write poetry after Auschwitz is barbaric'[23] seems misguided: if we take 'poetry' here to include all writing that aspires to high literary sophistication, there is no contradiction between writing well and writing truly. Writing well often renders the truth more compelling.[24]

The Scope of Australian Jewish Autobiography

The present study restricts itself to published volumes and essay-length autobiographical narratives. At time of writing, there are probably about 300 published volumes of Australian Jewish autobiography, together with perhaps 400 shorter, essay-length published autobiographical pieces in collections, journals or newspapers. This is a large and varied body of published (to say nothing of the unpublished) work produced over a period of almost 120 years by Jews from all walks of life, in strikingly diverse life-situations, and employing an impressive array of narrative forms. Because this literature comprises so many different text types, such a diverse array of chronological and other foci, and so many works by authors not skilled in conveying background information, the following account of salient trends can only be indicative. Absolute precision is just not possible in many instances, even in research like this where upwards of 90 percent of the available volumes have been consulted.

Chronological and demographic trends

I have been able to locate only one book-length volume published during the nineteenth century. Book-publication trends are approximately as follows: 1891–1900: 1; 1901–1940: 0; 1941–1950: 2; 1951–1960: 0; 1961–1970: 5; 1971–1980: 7; 1981–1990: 38; 1991–2000: 104; 2001–2007: 76. The sharp rise from the 1980s onwards occurs largely because survivors decide later in life to record their stories. They realize that there may not be much time left; and many feel better able to write than in earlier years, when trauma was still too raw and the hard work required to establish postwar lives left little room for reflection or writing. By the 1980s, too, survivors' children have reached an age at which autobiographical writing is possible and often tempting—especially in a culture becoming increasingly enamoured of non-fictional prose. Thus, since the 1980s many Jews not directly affected by the Holocaust have committed their lives to print, and a significant community of Australian Jewish writers has become established, many of them turning their hand to autobiography. Approximate figures for the decade of life in which Australian Jewish autobiographers have published are: 30s: 1 percent; 40s: 2 percent; 50s: 13 percent; 60s: 18 percent; 70s: 36 percent; 80s: 19 percent; 90s: 7 percent. In about 5 percent of cases one cannot be sure.

About 12 percent of the authors represented in this study were born in Australia. Of the total group, i.e. from Australia and elsewhere, about two-thirds are from observant Jewish backgrounds, the majority being Orthodox. Around 13 percent are from secular homes. In about one-quarter of cases it is difficult to determine the nature of authors' early Jewish home life. Among the texts by persons not born in Australia, the majority (about 63 percent) are by authors of eastern European origin, roughly two-thirds (66 percent) of whom are from Poland. More than half (58 percent) of the writers from eastern Europe are from cities; the remainder from towns and villages. Perhaps 25 percent of the latter category would generally be considered *shtetls* (in some instances it is impossible to state definitively whether a given place was or was not a *shtetl*). Over half of those writers from towns are from Orthodox or ultra-Orthodox milieus. Another 18 percent of books are by Jews of western European origin. Of these, some 70 percent are from large cities.

Approximately three-quarters (74 percent) of the texts by first-generation Australians are by Holocaust survivors. This may sound a lot but in fact it amounts only to about 0.5 percent of the total number of survivors who have settled in Australia. The vast majority of such people have not felt inclined, or able, to record their experiences. Of those who have done so in written form (as opposed to verbal and/or filmed testimonies), about 70 percent were in concentration camps. The remainder survived as fugitives (some in hiding, some by getting out of Europe; a small number fighting as partisans). An important and too often ignored sub-category is books by Jews who were deported to Russian labour camps: about 10 percent of the total of the Holocaust volumes. Books by children of survivors and by child survivors constitute perhaps 10 percent of the Holocaust writings, but there is a significant number of additional essay-length pieces in this category. Perhaps 11 percent of all these authors can be described as professional writers. The gender distribution across all texts is roughly 57 percent male, 43 percent female.

Traditions, themes and forms

To some extent, the structures of storytelling flow naturally from the way human reality is organized—from the fact, for instance, that events happen in sequences, sometimes with causal connections, sometimes with apparently distinct beginnings, middles and ends—but much storytelling follows, or is 'mediated' by, scripts or templates that derive from the writer's culture or cultures. This cultural provision of story begins in early infancy as we acquire language and notions of our role and place in the world, along with assumptions about what an individual self is and should be like. By the time an autobiographer starts to write, these templates have already played a massive part in shaping that person's internal 'story of self'. Some autobiographies—often the least interesting ones—simply replicate this already-existing story on the page; more dynamic and heuristic first-person narratives frequently display a tension between the established story of self and contrastive or even contrary ones that emerge during the process of writing. This kind of tension suggests that deterministic views of the relationship between template and author—views which see the author as almost completely shaped by cultural templates and ideological pressures—are simplistic. In principle, though not always in practice, there is a two-way relationship between template and autobiographical author; so much so that autobiographers like Augustine and Rousseau actually invent new plot configurations, or 'modes of emplotment',[25] in search of authentic self-representation.

Templates take a vast variety of forms, from simple 'generic' ones that might prompt an autobiographer to begin by announcing the date and time of her birth, through to more specialized and complex ones that might cause an author to employ a template encountered in a famous autobiography, or one that has become associated with rendering (say) psychological complexity or the nuances of vocation. Not surprisingly, examples of Australian Jewish autobiography exist all along the spectrum from the generic to the highly specialized. Because the majority of these texts are written by Holocaust survivors whose education was wrecked by the war, and because many of them write in a second language (English) in which they don't feel entirely comfortable even after many years in Australia, a sizeable number of these texts employ fairly conventional plot structures: family background, childhood, war, life in Australia (if described), in chronological order. Those who have not had the opportunity or inclination to read widely will naturally not draw heavily upon the more complex narrative models available in autobiographical and other literature. If we leave aside for the moment essay-length autobiographical pieces, some of which are written by well-educated Australian Jews who were invited to pen short life-narratives, something like 17 percent of the book-length autobiographies are written by folk who bring wide general reading to the process. An even smaller proportion—perhaps 8 percent—would bring significant familiarity with Australian literature and autobiography to the task; a similar number write books that reflect immersion in European literature and autobiography, including Yiddish writing. Perhaps surprisingly, a still smaller percentage of these books—it could be as few as 3 percent—are substantially indebted to the Jewish scriptures for their narrative forms and fields of reference.

Some examples. The professional writers—Arnold Zable, Lily Brett,

Andrew Riemer and others who figure in the second part of this study—are clearly widely read in various traditions. Jacob Rosenberg, also the subject of an essay in Part Two, is a retired businessman who began writing in his youth and has quite remarkably achieved eminence as a professional writer in his eighth decade. He is widely read in European literature, has some acquaintance with Australian literature, and writes books which are deeply influenced by Jewish scripture, Yiddish literature and folk tales. Itzhak Cytrynowski's fine self-published autobiography, '*And I Will Remember My Covenant...*',[26] is even more directly mediated by Jewish scripture than Rosenberg's works, but, Yiddish tales excepted, it does not reflect wide reading in European or Australian literature. It is important to note that a significant number of Australian Holocaust memoirists are not widely read in Holocaust memoir, whether Australian or other, and that some are largely unaware of the vast international archive of Holocaust writing that now exists. Their books owe little not only to literary and autobiographical tradition but also to other models of Holocaust narrative. Rosenberg, by contrast, has been profoundly influenced by Primo Levi, Elie Wiesel, Paul Celan and other masters of Holocaust literature. David Martin's *My Strange Friend*[27] (see Part Two) is the most striking example of an Australian Jewish autobiography written under the sign of European Romanticism; Mark Baker's *The Fiftieth Gate*[28] (also discussed in Part Two) is the book most obviously influenced by international literary modernism. Lolo Houbein's *Wrong Face in the Mirror*[29] is an instructive example of an Australian Jewish autobiography whose generic characteristics are heavily indebted to reading in particular traditions of Australian autobiographical narrative: by the time she wrote her autobiography Houbein was a respected scholar of Australian multicultural and migrant writing.

Given that autobiography reports on shared worlds, there will be large areas of thematic overlap between narratives, irrespective of whether particular authors have read a lot of autobiography or not. So, even if fewer than 11 percent of Australian Jewish autobiographers have read widely in non-Jewish Australian autobiography, there is bound to be significant commonality in themes. A standard list of themes in the Australian autobiographical 'tradition' might go something like this: bush and city; convict stories; the settler experience; childhood; place and space; race, ethnicity and migration; problems of belief; expatriate stories; gender;

romantic individualism; class and egalitarianism. Since most Australian Jews have lived in cities, or largish towns like Bendigo, their autobiographies have relatively little to say about the bush. (A welcome recent addition to the literature here is *Jewish Country Girls: A collection of memories*.[30]) There are few texts that would qualify as settler or expatriate narratives, though Lily Brett's writings clearly belong in the latter category. The other Australian autobiographical themes noted above are, however, all prominent in Australian Jewish autobiography, along with some that are specific to it: the Holocaust, Israel, particular issues pertaining to Jewish tradition, assimilation and religiosity.

Among the many narrative structures employed by Australian Jewish autobiographers, perhaps seven are especially prominent. First, and by far the most common, is the straightforward chronological first-person narrative which recounts life happenings but with little reference to the inner life of the author. Second, there are chronological first-person narratives which feature an added dimension of detailed introspection. A fine example here is Alida Belair's *Out of Step: A dancer reflects*,[31] where the author 'reflects' not just on her career as an internationally acclaimed ballerina but on the impact of that career on her emotional development, her self-esteem and her attitude to her body. Another notable instance is George Szego's *Two Prayers to One God*. Szego, a psychiatrist, subtitles his profoundly inward-looking narrative *A Journey towards identity and belonging*.[32]

Third, there are the generational chronicles in which the author's life is embedded in a third-person account of the family generations. Diane Armstrong's *Mosaic*[33] is the best-known example of this sub-genre. A fourth grouping comprises collaborative narratives. In works like Susan Varga's *Heddy and Me*[34] (see the essay on Varga in Part Two), Anna Rosner Blay's *Sister, Sister*[35] and Helen Max's *Searching for Yesterday*,[36] two generations of women work together to produce a narrative, usually occasioned by the Holocaust, that seeks to reconstruct family history and its meanings for first- and second-generation Australian Jews and their descendants. A related form features a biography of a parent, together with an account of the relationship between parent and offspring and reflections on what it has been like to be the child of such an adult. Narratives of filiation include Josiane Behmoiras's *Dora B*[37] and Richard Freadman's *Shadow of Doubt: My father and myself*.[38] Various forms of authorial partnership also occur: narratives by spouses, such as *Miracles Do Happen* by Fela and Felix Rosenbloom,[39] *Stepping into Life* by Moshe and Stefa Robin,[40] and Zoltán and Adi Schwartz's *Survivors*.[41] 'Ghosted' autobiographies, such as Henry Krongold's *Memoirs*[42] 'by' James Mitchell, are rare.

Fifth is a rather miscellaneous group in which the life-story is fundamentally structured through an account of career, be it in the arts, the professions, business, religion or government. Zelman Cowen's *A Public Life*[43] is one of few autobiographies by major Australian Jewish public figures. Many books, of course, fit into more than one category, so that Belair's volume belongs along with (say) June Epstein's *Woman with Two Hats*,[44] which describes the author's career but also her life as a wife and mother.

An important structural variant, a sixth grouping, includes autobiographies written primarily in the third person, or through alternating first- and third-person points of view. Narrative devices of this kind, by no means restricted to Jewish or Australian Jewish autobiography, can serve a variety of purposes. In Australian Holocaust memoirs such as Elena Jonaitis's *Elena's Journey*,[45] the third-person point of view can provide some emotional distance from traumatic events which might otherwise be too overwhelming to narrate.

Finally, in a very different key, there are the anthologies of shorter autobiographical pieces by Australian Jews. The remarkable Makor Library 'Write Your Story' program has produced three such anthologies.[46] Titles of other notable collections are *Strauss to Matilda: Viennese in Australia 1938–1988*; *Without Regret*; *Children of the Shadows: Voices of the second generation*; *On Being a German-Jewish Refugee in Australia*[47] (a volume of essays that includes two autobiographical pieces); *Silent No More: Melbourne child survivors of the Holocaust*;[48] and the aforementioned *Jewish Country Girls*. When compiled with care, such collections can achieve distinctive forms of structural sophistication.

Gender

In a recent summation of the current situation of Jewish women in Australia, Suzanne Rutland writes:

> Despite significant advances over the last few decades, Jewish women in Australia do not enjoy full equality with their male counterparts. Since most

take their domestic responsibilities seriously, full equality is definitely elusive. Women still bear the major responsibility for home and family, their traditional areas in Judaism. In addition, power, and community leadership, rest with those with money, who are mainly men.[49]

The 'advances' include professional and economic trends that have occurred throughout much of the Australian community, and the egalitarian ethos of Liberal Jewish religious life, where women can be ordained as rabbis and gender segregation in synagogues does not occur. Even here, however, full parity is inhibited by religious tradition: the *batmitzvah*, the twelve-year-old girl's rite of passage, is generally accorded less importance than the thirteen-year-old boy's *barmitzvah*. In Orthodox and ultra-Orthodox environments gender imbalances figure prominently relative to the wider Australian community. Feminism is a complex matter for many post-Holocaust Jewish women because the need and desire for emancipation can tug against powerful post-Holocaust feelings of loyalty to Jewish tradition. One consequence of this is a position that reflects wider post-1970s 'second wave' feminist commitments but does not challenge—at least not aggressively—gender imbalances within Judaism itself. A recent survey of Australian Jewish women finds that feminism is on the rise within this group but that such commitments bring with them conflicted 'pariah' feelings.[50] In light of this, it would not be surprising to find that when Australian Jewish feminists write autobiography their feminism tends to be directed 'outwards', towards patriarchy in general, rather than 'in' towards the still (in varying degrees) patriarchal worlds of Judaism. And this is in fact the case. But here, as with other aspects of Australian Jewish experience, we should not simply read autobiography as sociology by another name. These two discourses—sociology and autobiography—are intertwined in various ways, and autobiography's value lies partly in its ability to challenge or refine sociological generalizations, testing them against particular life-stories.

About 43 percent of Australian Jewish autobiographies are by women. Of the total, some 76 percent fall within the category of Holocaust autobiography. Across the board this body of work reflects Australian Jewish autobiography's prevailing ethos of realism—a point to which I will return. I have found few examples of radical narrative experimentation among these women's texts, though there is a good deal of subtle narrative innovation: for instance, the fusion of fairytale, realist narrative and poetry in Doris Brett's *Eating the Underworld* (see Part Two), Susan Varga's splicing of personal and maternal narratives in *Heddy and Me*, Helen Max's 'photographic essay' about her mother's Holocaust experience, and Kitia Altman's *Memories of Ordinary People*, with its powerful poetic style and its frequent shifts in perspective, genre and tonal register.[51] Anna Rosner Blay's *Sister, Sister* interleaves her mother's and her aunt's Holocaust narratives with her own recollections and ruminations, as in this transition from her mother Hela's description of a camp medical selection to Anna's italicized recollection of a childhood visit to the doctor:

> We had to strip and, clutching our clothes, run back and forth in front of a group of doctors who sat dispassionately at tables, shouting orders and selecting us into rows to the right or left, according to how healthy and useful we looked. Before each of these procedures we would pinch our cheeks to redden them, and we tried to move a little quicker without stooping our shoulders, in the hope that we would get into the right row.
>
> *We are going to visit another doctor. My mother holds my hand tightly as we march along grey footpaths, and my little legs try to keep up. We go in through a heavy glass door, then enter a dark lift smelling of stale food and antiseptic. We walk along endless corridors, following parallel lines on the walls of square white tiles with black grouting.*
>
> *The doctor looks pretty much like the others, with grey receding hair and glasses perched on the tip of his nose. My mother patiently repeats the problem to him: that I don't eat enough, that I am too thin.*
>
> *Everything depends on what he says. My mother's face is anxious. I study all the shiny metallic instruments laid out within reach of his hand, and terror engulfs me.* [52]

The passage works at several levels. There is Hela's intense concern about Anna's health, and in particular her levels of nutrition, an anxiety familiar among survivor-parents. There is the young girl's 'terror', a feeling precipitated by the surgical instruments, but perhaps also, and more subtly, by the anxiety that her mother unintentionally communicates to her. This anxiety is itself complex: its overt source is Anna's health, but deeper down—maybe even below the level of conscious registration—there are the echoes of the camp medical selections. The child has probably absorbed this unconscious anxiety from the mother. Later, as she witnesses and recounts her mother's Holocaust narrative, she sees the visit to the doctor from a still more layered vantage-point: there are the mother's conscious and unconscious feelings, the child's responses to these, and now the adult's reconstruction of the scene in the light of the knowledge of what her mother endured in the camp. She imagines, in a way the child could not, how difficult the visit must have been for her mother; what intense anxiety it must have occasioned. And perhaps she wonders at the mother's apparent trust in the doctor: '*Everything depends on what he says.*' Is this trust of a straightforward and remarkably sane kind; is it a trust bought at the expense of repressing memories of those camp selections; or—a darker possibility—a trust that owes something to the status of doctors in the camps, whose routine jobs included condemning some to slave labour and others to death?

Few among the Australian Jewish female autobiographers are academic feminists. Barbara Falk is an exception here, but in intellectual style her feminism predates the influential developments that have taken place since the 1960s. It is not therefore surprising that there is little evidence of influence from postmodern feminism, with its 'deconstructive' readings of the relationship between 'sex' and 'gender', its Derridean and Lacanian accounts of identity (an aspect of their rejection of humanist notions of self), its emphasis on 'performativity', on the relations between power and discourse, and so forth.[53]

Of course questions of gender—that is, questions about how a given culture interprets the physiological differences between the sexes, and creates social roles, expectations, myths and values based on its understanding of these differences—are not restricted to women's writing. Gender issues also embrace attitudes to bisexuality, homosexuality and lesbianism, including responses by 'straight' individuals to gender stereotyping. While many authors describe unease with conventional gender expectations (bookish Jewish boys having to negotiate school cultures dominated by Australia's obsession with sport), there is little detailed discussion in Australian Jewish autobiography of same-sex relationships.

Defying Gravity,[54] by academic and gay activist Dennis Altman, is the most detailed autobiographical life written here by a gay Jewish man. Susan Varga's account in *Heddy and Me* of her relationship with her partner Anne is one of few autobiographical treatments of lesbianism. In fact it is only in recent decades that such matters have been openly aired in Australian autobiography generally, and it is interesting to speculate why more Australian Jewish autobiographers have not followed suit. Most Orthodox Jews would not feel comfortable about discussing these matters in print, and perhaps some Liberal Jews fear that such self-revelations would be an unwarranted indulgence in the post-Holocaust environment. There is also a tendency towards social conservatism in some quarters of the Australian Jewish community which would discourage this degree of autobiographical frankness. Lily Brett's early stories include biting critique of what is after all a small community in which it is harder to go about one's heterodox business than it is in Chicago or New York.

Some scholars of women's autobiography have argued that the female autobiographical self is structured differently from the male one. The argument is that men tend to see themselves more as isolated individual egos than do women, and to derive their sense of personal identity principally from deeds, career and other external indices of selfhood. Women, by contrast, have a more 'relational'[55] orientation; that is, they are more inclined to see their identities as embedded within and defined by networks of connection to other people. As I have argued elsewhere,[56] the term 'relational' is currently used with bemusing variability. It is often not clear whether it is just a descriptive term that captures the connected ways in which women live and write their lives; a causal idea which argues that the individual's—in this case, the woman's—identity will be formed through interactions with others; or a normative notion according to which the life lived relationally is deemed to be morally superior to a solitary or self-centred one. The eminent American autobiography scholar Paul John Eakin has argued that personal identity in general is relational and that relationality is not particular to, or even particularly characteristic of, women.[57]

Another view, and one for which I find ample evidence in Australian Jewish autobiography, is that the term 'relationality' applies to both genders early in life, when personal identity is necessarily formed through interaction with others, but that later on, when many men have been socially conditioned to exercise greater autonomy and self-centredness than women, women will tend to live and write their lives in more relational ways than their male counterparts. Such generalizations are of course risky, but it does seem that among Australian Jewish autobiographers, especially first-generation authors, more women write in a detailed manner about interpersonal relationships than do men. They are also more inclined to write introspectively, and indeed these two tendencies are often intertwined: it is the perceived and felt complexities of relationships that often compel in these women an awareness of their own interior worlds. Kitia Altman's *Memories of Ordinary People* contains some fine writing of this kind. In addition to those I have already mentioned, there are a number of other moving relational autobiographies—that is, narratives which render the author's life in-relation-to another woman—including Helen Gardner, *My Mother's Child*, which focuses on the relationship between a child and her desolatingly distant mother; Elfie Rosenberg, *Serry and Me*, a tale of two sisters separated by the Holocaust; *Pola's Story*, the autobiographically inflected biography of a woman which is told collaboratively by her three daughters; and Lucy Gould, *Empty Corners*, a narrative containing a nuanced account of an increasingly fraught, Holocaust-afflicted mother–daughter relationship.[58]

Vera Schreiber, another innovative Holocaust author, uses italics to reconstruct her childhood feelings.[59] Hania Ajzner also recreates the inner world of the Holocaust child with great skill. As with many others, her case is complicated by the fact that as a child she had to assume a false identity in order to survive. Often, and quite eerily, she writes this experience of imposed, literal self-estrangement in the third person:

> Every now and then, as she had done in the past, she would feel a compulsion to see her real name, so she would write it down where no-one could see it, and then scribble over it before throwing the paper away. Seeing her name in black and white would reassure her as to her own reality, and the reality of her memories.[60]

Ajzner's fine book is a testimony to identity's terrible fragility, its vulnerability to sadistic ideological assault, but also to its remarkable resilience. That resilience, a kind of inner power, is apparent in the way she is able to reconnect with her real identity after the war—and in her capacity to bring these weirdly disjunctive phases of her life together between the pages of a beautifully integrated and crafted autobiographical narrative.

A particularly impressive story of resilience is Zelda D'Aprano's *Zelda*,[61] the most extended work of feminist autobiography by an Australian Jew. Born in working-class Carlton in 1928, D'Aprano was an important figure in the women's liberation movement for three decades. Her book chronicles her life in left-wing Australian politics—a world whose disposition towards feminism is shown to be fickle and often deeply disappointing—but it is also a remarkably fearless record of personal life. She writes openly of marriage, affairs, the experience of rape, confrontations with patriarchal authority in various guises, and with tremendous frankness about the female body—its cycles, its illnesses, its encounters with the patriarchal medical world. D'Aprano is not much concerned with Judaism or her Jewish identity. Nor was her family directly affected by the Holocaust. In these respects her book is atypical; but in others it is something of a compendium of concerns that appear in many other women's autobiographical texts. Writers like Alida Belair, Galina Kordin[62] and Lily Brett write at length about the female body and its discontents (including discontent at cultural constructions of the feminine); Robin Dalton[63] and Amirah Inglis[64] explore relations between female identity and class; while Helena Rubinstein[65] and June Epstein see female agency and its constraints in terms of professional life.

For many, though, life has been what one can make of it after the Holocaust. In this sense theirs are unusual women's narratives—unusual as lives, unusual as narrative accounts of lives. Here it is especially hard for a man to speak. We know that atrocities against women were committed on a colossal scale during the Holocaust and that significant domains of Holocaust experience were different for women than for men. Understandably sexual atrocities are almost never reported in these books. Sometimes humiliations of a gendered kind are mentioned, as when Rae Mandelbaum reports that she and other female inmates felt no embarrassment when having to shower in front of German soldiers, whom they saw as 'wooden statues'. 'However if one of our own men had to walk past (they were operating the showers), we would grab any bit of clothing to cover our bodies because they were men!'[66] So far as I can see—and I may be missing a good deal here—Australian accounts of Holocaust suffering are not strongly gendered: for the most part, the emphasis seems to be on general human degradation, an assault on one's humanity and one's Jewishness, rather than on one's gender.

A partial exception to this rule is Maria Lewitt's *Come Spring*. This book is a distinguished example of what might be called the 'narrative of the curtailed life'. Such narratives constitute an important sub-genre of Holocaust literature. They recount the forms that life takes when one must go into hiding or endure other deprivations occasioned by war; the ways in which people—often young people—adapt, make do, put a fuller, normal existence on hold. Perhaps the greatest example of such writing is *The Diary of Anne Frank*. The parallels between that astonishing text and *Come Spring* should not be pressed too hard because there are significant generic and other differences between the two works; nevertheless there are some striking similarities. Each gives us the world through the eyes of an adolescent girl during the Holocaust. Anne is thirteen when she goes into hiding; Maria is fifteen at the outbreak of war. Each girl has a complex relationship with her mother which must be managed in an artificially confined and stressful environment; each comes to sexual maturity in that environment and becomes emotionally involved with a young man who is confined in the same place. Both girls are intense, bright, unusually self-aware, literary, and have an immense appetite for life. The miracle of Anne Frank's life in hiding is that in many ways her life is not curtailed at all.

Maria hides in a property outside Warsaw in which her Aunt Olga lives with her husband Boyarski, an impoverished antisemitic Polish aristocrat. When retreating German troops torch many of the houses in the district, this one is among those that are spared, a battered but enduring monument to resistance and survival.

The spirit of resistance is beautifully captured in an early scene which also reflects the book's preoccupation with time. Every Sunday Maria's father would wind up the grandfather clock in the family home, warning Maria and her sister, 'You can't move the arms back... Because you can't bring back the time which has passed.' After her father's death, Maria reaches for the key to the clock:

Rattling the lock, I opened the door. 'Remember, never backwards,' my father said many lives ago. So I turned the large hand in the opposite direction, feeling the resistance of the movement. Faster, faster. I cried for my father. Silent anger couldn't bring back to me the times which had passed, so I pushed the hands backwards until they clicked and hung loosely, swaying lifelessly.[67]

The symbolism is typically subtle. The clock resists the girl's attempts to wind back time and recover her father, an innocent victim of the remorseless march of history; but her attempts are themselves a form of active resistance, a refusal of the horror of the historical moment in which she finds herself. Resistance, this moment seems to tell us, must emanate from each individual human heart. It is one of many signal moments when Lewitt admits us inside her younger self, offering the reader an internal history of her moral being, a history lived through circuitous trajectories of a time disfigured by lunacy, but never quite bereft of hope. Better will come, 'come spring'.

The Australian Jewish Diaspora

Australia's is geographically the second-most-remote Jewish diaspora from Israel: only New Zealand's is farther removed from the ancestral home. One important study of Australian Jewish history is aptly entitled *Edge of the Diaspora*.[68] It is surprising that this diasporic community is not accorded a section in Ember, Ember and Skoggard's recent *Encyclopedia of Diasporas*,[69] given the numerical size of the Australian Jewish population (now about 100,000), its vitality (it is one of the most diverse and dynamic among Jewish diasporic communities), its high number of Holocaust survivors, and its contributions to international Jewish life.

Defining diaspora

In order best to understand the Australian Jewish diaspora and its bearing on Australian Jewish autobiography it will be helpful to consider the question of diasporas more generally. As leading diaspora scholar Robin Cohen points out, the Jewish diasporic experience is generally associated with catastrophe,[70] and with good reason given the Jews' 2000-year history of deterritorialization. However, Cohen also rightly makes the point that a significant amount of Jewish dispersion—some of it voluntary, some not— has been productive, resulting in creative new forms of cultural synthesis and opportunity. The history of the Australian Jewish diaspora, which on the whole has been a place where Jews can thrive, and has received many Jews who were not victims of tragedy, should caution against a too sweeping equation of diaspora and catastrophic dispersion. Indeed the very word diaspora, which is derived from the Greek *speirein* (to sow) and *dia* (through), contains an ambiguity: it suggests dispersion from a source, but also fertility, seeds that will flower elsewhere.

What then is a diaspora? There are various definitions, but Cohen provides an authoritative and appropriately flexible one:

> Normally, diasporas exhibit several of the following features: (1) dispersal from an original homeland, often traumatically; (2) alternatively, the expansion from a homeland in search of work, in pursuit of trade or to further colonial ambitions; (3) a collective memory and myth about the homeland; (4) an idealization of the supposed ancestral home; (5) a return movement; (6) a strong ethnic group consciousness sustained over a long time; (7) a troubled relationship with host societies; (8) a sense of solidarity with co-ethnic members in other countries; and (9) the possibility of a distinctive creative, enriching life in tolerant host countries.[71]

In the case of any particular diaspora, some of these features will mutually reinforce or otherwise impinge on others. A more comprehensive characterization might group diasporas into kinds: for instance, 'classical', 'new' and 'incipient'[72] diasporas; or might give an expanded version of Cohen's points (1) and (2) which specifies particular causal factors that precipitate the formation of diasporas. Cohen groups the diasporas he discusses under the following causal rubrics: victim, labour, trade, imperial, and cultural.[73]

As Cohen acknowledges, categorizing diasporas in this way is an inexact science,[74] partly because any diaspora will differ in some respects from any other, but also because diasporas change over time. Internal forces cause modification or transformation, as do external ones, and change is often precipitated by interactions between internal and external factors. External influences can range from local trends to international phenomena such as war, colonialism, globalization, transnationalism and multiculturalism.

Lists of defining factors are one thing, but ascribing weight to these factors can be another. For example, how much weight might or should be given to Cohen's third factor, 'a collective memory and myth about the homeland'? Popular perceptions of the Jewish diaspora generally give this factor enormous, even overriding or determinative weight: many would assume that Zionism is the core defining feature of a Jewish diasporic community. But as the history of the Australian Jewish diaspora shows, this is not necessarily the case—certainly not at all times. The prominence of factor (3), like so much else in diasporic communities, is subject to change across time.

Collective memories and myths about the homeland can vary from person to person within a diaspora at a given time. As we shall see, the overwhelming majority of Australian Jews are now Zionistic, and this fact might—albeit reductively—be thought definitive of the Australian Jewish diaspora. But it does not follow that every contemporary Australian Jew is a Zionist, or that those who are Zionists espouse the position with the same emphases or degrees of commitment. Some secular and entirely non-observant Australian Jews are Zionists for political and humanitarian reasons alone: they feel that after the Holocaust and the history of persecution that preceded it, the Jews must have a political home and Israel must survive as that place. Then there are Orthodox Jews who believe this, but also that Israel is God's appointed home for the Jews. However, there are ultra-Orthodox Jews who do not believe that the modern state of Israel constitutes the divinely ordained home of the Jews. For them, this blessed place can only come into being with the coming of the Messiah.

Such variations will in turn contribute to differences in how it *feels* to be a diasporic Jew, and in how that status actually enters into and helps define an individual's sense of personal identity. For the secular Zionist, being a 'Jew' may be a highly important aspect of personal identity, but Zionism may be more important to that aspect of the individual's personal identity than other components of Judaism (say, religious belief). Such a person might regard his Jewishness as being important, but not of overriding importance, to his personal identity—he might, for instance, define himself as an Australian Jew rather than as a Jewish Australian—but within the Jewish dimension of his identity Zionism might have a dominant position. There is, then, a vast range of possible connections between diaspora membership and personal identity, and even the links themselves can be subject to alteration.

The Australian Jewish diaspora

The history of the Jews in Australia has been amply documented and debated and there is no need for more than a brief, thematized sketch here. Those who wish to read more widely will find a range of treatments, the most detailed being Hilary and Bill (W. D.) Rubinstein's two-volume history, *The Jews in Australia*[75] and Suzanne Rutland's *Edge of the Diaspora*. Rutland's recent *The Jews in Australia* provides an admirable and up-to-date shorter treatment.[76]

Jews have been in Australia from the beginnings of European settlement, with an uncertain number (between eight and fourteen) arriving on the First Fleet in 1788.[77] The first free Jewish migrant arrived in 1816, and religious observance commenced around 1820. Gradually Melbourne overtook Sydney as the main centre of Jewish life and most Jews lived in cities; but regional communities also formed, particularly during the goldrush era. Traditionally the Australian Jewish community was strongly Anglo-Jewish in character. Its style of religious observance was shaped by a modernized form of Orthodoxy that developed in England in the nineteenth century, and most of the community felt a powerful allegiance to that country—England, rather than Palestine, constituted 'home'. The majority saw themselves as Australian Jewish citizens of the British Empire, though a significant minority were of German origin. Until the 1920s there were few eastern European Jews in Australia (the mass flight of persecuted Jews from Russia to America in the period 1881–1920 was not replicated in Australia; they came here in relatively small numbers). This meant that little Yiddish was spoken, that with some notable exceptions[78] the culture of *Yiddishkeit*—the world of eastern European Yiddish Jewry— took only limited hold, and that eastern European ultra-Orthodox Judaism had little impact on patterns of Jewish observance. The nineteenth-century Anglo-Australian Jews pursued a policy of 'non-distinctiveness', their wish being to blend unproblematically with mainstream society—but without assimilating. In the first part of the twentieth century this policy gradated into one of 'inconspicuousness bordering on invisibility'.[79] Yet still the pattern was one of acculturation, of adapting to but not losing ethnic identity within 'mainstream' Australian culture. As a result of their geographic remoteness, their comfortable adaptation in a place relatively free of antisemitism, and their success in various spheres of Australian life, these Australian Jews tended to be socially conservative, rather cut off from Jewish communities elsewhere, apprehensive about the impact that 'rough-mannered' eastern European Jewish migrants might have on their situation, and lukewarm, indifferent or even hostile towards Zionism.

Revelations of the full scale and horror of the Holocaust, and the foundation of Israel in May 1948, transformed the Australian Jewish diaspora, partly through shifts in opinion among already settled Jews and also through postwar migration. Something in the order of 35,000 eastern and other European survivors arrived through the late 1940s and the 1950s, as did subsequent migrants from the Soviet Union, the Middle East and South Africa. Now there were effectively two wings of the Australian Jewish community: the older Anglo-Jewish elite and the rapidly expanding eastern European group.

Herein lies the most troubling aspect of this diaspora's history. Though the details and their wider implications are still debated, it is clear that Australian Anglo-Jewish reservations about eastern European Jewish migration persisted prior to and into the war years when, in W. D. Rubinstein's words, the old elite 'failed the Jewish people in its greatest hour of need in modern history, by virtually declining to lift a finger to assist more of the beleaguered Jews of Nazi-occupied Europe to find a place of refuge in a practically unoccupied continent'.[80] Indeed the Anglo-Jewish elite, which was sometimes guilty of applying antisemitic stereotypes to its eastern European brethren, generally supported Australian governmental immigration quotas on the eastern European refugees through that period.[81] Once the magnitude of the Holocaust became widely understood and these refugees had put down some roots, the balance of power in the community effectively shifted to the newer—and now more numerous—group, and virtually the entire community became Zionistic. The old ethos of minimal visibility has gone. The contemporary Australian Jewish community, assisted by the implementation of Australian multicultural policy in the early 1970s,[82] is now assertive with respect to its distinctiveness and its response to antisemitic pressures.

It will be clear from this briefest of outlines that the Australian Jewish diaspora is by no means a homogeneous or static entity. As we have seen, diasporas are seldom either homogenous or static, however much we might be inclined to generalize about 'American Jews', the 'Irish Americans', or any other group. Such communities should not broadly be seen—and certainly not in the Jewish case—as mere outgrowths of monolithic earlier cultural narratives. Many micro-narratives coexist, and sometimes clash, in such communities. Thus, while many Australian Jews of eastern European origin would have been raised as Zionists in Europe, and would have brought such attitudes to Australia, many were not. An appreciable number were raised in the anti-Zionist socialist tradition of the Bund, which believed in progressive emancipation of Jews in the diaspora.

There are variations, too, according to location. The Melbourne and Sydney Jewish communities differ significantly,[83] as do the regional communities from the major city ones. Other differences are occasioned by migration and travel flows between the diaspora and Israel: some Australian Jews have migrated to Israel, and there has been significant recent migration from Israel to Australia. Across the Australian Jewish community the sense of 'home' has been and continues to be variable. It inevitably dilutes and changes as post-migrant generations become more embedded in the host culture. Attitudinal shifts can also be occasioned by changes in Israeli policy and in Israel's geopolitical environment.

Thus the Australian Jewish community has evolved in a variety of ways and along a variety of trajectories: ethnic, religious, political and linguistic, among others. Like most diasporas it has a marked degree of internal differentiation: it is more heterogeneous than it might look from the outside or when seen, as it too often is, through the lens of cultural stereotypes. Because Jews have resided in so many different places, spoken so many different languages and lived so many different versions of 'the Jewish life' over two millennia, the cultural roots of the Australian Jewish community are extremely diverse. The Holocaust, the birth of Israel, and subsequent events in the Middle East have been powerful sources of unification along some axes, but divisions of orientation—say, between Orthodox and Liberal Jews, or in attitudes to Israeli policy—are very much in evidence. The Australian Jewish diaspora certainly exhibits several of Cohen's proposed characteristics; but it must be added that a substantial number of Jews came here in search of work and other forms of economic and personal prosperity without any catastrophic precipitating cause, and that broadly speaking—certainly relative to Jewish experience in most other places—Jews here have not experienced 'a troubled relationship' with the host culture. For the most part, they have experienced 'a distinctive creative, enriching life' in what is on the whole—though not wholly—a tolerant host country.

In the discussion so far I have tried to suggest that there is usually an imprecise 'fit' between any given definition of diaspora and any particular diasporic community, and between generalized perceptions of what a given diasporic community might be like and the characteristics of particular individual diasporic citizens. Here again, generalizations will take us only so far; the best source of insight is a shuttling process between general sociological characterizations and the autobiographical narratives (whether verbal or written) of particular individuals. Indeed, generalizations are themselves heavily indebted to such narratives.

Even generalizations about perceptions of Israel have to be made with care. Many Australian Jewish autobiographers refer to Israel, but with varying degrees of emphasis. The birth of the nation is of course often noted, and a considerable number of volumes feature travel descriptions that include visits to Israel or, as in Lucy Gould's *Empty Corners* and Kathy Reisman's *More Than Nine Lives*,[84] years spent in Israel prior to settlement in Australia. Few of these descriptions are strikingly accomplished in aesthetic terms. However cherished the idea of Israel may be, its cultural remoteness from Australia, and from some of these authors' European roots, seems to constitute a barrier to sophisticated and assured autobiographical writing.

Leo Cooper, a Pole who came to Australia after the war, is typical in recounting his strong feelings upon first setting foot on Israeli soil in 1955:

> Our emotions were very intense when the pilot announced that we would begin the descent toward Tel-Aviv and we saw the first lights of the city below. We arrived late at night. We were not alone in being emotional. Stepping down from the plane, I saw a couple of people kneeling and kissing the ground.[85]

Zionism is important but not predominant in Cooper's narrative, and the same applies to his sense of personal identity. The contrary is true of Max Freilich, whose autobiography is entitled *Zion in Our Time: Memoirs of an Australian Zionist*. As the title suggests, Zionism is the core and organizing theme of this book and it runs very deep in Freilich's sense of himself as a

Jew, for whom: 'The survival of the Jewish people in the face of inconceivable physical and spiritual suffering throughout its long and dark history of nearly twenty centuries in exile can only be conceived as transcendental.' [86] Freilich, a Jew of Galician extraction who arrived in Australia in 1929, first visits Palestine in 1932. Writing thirty-five years on he finds it 'difficult to recapture and describe adequately the emotions and the internal excitement we experienced'.[87] Later, when the horror of the Holocaust dawns in Australia, his commitment to his 'Zionist task' [88] takes on a tremendous new urgency. He reports that with the birth of Israel, 'The Australian Jewish community, like all Jewish communities the world over, was electrified by the unprecedented historical phenomenon of the re-emergence of the sovereign Jewish nation'.[89] Freilich encountered and became committed to Zionism before he left Europe. He knew the movement and its cultural roots from the inside and was ideally prepared to become one of its most powerful Australian advocates.

In his *The Five Books of Boas*, the Australian-born psychologist and Jewish community identity, Bernard Boas, describes his first visit to Israel in 1955. After commenting on the physical dangers of the environment he recalls his arrival at the King David Hotel in Jerusalem:

> We had arrived at *Chanukah* and a *Menorah* was lit in the hotel foyer. To us this was a revelation. In Australia, this was done only in private, at home or inside a *shule*. In a night-time procession down the streets, children were singing at the top of their voices '*Maoz Tsur*', the war song of the Maccabees of ancient times, when the Hebrews were struggling with the forces of Greece. Deeply moved, we began to see that Jews really are a different people. I began to feel that I was a Jew!
>
> The whole country is about as big as East Gippsland, or half the size of Tasmania...[90]

The references to Australian geography show how far Boas experiences Israel through the frames of his Australian identity and experience. There is a cultural remoteness about the description, and yet it is precisely this remoteness, this sense of encountering an authentic religiosity that is also in some ways alien, which precipitates the transformative experience that, almost mystically, enabled Boas to take possession of his Judaism.

One could elaborate differences of this kind at great length, so various are Australian Jewish perceptions of Israel. A very different example is Josiane Behmoiras's moving account of her psychologically disturbed mother, *Dora B*, which is set first in France and then in Israel, where the pair moved when Josiane was eight. In this instance the narrative's focus is squarely on the mother–daughter relationship and its consequences for the adult author. Israel is described in often sensuous yet menacing prose vignettes—'I see pink flowers with wolves' teeth blossoming in the dark wood along a country road'[91]—but the place itself has little intrinsic, still less Zionistic, importance in the narrative. Indeed it is a place that Josiane must leave in order to find adult identity away from her mother. She settles in Australia in 1985.

Recent developments in theories of diaspora

Postcolonial studies[92] are concerned with colonialism and its aftermath; that is, with the nature of colonialism and with the cultural and political situations and movements that obtain in former colonies. Though it has important things to say about a former—or almost former—white first-world colony like Australia, postcolonial scholarship tends to focus its powerful political analyses on third-world, non-white former colonies, where the ravages of European colonialism have generally been most extreme. It takes issue not just with the political and military dimensions of colonialism but also, and very centrally, with its cultural and intellectual aspects—with the ways in which it attempts to shape, but also to *represent*, the non-European world. The American-Palestinian intellectual Edward Said uses the term 'orientalism' to describe how the 'orient' has been pictured, mythologized and to a very great extent invented by the West.[93] Said notes that this intellectual-cultural dimension of imperialism needs to be understood in terms of particular imagined versions of the orient, but also with respect to how European ways of seeing and talking about the world predominate in these representations. They are 'Eurocentric' in that they see the world through European eyes, values and discourses.

Said was heavily influenced by the French postmodern theorist Michel Foucault's[94] account of how our ways of knowing are shaped by power-driven agendas. Thus, a colonial power might mythologize, or claim to 'know', a subject-society as 'primitive' because such a view serves colonial self-interest. Colonialist economic exploitation can be rationalized as humane 'modernization'; Christianity can be imposed because Western 'knowledge' categorizes indigenous spirituality as 'pagan'. Said's thought owes less to another one of the major postmodern thinkers, the French philosopher Jacques Derrida. I will have more to say about Derrida, and about postmodernism generally, in a later section on Holocaust autobiography; suffice it to say here that Derrida has had a major influence on some traditions of postcolonial scholarship, not least on diaspora studies, and that what we might call Derrida-influenced diaspora studies are markedly different in style from the approach I have adopted in this discussion of the Australian Jewish diaspora—an approach that is under challenge in some academic quarters.

A Derrida-influenced view would tend to see my discussion as Eurocentric in the sense that its very terms derive from Western liberal humanism. This would apply, for example, to the way I have pictured individual selves. A Derridean reading would agree that individual identities are comprised of various dimensions, but it would lay much greater emphasis than I have on the heterogeneity of these component aspects of identity. So much so, that it would tend to see identity as fragmentary rather than cohesive, and the self as a kind of psycho-cultural miscellany rather than a unified being which is orchestrated from a stable 'core'. In fact, in such work the notion of 'self' is generally replaced by the more overtly political term 'subject' (a term which indicates that selves are subject to networks of social and political power); similarly, the notion of 'individual psychology' tends to be supplanted by the term 'subjectivity', the implication being that our inwardness is powerfully shaped by external—social and cultural—factors. Thus, in a recent collection of essays, *Theorizing Diaspora*, many of them postmodern, the editors refer to 'diasporic subjectivities',[95] meaning (roughly) typical forms of historically shaped diaspora consciousness.

The Derridean perspective emphasizes the fluid and constantly evolving nature of diasporic (and other) communities; the sense in which 'the final story' of a given society is never told, is always unfolding, and should never be the exclusive property of a ruling elite. *Theorizing Diaspora* features an essay by the postmodern critic Stuart Hall, entitled 'Cultural Identity and Diaspora', which links Derrida's scepticism about accurate representation with this notion of an always-unfolding story whose authority is not beholden to settled structures of social authority and power. Derrida's compound term *différance*—a play on the relationship between 'differ' and 'defer'—can be taken to imply that the story of social relations, of the composition of a society, can never be definitively narrated; will inevitably and always be deferred. Social identities, then, are never finally settled. Hall inquires: 'Where, then, does identity come into this infinite postponement of meaning?' He responds: 'Derrida does not help us as much as he might here, though the notion of the "trace" goes some way toward it.'[96] I will defer discussion of the notion of the 'trace', and note here that in this passage Hall is drawing attention to a much debated issue in anti-humanist diaspora studies: how does one derive meaningful notions of personal and collective identity from a theoretical perspective whose overwhelming emphasis is on radical difference, on never settling for a story about who one is and where one belongs? Though the Derrida-inspired approach to diaspora studies has yielded powerful, politically engaged work by the Hong Kong–American scholar Rey Chow[97] and others, it seems to me to function best as a critique, and less well as a way of capturing the experience—highly differentiated though it is—of individuals in a community like the Australian Jewish diaspora.

Australian Jewish autobiographers are of course greatly concerned with antisemitism, but they write about it from a new-world perspective, a place remote from European antisemitism's roots and horrors. The majority see democratic institutions and a culture that is inclusive but respectful of ethnic difference as the best antidote to the cultural violence that comes with antisemitism and other forms of discriminatory social categorization. Because of this, and because of my own reservations about Derridean theory as an approach to Western autobiography, I have taken an essentially humanist and empirical approach to this discussion of the Jewish diaspora in Australia.

Australian Jewish Migrant Autobiography

Some of the intellectual complexities associated with theories of diaspora also apply to the genre of migrant autobiography.[98] It can be argued, for instance, that migrant autobiographers run the risk that their original cultural perspective will be ignored or insufficiently valued by readers who see such stories only, or primarily, in terms of the perspectives of the adoptive culture. This is of course true in some cases, but it is also true that migrant autobiography in Australia—even in John Howard's Australia—is playing an important part in broadening local perspectives and helping to bring about a multicultural community that recognizes and respects ethnic and religious difference. This is certainly the tenor of most post-Holocaust Australian Jewish autobiography, Arnold Zable's work (see Part Two) being a prime example.

Migrant autobiography

It is not necessary for our purposes to belabour the term 'migrant'. I construe it as a synonym for 'immigrant'. I do not assume, as some definitions do, that a migrant necessarily changes places through an act of free choice. Of course, many migrants do freely choose to move—though degrees of freedom vary from case to case—but some, like many Holocaust refugees, came to Australia by sheer happenstance when there was no longer a 'home' to go back to. In the present discussion, 'migrant' covers the whole spectrum: from those who chose freely to leave (sometimes called 'voluntary migrants'), to victims of catastrophe who have no choice at all ('involuntary migrants'). It refers to people who live in an adoptive culture for an appreciable time—but without specifying what 'appreciable' means in months or years.[99] I will use the term 'migrant autobiography' in a rather narrow way, such that it refers to autobiographies that deal in some detail with 'the migrant experience'; that is, with the experience of cultural transplantation. Some of these—though only a small minority in the case of Australian Jewish migrants—also offer analysis of Australian society as they find it.

My use of the term 'migrant autobiography' means, perhaps surprisingly, that not all migrants who write autobiography are writing in the genre of migrant autobiography. If a Sicilian migrant writes an entire autobiography about his business life in Australia but says little or nothing about his journey here and the adjustments it required, nor anything analytical about Australian society, he is not writing migrant autobiography as I have defined it.

There is an important distinction to be made between migrants who transplant to places which speak the same language as their place of origin, and those who move to different language worlds—that is, to places where their native language is either not spoken or not the predominant medium of communication. In her fine study of migrant autobiography, *Translating One's Self*, Mary Besemeres terms the second group 'language migrants'.[100] The notion of a 'language world', often associated with the twentieth-century philosopher Ludwig Wittgenstein, is very important here. It's easy to assume that human communities somehow spring into being, and that they then manufacture their languages rather as the mint manufactures currency. Wittgenstein and others remind us that this is not the case; that in fact a human community, which comprises assumptions, practices and values, develops with and through language. Language powerfully influences the kinds of individuals we are, the narratives we believe about the world, and much more. To depart one language world for another is, then, a major step, though how major will depend on a variety of factors, particularly age. In very broad terms we might say that young children are more adaptable to new cultures than their elders, not just because they 'pick up' language more readily than adults but because an adult's native tongue has had much longer to shape, express and define that person's identity.

Besemeres reads migrant autobiography as a way of understanding the linguistic and personal lives of 'language migrants' who depart the language of their place of origin for a new language world. Her pivotal concept, 'self-translation',[101] refers to the process by which the language migrant seeks to write an autobiographical narrative that encompasses both the inaugural and the relocated cultural-linguistic self. Such writers, working in their adoptive language, must 'translate' the inaugural language-self into a verbal artifact that will be intelligible to readers in the adoptive culture.

Besemeres conceives of selves as substantial, discriminating, decision-making individuals who take shape in but also creatively *use* language. The relationship of self and language is a dynamic, two-way process. One of the things people do through language is create a sense of self—through conversation, reflection, written narrative, and other means. Besemeres refers approvingly to Polish-American Jewish autobiographer Eva Hoffman's 'reflexive metaphor of "self-translation", where the self is understood as both struggling agent and elusive object of the enterprise'.[102] For Besemeres, as for Hoffman, the autobiographical storying of the self's psychic and circumstantial discontinuities can help heal rifts and promote integration. Neither wishes to surrender the concept of self to generalized poststructuralist accounts that insist on its inevitable and radical fragmentation. As we will see, this notion of harmonization through narrative has important applications for Holocaust autobiography.

Gratitude and resentment

Australian Jewish migrant autobiography has been discussed under various headings, including migrant writing, multiculturalism and ethnic minority writing. But some recent academic discussions of such writing in Australia don't adequately fit the Jewish case. One of the most influential is Sneja Gunew's *Framing Marginality*, a study that speaks of the need 'both to assemble the work and to find the conceptual tools to analyse it'.[103] Her own conceptual tools comprise a blend of several forms of postmodern theory, including Derrida, Foucault and the French Marxist, Louis Althusser. Gunew emphasizes the ways in which ethnic minority writing deconstructs—that is, challenges, erodes, shows up contradictions within—aspects of 'mainstream' Australian society, especially its networks of power and authority. For her, such writing is a sort of writing back from the margins which subverts dominant cultural discourses, literary and other, including discourses that reproduce dominant modes of identity-formation. She wants to reconceptualize multicultural writing in order, as she puts it elsewhere, to achieve an

> allegorical palimpsest where texts are read through each other and none is particularly privileged. Here the primary impulse is not the hermeneutic one of recovering an original meaning. Instead each reading functions as supplement; but, as we know, supplements [i.e. Derridean supplements] redefine the whole.[104]

Derrida's notion of the 'supplement' is a concept that calls into question language's capacity to furnish a reliable description of the world. Gunew's point here is, roughly, that we should not read texts as authoritative accounts of the world—definitive representations springing from the intentions of their authors—but rather as a sort of endlessly growing and rearranging gallery of stories about reality. The stories, which are to be read with reference to one another rather than to the world they seek to describe, should all be thought of as having equal cultural authority. This shifting and non-hierarchical gallery challenges existing notions of cultural authority—for instance, the assumption, so often an organizing principle among those who design galleries and exhibitions, that some artworks are better or more central to a given cultural tradition than others, and that artworks can reliably reflect certain aspects of reality. Not surprisingly, this orientation predisposes Gunew to favour 'ethnic minority' texts that exhibit a high degree of ideological ambivalence and have a subversive disposition towards mainstream Australian writing. This subversive disposition is generally associated with anti-realist aesthetic experimentation. Early on, she refers to Judah Waten's quasi-autobiographical realist classic, *Alien Son*. But in fact Jews scarcely figure in *Framing Marginality*, and the reference to Waten is there largely to disparage what Gunew considers a misguided tendency on the part of many academics to see migrant writing as fundamentally realist in its ethos and methods. She adduces scholarly discussion of *Alien Son* as the 'paradigmatic'[105] example of this mistaken characterization of migrant writing.

Yet, as David Carter has noted in a fine study of Waten's literary and political career, his adherence to realism was itself revolutionary in character: it reflected Russian Marxist opposition to modernist aesthetic doctrines which construed art as an autonomous realm distinct from the world of political 'praxis', or action.[106] Moreover, Waten's realist aesthetic is consistent with most of the Australian Jewish autobiographical writing that was to follow. In this respect, as in some others, Gunew's transgressive model of ethnic minority writing does not work well for Jewish autobiographical texts. There are several reasons for this. First, the anti-realist deconstructive stance undermines what matters most to Holocaust memoirists—the opportunity to bear truthful witness, and to be believed. Kitia Altman writes of her televised encounter with Holocaust denier David Irving that his denial of her story 'was equal in its horror to my other experience, that of selection in Auschwitz'.[107] Second, it suggests that ethnic minority writing in Australia should be seen as fundamentally rebellious and experimental; yet such experimentation is almost entirely absent from first-generation Jewish autobiographical narratives and is not prominent even among second-generation ones. Finally, Gunew's emphasis on resentful, alienated and transgressive writing back from the margins misses what is perhaps the most fundamental disposition towards Australia in first-generation and even—albeit more ambivalently—in second-generation Jewish autobiographical texts. This is a disposition of what can simply be called gratitude.

Gratitude may seem an unspectacular, even obeisant sort of ethnic minority disposition, but its importance in post-Holocaust Australian Jewish autobiography can hardly be overstated. In his preface to *Strauss to Matilda*, an anthology of writings by Viennese Jews who fled Hitler and settled in Australia, the editor, Karl Bittman, characterizes the impetus for the book thus: 'the Austrian immigrant community needed to express its gratitude to Australia for receiving it after its life and prospects in Austria were shattered'.[108] While Bittman speaks for central European Jews, who have often found assimilation in Australian society less fraught than their eastern European counterparts, the sentiment is no less apparent in autobiographical writing from that latter group. In an important text, Israel Kipen, a Jew of Polish origin, expresses sentiments that recur again and again in post-Holocaust Australian Jewish autobiography:

> The most profound of all impressions made upon me by the new country were its democratic attitudes, tradition and practices. Nothing else about Australian life, no matter how novel or startling it may have been, affected me so positively as the equality accorded to every citizen in theory and in practice—a reality so ingrained as to be taken for granted and perhaps hard to appreciate fully, except by one who has known life in a police state or under the heel of a totalitarian regime. The simple incident of hearing a mother tell her child that a policeman was a friend whom one could always trust and ask for help was, to one like myself who had been raised in a milieu where mothers would mention the police to frighten recalcitrant children, extraordinary and almost unbelievable... For a time, I was not only geographically, but also philosophically displaced. To be seen as human in my own right and never having to prove my innocence against presumed guilt were, at once, liberating, revolutionary, and reassuring.[109]

And again later: 'I remain grateful for the rootedness of the democratic tradition of the country.'[110] It is striking that when Kipen talks of 'displacement' he is not referring—as one might expect—to the pain and threatening existential disorientation we often associate with the 'migrant condition'. In fact, exilic nostalgia is much more common in second-generation Australian Jewish narratives, where authors have not known the horrors of European antisemitism first-hand but have a yearning to reconstruct their ancestral roots and the world Nazism destroyed. Kipen is alluding to the almost unbelievable relief, the cessation of dread, that comes with being 'displaced' from a place where one was hunted like an animal to a culture in which one can relax into life and enjoy basic human rights. The acquisition of such rights occasions a particular and powerful emotional turning-point in many post-Holocaust Australian Jewish autobiographies.

I presume that this sentiment of gratitude occurs in other refugee, migrant and exilic Australian autobiographical literatures as well. Tragically and deplorably, in Howard's Australia such rights are being withheld from people who are in dire situations. Indeed let us not sentimentalize Australia's multicultural and migrant history: indigenous Australians, victims of a history of racism, brutality and neglect, still do not have an official apology for the past practice of state-sponsored forced removal of children. The Jews too have at times suffered bitterly at the hands of Australian migration policy.

I don't of course deny that Gunew's reconceptualization of multiculturalism and its literary implications works for some ethnic minority writing in Australia. It is clearly relevant to work in other genres by contemporary 'Australian Jewish' writers like Brian Castro, Dorothy Porter and Ania Walwicz. My point is simply that there are important classes of texts for which it does not work and that we need to be careful not to mandate a new centrism in these matters—a centrism wherein academics take the possession of certain rights, freedoms and entitlements of selfhood so much for granted that they overlook the experience of people who have not been so fortunate. Our theories ought not to obscure or distort the empirical histories they are there to help explain. The Aboriginal autobiographer has every reason to 'write back' angrily from the margins, but most Australian Jewish autobiographers feel no such need.

Australian texts and trends

There are about twenty published works of Australian Jewish migrant autobiography as I have defined it. The most accomplished author in this genre is perhaps Andrew Riemer, whose multi-volume autobiographical project, comparable in depth and interest to Eva Hoffman's, is discussed in Part Two.

In the broader category of autobiographies by Australian Jewish migrants, the majority were written in English; most of the remainder have been translated into the adoptive tongue. About 20 percent of those originally published in English display what might be termed sophisticated English-language skills. As one would expect, a high proportion of these are second- or later-generation narratives.

Besemeres's emphasis on 'the whole inner life'[111] is apt because many migrant autobiographers simply tell their story without being particularly concerned about matters of identity. As Lolo Houbein says: 'I would even dare to suggest that being a migrant is marginal to the lives of most migrants. They sought space for their pursuits and only if the pursuits do not work out does being a migrant take a central place in their perception of themselves.'[112]

Does one think of oneself as an Australian Jew or a Jewish Australian? The question matters to an intellectual and self-conscious autobiographer like Amirah Inglis, whose self-image was powerfully shaped by the migrant child's experience of leading a 'double life'.[113] But for many, such questions are not particularly important and don't loom large in their autobio-graphies. They write their stories, often in a relatively unselfconscious way, revealing aspects of their 'inner life', but often concentrating more on the 'outer' life of profession, social adaptation and family. In fact, a sizeable proportion of such writers—particularly the men—reveal very little indeed about their inner lives. Their narratives focus almost entirely on external events and developments with only the most cursory references to how things felt at a given time. Sometimes this is because the author does not have the confidence or the command of English required to express the nuances of feeling and reflection; but there can be other reasons as well. Some people, as we know, are just temperamentally less inclined to self-revelation than others. Another and very important factor is that elaborate self-awareness of the kind now so familiar in the Western world is by no means a universal cultural phenomenon. Woody Allen's colossally self-conscious, identity-obsessed humour is often thought to be quintessentially 'Jewish', and in certain ways it is. It has deep roots in eastern European Yiddish culture. However, that culture itself was not on the whole deeply introspective: the driving concern in that world was not 'Who am I?' but rather the ethical question 'Am I living the good Jewish life?'. Woody Allen's self-consciousness is a later elaboration, deriving partly from metropolitan central and western European culture (Jewish and other) and of course from American individualism. The majority of the migrant autobiographies written by Australian Jews are by people from eastern European cultural worlds which did not encourage psychological—as opposed to moral—introspection. This disinclination to introspect often marks these autobiographies, even though in many cases they are written after long settlement in Australia—a culture traditionally reticent about introspection and self-revelation, but more given to such tendencies in the postwar period with its increasing cosmopolitanization and Americanization.

In texts of this kind, it is perhaps more helpful to speak of 'transition' than 'translation', in the sense that these authors are less concerned to probe cultural variations in selfhood and the adaptations they require, than to narrate the logistics of transition to another culture. Some of these logistics naturally involve the encounter with a new language; but with notable exceptions like Jacob Rosenberg, these reticent migrant autobiographers do not generally assert deep interconnections between language and selfhood. Moving countries requires that the self, which for them is largely already-formed, learn a new language. They see this as a pragmatic requirement rather than an existential conundrum or challenge. This of course does not necessarily mean that they aren't changed in subtle ways by their new language world—change of this kind is to some degree inevitable; it simply means that such change does not feature as an issue in their autobiographies.

Australia figures in varying degrees in post-Holocaust Jewish autobiography. In many first-generation texts it scarcely features at all. Zyga Elton's *Destination Buchara*,[114] for instance, ends at the point of arrival here. Other narratives deal predominantly with the gone prewar world and the Holocaust experience, devoting a coda of perhaps fifteen to twenty pages to life in Australia. Narratives in this category include Abraham Biderman's *The World of My Past*, Mark Verstandig's *I Rest My Case*, Richard Seligman's *Very Convenient Everywhere*, Joseph West's *Survival*,

Struggle & Success, and Max Heitlinger's *In the Nick of Time*.[115] In cases like these there is little if any analytical reflection on Australian society. That society functions largely as an enabling environment and a backdrop to the rebuilding of a life, albeit one in which the sense of self derives certain nuances from the new milieu. Emphasis tends to be on professional success, the family, life in the local Jewish community. In a third category of texts, however, Australia does figure prominently and can be the subject of quite detailed reflection. Until recently, such texts were very much in the minority. This has changed, and continues to do so, partly as a result of a remarkable community writing project based at the Makor Jewish Community Library in South Caulfield, Melbourne. The Makor 'Write Your Story' project (see Part Two for a detailed discussion) often encourages its autobiographical authors to include in their narratives descriptions of their life in Australia.

Paul Kraus's *A New Australian, a New Australia* is one of the most focused and anguished of Australian Jewish migrant autobiographies. This book had an earlier manifestation under the title *The Not So Fabulous Fifties: Images of a migrant childhood*. As that title suggests, Kraus set out to write in detail about Australia, and he does so from the vantage-point of a migrant. His cultural situation is especially complex. His father, who was dying in Mauthausen when that concentration camp was liberated, was a Liberal Jew with a strong sense of Jewish identity. Paul's mother, who had been in Budapest in hiding with her two boys during the Holocaust, underwent a conversion to Christianity late in the war. It is Christianity which eventually meets Paul's religious needs; yet his identification with the Jewish fate is the most powerful motivating factor in the narrative: 'Judaism, I came to realise in later years, was all about belonging, whereas Christianity, certainly the Anglican persuasion, was all about believing.'[116]

Paul is five when in 1949 the family arrives in 'that far-away, unknown Australia'.[117] He is critical of various aspects of this place as he finds it in the 1960s. Some of his criticisms—for instance, of burgeoning consumerism—don't relate directly to his status as a migrant. But others do: his caustic discussions of parochialism, monoculturalism and its assimilationist ideology,[118] and his experience of antisemitism at school. Kraus lacks the narrative range and sophistication of the more 'literary' Australian Jewish autobiographers, but like other second-generation authors he assays both sociological and introspective psychological analysis and reflects on linkages between the two. He writes repeatedly about his own lack of 'self-esteem', a deficit he in part attributes to 'being different' in 1960s Australia.[119] In his early twenties he spends fourteen months in Europe seeking a more secure sense of identity. But it is not until he returns to Australia that feelings of resolution come, thanks particularly to marriage and Christianity. By now the family is thoroughly assimilated in Australia—'a place which I had only ever provisionally called home'[120]— and Judaism has largely ceased to define Paul's sense of self and his destiny.[121]

Perhaps the most sociologically searching of the migrant narratives is Israel Kipen's *A Life to Live* ... . Kipen was born into an Orthodox family in Bialystok, Poland, in 1919. He survived the war by escaping through Russia, Shanghai and Japan, reaching Australia in 1946. Like many survivors, he made his living here in the clothing trade. He did well in business and was also a prime mover in facilitating primary, secondary and tertiary Jewish education in Melbourne. Indeed much of the Australian part of his story is focused through life in the Jewish community. In his retirement Kipen attained honours and MA degrees in History at the University of Melbourne. *A Life to Live* ... contains a detailed chapter entitled 'Australian Society' which comments, sometimes critically though always forgivingly, on his adoptive culture. (In this vein, see also Sabiha Jawary's thoughtful and charming volume, *Baghdad I Remember*,[122] for its reflections on Australian multiculturalism.) Kipen's moral, political and sociological gaze surveys our postcolonial condition, our history with respect to indigenous Australians, and our postwar insularity and xenophobia. He writes admiringly of the Australian ethos of decency (a central theme in Freadman's *Shadow of Doubt*). It takes him some time to adjust to the fact that when an Australian public servant inquires 'Can I help you?', the voice does not cloak totalitarian or sectarian menace. But there is admirable firmness in his less flattering observations, as when he recalls his first encounter with an Aboriginal person, which stirred him

> to seek to learn more about the Aborigines' origins, culture and lifestyle, and of the impact of white settlement upon them—a lesson that opened out on many issues, among them the less salutary ones of shameful dealings, national guilt

and political expediency, which remain to this day on the front burner of Australia's political dilemmas.[123]

Though neither particularly literary nor notably introspective, Kipen's book constitutes something of a bridge between first- and second-generation narrative modes and is exemplary in its determination to make a balanced assessment of the adoptive culture.

The term 'migrant' is a sociological category, and a sometimes ideologically charged form of social labelling. It is also a state of mind. Australian Jewish migrant autobiographies remind us of just how variable this state of mind can be and how variable are attitudes to the label itself. Holocaust survivors often possess enormous strength of will, huge powers of resistance to the forces that would label, denigrate or otherwise marginalize them. Survivor Andor Schwartz writes of his early days in rural Australia thus:

> I became, after a year of living in Nar Nar Goon, a full Australian. I was never an ethnic. Even though I couldn't speak well, I was accepted as if I had been born here. Everything depends on you. [124]

This might seem unconvincing at first, but it has a certain resonance. Schwartz is one of many migrants who see adoptive cultural identity as something they can will into being. Given how many Australians are from elsewhere, there is good reason for this perception. And after all, personal identity is in part a matter of whom one wills oneself to be. Schwartz is no philosopher (though he is a mystic), but he has an instinctive distrust of the third-person point of view and an indomitable sense of his own transcultural authenticity.

Reading Holocaust Autobiography

Holocaust survivor and celebrated author Elie Wiesel has argued that 'If the Greeks invented tragedy, the Romans the epistle, and the Renaissance the sonnet, our generation invented a new literature, that of testimony'.[125] Of course many autobiographers before the Holocaust had recorded horrific accounts of war, slavery and other evils, but Wiesel argues that the

Holocaust was an event of such unprecedented enormity that new means were needed to recount experiences which seemed to demand—but also to defy—representation:

> What kind of words? That, too, became a difficulty the writer had to solve and overcome. Language had been corrupted to the point that it had to be invented anew and purified. This time we [survivors] wrote not with words but against words. Often we told less so as to make the truth more credible. Had any one of us told the whole story, he would have been proclaimed mad. Once upon a time the novelist and the poet were in advance of their readers. Not now. Once upon a time the artist could foresee the future. Not now. Now he has to remember the past, knowing all the while that what he has to say will never be told. What he hopes to transmit can never be transmitted. All he can possibly hope to achieve is to communicate the impossibility of communication.[126]

Wiesel's comments suggest that however graphic and apparently reliable Holocaust autobiography might appear, this genre of writing is fraught with complexities. These complexities include problems of definition.[127]

Other complexities pertain to the supposedly unprecedented nature of this form of writing, the limits of language, the sheer strangeness of much Holocaust experience, and the varying contexts within which Holocaust and other forms of testimony are read.[128] The notion that to communicate these things might be 'impossible' seems to fly in the face of the common-sense assumption that we can simply pick up such narratives and read them as transparent windows on Holocaust realities.

Some readers may feel that Wiesel's concerns unnecessarily complicate matters and that common-sense readings of Holocaust autobiography are quite in order. There is a lot to be said for this view, not least because most survivor-authors write in the hope that their narratives will be taken at face value as reasonably accurate accounts of first-hand experience. I think it is fair to say that many of them would not expect or want their writing to become the subject of high-level philosophical speculation about the nature of language, reality or genre. They want to be read—and believed, as they generally are—by Jews, the general reading public, historians and others. Nevertheless, Wiesel's remarks indicate that there are real issues to be considered and that it is quite appropriate for such considerations to be aired, alongside—and in conjunction with—more 'common-sense' approaches. After all, academic discussion of the Holocaust concerns not just what we know but *how* we know it. This isn't intellectual self-indulgence, because here, as in a court of law, information must be weighed according to its sources and its status as evidence.[129]

Humanist and postmodern approaches

It is useful at this point to draw a rough—and it *is* rough—distinction between so-called humanist and postmodern views. In broad terms, humanists tend to assume that narrative in general, and therefore Holocaust narrative in particular, can give reliable descriptions of the world. This confidence in the possibility of narrative reliability assumes that differences in how particular individuals see the world do not necessarily prevent us from arriving at reliable consensus about the truth and meaning of particular events. Such a belief is usually associated with the aesthetic creed of 'realism'. Humanists also tend to believe that there is such a thing as human nature, and that human beings possess—at least potentially—profound internal psychological coherence and innate moral propensities. When humanists read literature or autobiography their emphasis is apt to be on the experience and moral behaviour of individual people. Some humanist readings may leave it at this; others include historical considerations such as how and how far individuals and individual behaviour are shaped by cultural and historical forces. Humanism has a long and diverse intellectual history, but it has deep roots in classical, Renaissance and Enlightenment culture.

In some respects postmodernism, which came to the fore in the 1960s, is a mirror image of humanism. Its ethos tends to be 'anti-realist' in that it denies, or is sceptical about, the capacity of narrative to furnish reliable descriptions of the world; it also denies or is sceptical about our ability to derive consensual understandings from divergent individual perspectives. It generally rejects the notion of human nature, believing instead that human beings become what they are through cultural causation. This leads them to deny that people possess inherent moral proclivities: rather, on this view, their ethical behaviour, like other aspects of their conduct, will be profoundly shaped by cultural forces (but also by aspects of individual life-history). Postmodernist readings of narrative are inclined to question modern Western culture's so-called 'cult of the individual', with its emphasis on the uniqueness and coherence of individual selves, and its assumption that individuals possess a highly developed capacity to make assessments, and to make choices in the light of those assessments. Postmodernism tends to see such conceptions of individuality as themselves cultural products. Thus postmodern readings, rather than focusing on (say) the moral conduct of individuals, will often highlight alleged contradictions in the way such individuals are presented in a narrative (contradictions that are thought to reflect contradictions within the cultural 'cult of the individual'), and inconsistencies in the moral codes they are embedded in. Postmodernism is a self-styled critique of many aspects of Western thought and culture, and is often particularly hostile to humanism and its supposed apotheosis during the Enlightenment.

Because the present study of Australian Jewish autobiography is heavily literary in emphasis, and because postmodernism has had a significant impact on the study of narrative, I will speak at some length about post-modernism and its attack on the more traditional ethos of humanist literary study. It should not however be assumed that postmodernism now dominates discussions of Holocaust autobiography across the board. Its influential position in English and cultural studies departments, where Holocaust memoir is often discussed, is not matched elsewhere. Most historians and others still assume that some version of humanistic realism is appropriate to the study of these texts.

Key issues in recent discussions of Holocaust autobiography include: (1) Can language give us accurate representations of history and of the world in general? (2) Was the world of the concentration camps fundamentally different (or 'discontinuous') from the world at large, or was it just an extreme form of the world beyond the camps and therefore 'continuous' with it? (3) Should our assumptions when reading Holocaust memoir be 'realist' or 'anti-realist', or perhaps a combination of the two? (4) Is it possible or ethically proper to identify closely with the experience of others, and in particular with the extreme experiences suffered by people in the camps? (5) Does the fact that no two people see anything in exactly the same way mean that we cannot agree about the 'truth' of certain representations of the world? (6) Is there such a thing as human nature, or are human beings fundamentally shaped by their specific cultural worlds?

(7) In what ways and to what degrees does the experience of trauma affect victims' capacity to reliably narrate events that caused or accompanied that trauma? Issues 1, 3, 5 and 6 relate in very visible ways to the debates between humanism and postmodernism outlined above. Issues 2, 4 and 7 also have connections to these debates, but in more indirect ways.

Let us now take each of these questions in turn.

(1) Can language give us accurate representations of history and of the world in general?

In the present context, 'representation' refers to the processes and complexities involved in narrating actual historical occurrences. Such narrating goes beyond mere physical 'facts': it involves, for example, subjective individual feelings, and interpretations of what various 'facts' mean in historical, moral and other terms. Most current academic studies of Holocaust autobiography assume that written testimonies cannot simply hold a mirror up to life in the concentration camps. One reason for this is the assumption that *narrative in general* cannot be one hundred percent accurate because, for instance, no writer can include every detail and nuance of an experience. Another reason has to do with the nature of the medium in which memoir is written—language.

Jacques Derrida is the most important figure in a movement that expresses scepticism about the representational powers of language. Derrida termed this position, and the techniques of reading associated with it, Deconstruction. Detailed accounts of Derrida's thought are readily available,[130] but a preliminary statement of his view of language might go like this: Meaning can't just pass from me to you like a dollar coin. Meanings leak and change in transit, so that what I 'meant' will never be the exact meaning you receive. This is partly because words aren't snapshots of the world: they are a conventional and often biased means of referring to a world they cannot adequately capture. One reason for this is that 'the world'—or our sense of the way things are—is itself created and filtered through language. Beyond this, linguistic communication (and note that, strictly speaking, not all forms of linguistic communication involve acts of representation) entails complexities at the points of saying and receiving. I may have the feeling that I 'know' precisely what I want to say, but Derrida (like Freud) thinks that many of my intentions, linguistic and otherwise, are actually more mixed and opaque than I realize. What I 'mean' to say, at least in cases of complex communication, will never simply be what I thought I meant. When you 'receive' what I've said or written, the process is not like etching, where (say) words are simply engraved in an inert surface; it's more like a process of interpretation, of 'putting my own spin' on things. You'll process what I say in terms of your own experience. Derrida believes that linguistic communication is always like this to some extent, regardless of whether we're communicating face-to-face or via a written text.

Many readers of Derrida, myself included, have interpreted his views as meaning that language cannot reliably report on historical reality—such as the actualities of the Holocaust. I will not repeat here certain philosophical objections to his theories which a co-author and I have made elsewhere,[131] save to say that it is philosophically quite possible to explain how and why an adequate degree of reliability can be attained in certain verbal and written communications, including various forms of testimony, given that such communication is guided and governed by shared conventions and that the parties to the communication share, at least to some degree, a sense of wider cultural context. Such demonstrations can focus on the way people actually use language; they can also focus, as does the philosopher C. A. J. Coady's work on testimony,[132] upon the way testimony actually functions. As Coady shows, social life is possible only because we take on trust all manner of information that comes from the testimony of others. Testimony, in other words, is not restricted to reports of strange and horrific experiences; it frequently occurs in everyday life. If I ask someone who regularly travels the route how heavy the freeway traffic tends to be at 7.45 a.m. and she replies 'Very heavy: it takes fifty minutes to reach the city', I am seeking and receiving first-hand testimony from her.

Derrida strenuously denies that his position excludes the possibility of reliable representations of historical reality. He has argued that deconstruction is a philosophical investigation of the ultimate complexities and limitations of language, but not one which denies language's ability to 'get the job done' in less ultimate, everyday contexts. This view is somewhat akin to Wiesel's notion of communication that occurs even as it knows itself to be in some ultimate sense 'impossible'. Those who remain unconvinced by Derrida's disclaimer on this point may wonder why, if he does not deny the possibility of accurate representations of historical actuality, his work is so massively—almost obsessively—preoccupied with linguistic limitations and complexities, and apparently so much less interested in the ways language does indeed 'get the job done'. In very general terms his answer here seems to be that we don't just need to talk about the world: we must also keep under review our *ways* of talking, since they may be implicated in some of the problems that our talk about the world reveals. A further suggestion seems to be that postmodern linguistic innovations can provide more nuanced ways of talking about Holocaust and other complex experiences than more conventional forms of expression allow.

The postmodern French writer Maurice Blanchot is much admired for the way in which he uses a paradoxical but poetic style to write about the Holocaust, as in this passage from his *The Writing of the Disaster*:

> Weakness is grief weeping without tears; it is the murmur of the plaintive voice or the restless rustling of that which speaks without words, the dearth, the exhaustion of appearance. Weakness eludes all violence, which, even if it is oppressive omnipotence, can do nothing to the passivity of dying. [133]

One might admire such prose, but it raises two broader questions about Holocaust representation. First, if this approaches some sort of adequacy in representing the subject-matter, does it not suggest that it isn't language *per se* but rather particular kinds and traditions of language use which set limits on representation in general, and Holocaust representation in particular? Second, is it really the case that existing languages are so profoundly inadequate for these purposes? Surely one ought not to be too sweeping here. What we might call 'ordinary', 'everyday' language, limited in its poetic and descriptive depth, may well be restricted in its ability to convey Holocaust experience. But great writers like Primo Levi and Paul Celan manage to write with tremendous power and penetration about the Holocaust, because they have the linguistic range and creativity required for this daunting task. Their linguistic powers already challenge existing expressive forms. They did not need poststructuralist scepticism about language in general, nor poststructuralist expressive styles. This (admittedly rough) distinction between 'everyday' and 'literary' language runs deep in the present study of Australian Jewish autobiography, partly because the better the writing the deeper it goes—whether into Holocaust or other experience.

One reason for possible concern about Derrida's views is that they may seem to play into the hands of Holocaust deniers who will be only too pleased to hear that a famous modern philosopher—and a Jew to boot—says that we cannot write accurate accounts of history. Derrida, a deeply compassionate man who said that '"Auschwitz" has obsessed everything that I have ever been able to think',[134] loathed Holocaust denial and was horrified by the suggestion that his theories might be in any way compatible with it. In fact he wrote a good deal about Holocaust testimony and testimony in general. In a typically complicated but representative formulation he writes that 'testimony remains irreducibly heterogeneous to proof';[135] in other words, that we would look in vain for some utterly definitive, infallible proof of the ultimate truthfulness of any individual testimony. However, he does not believe that this renders the quest for truth—for instance, the painstaking reading of Holocaust testimonies to piece together the closest possible approximation to truth—pointless. If this is indeed what he is saying, it may not be particularly controversial, and we might wonder why his accounts of language and epistemology have been regarded as so radical: after all, many non-philosophers and non-postmodernists would agree that one hundred percent truth—whatever that means—is beyond the reach of mere mortals and that the best we can do, with respect to the Holocaust or any other domain of experience, is to get as close as we can to what seems to be the 'truth'. Whether one is convinced by Derrida's claims here will in part depend on how one understands the impact on his thought of one of his major intellectual forebears, the nineteenth-century German philosopher Friedrich Nietzsche, whose notion of 'perspectivism' proposes that we cannot derive definitively reliable consensus about the world from individual people's subjective perceptions of it.

In his recent book *The Holocaust and the Postmodern*, Robert Eaglestone argues that 'postmodernism… is a response to the Holocaust',[136] by which he means that the work of many of the key postmodern thinkers has been centrally motivated by Holocaust anguish and by a wish to open up possible new cultural directions for the post-Holocaust world. Eaglestone's book has none of the freewheeling verbal pizzazz that characterizes much postmodern writing and one is grateful for the judicious clarity with which he presents his case, not least in his expositions of Derrida, Levinas, Blanchot and other postmodern thinkers. Nevertheless, his case is a bold one: far from conceding that, as many think, postmodern theories, with their scepticism about the adequacy of linguistic representation, complicate and even disable our efforts to understand what actually happened during the Holocaust, Eaglestone claims a particular affinity between post-Holocaust anguish and postmodern thought. Indeed he argues that postmodernism can help deliver us from the historical evils that caused the Holocaust.

This last claim is by no means new. As Eaglestone readily acknowledges, there has long been a school of thought, most famously articulated by the German social theorist Theodor Adorno,[137] that the Holocaust was in some way a peculiarly modern occurrence; that it was the culmination of certain trends in modern history, in particular a confluence of late capitalism, modern technology and a certain kind of calculating rationality sometimes associated with the Enlightenment. I for one find such views unconvincing. Genocide is age-old and in no sense necessarily the product of modernity. Whilst the Enlightenment does in some respects feature cool, 'instrumental' kinds of rationality, it also highlights other, much more empathetic kinds—the Holocaust scholar and historian Dominick LaCapra calls this 'substantive' as opposed to 'technical' rationality[138]—and it was, after all, a period of immense democratization and moral awakening, not least in terms of Jewish emancipation. In spite of this, much postmodern thinking is hostile to the Enlightenment. Where then does someone like Eaglestone, who shares this hostility, direct us for alternative cultural and philosophical possibilities—ones whose pedigrees are not sullied by entanglements with the Enlightenment, capitalist democracy, humanism and the like? One answer is the Jewish philosopher Emmanuel Levinas. Another, as we have seen, is Derrida. Still another is the German philosopher Martin Heidegger, whose work had a massive influence on Derrida.

In order better to grasp the intellectual contexts of Derrida's work, it is useful to add that his thinking draws heavily upon two traditions (among others): one, a tradition of language theory that owes much to the Swiss linguist Ferdinand de Saussure, the other a philosophical tradition known as phenomenology, of which Heidegger is the most influential exponent.

Eaglestone's case for Derrida rests heavily on one of his central concepts, an inherently elusive idea known as the 'trace'.[139] But as Eaglestone admits, Derrida inherits that notion from Heidegger—and Heidegger was a National Socialist who was famously reluctant to denounce the Holocaust, even after the war. What sort of cultural pedigree, we might ask, is *that*?[140] Eaglestone is right to see 'a terrible irony'[141] in the fact that post-Holocaust culture might have to turn to a Nazi sympathizer for help. One might equally see a 'terrible irony' in the fact that the Holocaust was perpetrated from the centre of post-Enlightenment Europe, without suggesting that Holocaust blame should therefore be imputed undiscriminatingly to the Enlightenment. In matters like this I think that Yehuda Bauer, a renowned and admirably balanced Holocaust historian, is much closer to the mark when he writes that in order to pursue their lunatic utopian racial vision it was necessary for the Nazis

> to revolt against everything that had been before: middle-class and Judeo-Christian morality, individual freedom, humanitarianism—the whole package of the French Revolution and the Enlightenment.[142]

Whatever Derrida's philosophy of representation amounts to, there is the question—as there always is in the case of powerful original thinkers—of how his thought is understood and deployed by others. Thus James E. Young, an influential figure in Holocaust studies, writes that in the case of a crime reported in a Holocaust diary, 'what was evidence for the writer at the moment he wrote is now, after it leaves his hand, only a detached and free-floating sign, at the mercy of all who would read and misread it'.[143] And again: 'The fictiveness in testimony does not involve disputes about facts, but the inevitable variance in perceiving and representing these facts, witness by witness, language by language, culture by culture.'[144] Young is taking at face value Derrida's suggestions about the leakiness and inadequacies of linguistic communication (the notion of a 'free-floating' linguistic sign which is not anchored in reality is a *sine qua non* of poststructuralist language theory), and the limits imposed by personal perspective. So much so that he seems to conclude that written survivor accounts must *of necessity* be seriously—disablingly—unreliable. Such a view is deeply problematic in philosophical terms; it is also deeply objectionable in moral terms, given that survivor-authors want so desperately to tell the world what happened. Young is clearly anguished by his conclusions; indeed, like Eaglestone, he sees in them 'the horrible irony... that, as nearly all the diarists and many of the survivors remind us, their insights, interpretations, and eyewitness descriptions may even be less reliable in a factual sense *because* of their proximity to events'.[145]

I do not know whether Young is right to claim that 'nearly all the diarists and many of the survivors' see the accuracy of their recollections as being compromised by their proximity to the Holocaust. I can only say that my reading of Australian Holocaust memoir does not confirm this observation. Whether right or wrong, the observation is based not just on assumptions about language, but also, and very importantly, on assumptions about trauma—a topic to which I will return.

(2) Was the world of the concentration camps fundamentally different (or 'discontinuous') from the world at large?

As is evident from the Wiesel passage quoted above, the complexities of representation don't concern only the medium (language) in which the representing is to be done: in the case of the Holocaust the complexities extend to the nature of the events and feelings that are to be represented. Does the everyday world provide languages capable of communicating about such horror? Will people who have been spared such experiences be willing to face others' accounts of them? Can a person not directly acquainted with the sheer strangeness of what is sometimes called 'the concentrationary universe'[146] adequately process descriptions of it? Here, as in so many areas of Holocaust scholarship and memoir, there are differing views.

Elsewhere, with memorable succinctness, Wiesel puts what might be called 'the discontinuity view'—that the camps were radically unlike other human worlds: 'We speak in code, we survivors, and this code cannot be broken, cannot be deciphered, not by you no matter how much you try.'[147] Nevertheless the desire to transmit the story can be very powerful (even if only a small percentage of survivors have done so in written form[148]). In his memoir *After Forty Years Silence*, the Australian autobiographer Alex Colman explains that he has 'resolved to break the silence of forty years'[149]— his silence—in particular because he is haunted by a question:

> Could it happen again? I shudder to think what may come. I feel so deeply that
> the world is poised on the brink of disaster, that I must do my utmost to remind
> the world of the pain, the misery, the suffering and the agonising torture that
> I, with millions of others, was forced to endure—simply because of being born
> Jewish.[150]

Such long silence is a common pattern, but it is not the only one: some
survivors recounted their experiences in various settings—writing, family,
lecturing, oral testimonies—sooner than this. Abraham Wajnryb speaks
for a significant group of Australian survivor-authors when he says
that during the war 'each of us developed a compulsion to tell our story',
and that the drive to get the story told in fact became one of the principal
motivations for survival. 'The idea that one had to remain alive in order to
tell the world what had happened in the ghettos and in the camps bothered
us all a great deal.'[151] Whatever the pattern, it is clear that when they do
speak, these survivors, like their counterparts elsewhere, are driven by an
overwhelming need to be heard and believed. Many will concede that their
memories are not perfect. Kitia Altman writes with special power about the
ambiguities and terrors of memory:

> What does it mean to remember?
>
> Is it to look at a photograph of people or places that were once familiar?
>
> Or is it more like finding a misplaced precious object? And once the object
> is in your hands again, you start to marvel at the many details obliterated by the
> passage of time and buried under an avalanche of new images.
>
> Or is remembering like an archaeological dig—the geography more or less
> familiar but still requiring will and determination to find something?
>
> That's how it was with this memory.
>
> A memory at first difficult to place, a chaos of details from which, piece by
> tiny piece, image by image, I gleaned a shape. A shape without a face, a body
> without a name. I probably never knew the name. The face was the same as
> thousands of others in this place cursed by God and man alike.[152]

This superb passage contains a fine psychological insight. Freudian theories
of the mind too often tend to draw a rigid distinction between things we
can know and remember, and things which, because they are allegedly

'buried' in the unconscious, we cannot access, at least not without the help of a psychoanalyst. But, as Stephen Mitchell[153] and some other psychologists have argued, such rigid differentiations ignore the part the will can play in penetrating opaque or frightening memories. It is perhaps not so much a matter of what one *can* know, as of how much, and in what ways, one *wants* to know. Like many survivors, Altman both wants and does not want to remember; but the fact that she chose to write autobiography suggests that the wanting is more powerful than the not-wanting, and that she is prepared to engage her will in the very difficult business of remembering. It seems to me that few of these writers seriously doubt the essential veracity of their own recollections. Schmul Schwartz is typical in saying that his memoir 'contains facts etched into my memory with blood'.[154] Like Wiesel they are often haunted by the fear of not being believed—because the world will not want to know, or because their stories almost defy belief. As Lawrence Langer writes in his study of Holocaust oral testimonies, 'One of the regrets of anguished memory is its premonition, during the very process of testifying, of the absence of a common ground between *its* reality and our attempts to imagine it.'[155] Still, testimony is among other things a testament to the overpowering need to tell, however fraught that process might be.

Arguments for the continuities between normal and camp experience take various forms. This is as it should be: generalizations about similarity and difference between camp and other realities are far less helpful than comparisons along particular axes. Tzvetan Todorov's *Facing the Extreme: Moral life in the concentration camp*s, a work which identifies with 'the philosophy of humanism',[156] offers one of the best-known affirmations of 'the continuity between ordinary experience and that of the camps',[157] an affirmation that stresses the enduring presence of moral life under extreme circumstances. (Unlike Adorno, Todorov sees the Holocaust as a natural outgrowth of totalitarianism, not of capitalist modernity.) Viktor Frankl, survivor, psychiatrist and author of a famous Holocaust memoir, *Man's Search for Meaning*, also argues the continuity case in fundamentally humanist terms. According to Frankl, human beings possess an inalienable capacity for decision, a power of the *will*, whereby they can choose what attitudes they will adopt towards a given situation, and what meanings they will derive from it, even in a hell like Auschwitz. He argues that a certain 'spiritual freedom'[158] was possible even in the camps. 'Fundamentally, therefore, any man can, even under such circumstances, decide what shall become of him—mentally and spiritually.'[159] This emphasis on the individual's power of decision, in particular a will to meaning in life, was to shape Frankl's postwar therapeutic practice of 'logotherapy'.

Dori Laub, child survivor, psychiatrist and witness to many verbal Holocaust testimonies, sees deep continuities between the existential challenges that faced—and face—Holocaust survivors and those that most of us encounter:

> The survival experience, or the Holocaust experience, is a very condensed version of most of what life is about: it contains a great many existential questions, that we manage to avoid in our daily living, often through preoccupation with trivia. The Holocaust experience is an inexorable and, henceforth, an unavoidable confrontation with those questions. This listener [to Holocaust testimony] can no longer ignore the question of facing death; of facing time and its passage; of the meaning and purpose of living; of the limits of one's omnipotence; of losing the ones that are close to us; the great question of our ultimate aloneness; our otherness from any other; our responsibility to and for our destiny; the question of loving and its limits; of parents and children; and so on.[160]

Laub's formulation is powerful but also general. Elsewhere he speaks of particular cases and of the variations that occur from one instance to another. This is important because, in my view, one of the great perils of Holocaust analysis is the tendency to over-generalize. One of the inestimable values of Holocaust autobiography is its ability to take us beyond generalizations and help us to learn (within admitted limits) how particular people experienced these events. This cautionary note about over-generalization is not a theoretical but rather an empirical matter. After all, conditions were not the same in all camps, or even in all parts of particular camps. Some people were able to tolerate some conditions more robustly than others, thus perhaps retaining a stronger grasp of continuities between camp and normal life, and thus being better equipped later to bring these two realities into meaningful conjunction in their written autobiographies. Some people were less abused than others for pragmatic reasons—Primo Levi frankly admits that he fared better than many because as a trained chemist he was less expendable to the Nazis—and in this sense they did not experience entirely the same conditions as less fortunate victims. It is important to note that we know about such variations principally *from* written and verbal Holocaust testimony, and because we feel that having satisfied ourselves as to the reliability of certain survivor-narrators we can take much of what they say on trust, as the ethos of 'realism' encourages us to do.

With respect to Holocaust autobiography it's also important to remember that many volumes do not restrict themselves to camp life. Where they also describe prewar—and sometimes postwar—life, there are opportunities for authors to create stylistic and other continuities between their descriptions of camp life and what occurred before and after. And of course written testimony, unlike oral forms, provides opportunities for revision and for seeking greater integration between various parts of the narrative. The majority of Australian examples feature description of prewar life; some also narrate life after the war, though such narratives are very much in the minority. About 40 percent of the total author group devote 25 percent or more of their narratives to their lives in Australia; perhaps 35 percent allocate at least half of their pages to life in the Antipodes. Of those authors who were in concentration camps, about 20 percent devote one-quarter of their text to life in Australia, while about 10 percent devote half or more of their pages to the Australian portion of their lives. Those who survived the Holocaust as fugitives and were spared the horrors of the camps are more likely to devote substantial proportions of their books to the Australian phase of their lives: about 40 percent allocate one-quarter; upwards of 30 percent a half or more. Some authors achieve stylistic continuity between Holocaust and peacetime descriptions; in other cases there is a discernible shift from the often affectionate and lyrical reconstruction of the prewar world to a more mechanical reportage of life in the camps. Guta Goldstein writes thus of an early childhood memory:

> My mother taught me nursery rhymes and songs. I can still remember and sing them. I loved to hear her voice. She made my clothes and placed large ribbons in my hair. She made me daisy chains and plaited baskets from fragrant-smelling heather. When she bathed me, her wedding ring knocked against the wall of the bathtub making a sonorous sound.[161]

And thus of Auschwitz-Birkenau:

> It was late summer and the afternoons were hot. Always five abreast, we sat on the sun-dried, hard, clay ground in the hot sun between the barracks. We just sat. With a hard little stone, sometimes a splinter of wood, I would scratch out some sums on the yellow ground and practise my math, so that I would not forget it when I went back to school at war's end.[162]

A tonal shift such as this perhaps suggests a pattern of rupture-within-continuity: continuity, insofar as the description places horrific events in a larger life-sequence and, in this case, includes imaginative leaps forward into a postwar future; rupture, in that the events are so desolating that they threaten the sense of sequence and drain the narrating voice of some of its distinctive tones, rhythms and self-assurance.

(3) Should our assumptions when reading Holocaust memoir be 'realist' or 'anti-realist', or perhaps a combination of the two?

The notion of a rupture-within-continuity suggests that it may be too simple to think in terms either of absolute difference between Holocaust and other experience, or of unqualified continuity between the two. Michael Rothberg's *Traumatic Realism: The demands of Holocaust representation* attempts to steer a course between these poles and propose an accommodation between the radical-discontinuity and continuity theses. The book is also a critique of postmodern scepticism about the possibilities of accurate representation. Rothberg rejects 'the postmodern version of the [Holocaust] bystander's lament whereby "we didn't know" is transformed into "we can't know"'.[163] He rightly insists that we do in fact know a lot about the concentrationary universe and that, for the most part, we have obtained this knowledge from conventional historical scholarship and realist techniques of narration in Holocaust autobiography. However, he also concedes that traditional literary realism—say, of the kinds we find in Jane Austen or George Eliot—cannot cope with certain extreme aspects of Holocaust experiences which are light-years removed from the worlds Austen and Eliot write about. To the extent that Holocaust memoir exceeds 'the frameworks of both classical realism and the poststructuralist critique of representation',[164] we need a conception of the genre's methods that accommodates both the communicability *and* the alien extremity of much Holocaust experience. Rothberg terms this conception 'traumatic realism'. This sort of realism invites the reader of Holocaust memoir to identify where possible with the author's experience, but it also compels him to acknowledge the strangeness of what he reads and to be conscious of his obligations and responses as a reader-citizen of the post-Holocaust world. Rothberg proposes, then, a concept of 'realism under the sign of trauma';[165] a realism which takes account of the fact that virtually all who experienced the world of the camps suffered some degree of trauma, and that trauma can disturb the faculty of memory upon which reliable historical representation depends. To put it another way: while non-traumatic memory will tend to see things in sequence, and to relate various memories and remembered realities to one another, trauma can blast things out of sequence, can destroy the sense of connection between traumatic and other experiences. Rothberg admits that this puts strain on realism, which tends to work through sequence, connection and familiarity; but because realism is so essential to our knowledge of the Holocaust, he is not prepared to repudiate it. Instead, he proposes a form of realism that can accommodate the devastating disorientation that trauma often causes. This is 'traumatic realism'.

In effect, Rothberg thinks that we should exercise compassionate identification when we read Holocaust memoir (how, one might ask, could we *not*?), but without reading in a way that denies the gulf that separates those who have suffered horrific experiences from those who have not. (All such discussion, of course, applies to a whole range of horrific experience, not just to Holocaust suffering.) One reason Rothberg insists on this distinction is that we live in a post-Holocaust world and that the very notion of 'post-Holocaust' is ambiguous: at one level it suggests that the Holocaust is over and that we are now living in a time after its occurrence; but there's a very important sense in which it is not over, in which 'post' has the force of 'still shadowed by': the trauma remains for survivors and their families, while a wider human community continues to be horrified by the systematic and sadistic barbarity of this attempt to annihilate an entire people. Inevitably, that community has lost some confidence in human nature and the world more generally. In this sense, the Holocaust is more than a historical occurrence: it is one of those vast events that actually challenge or transform our sense of what human beings are like and of how, therefore, we should represent their histories. Innovative Holocaust historians like Saul Friedlander[166] try in their work to take account of this dual sense of the Holocaust's so-called 'historicity': its historical character, but also its transformative impact on our sense of what history is and how it should be written.

To live in a post-Holocaust world is then, for some at least, to live *with* the Holocaust, but also with the associated fact that the Holocaust is still widely represented in various modern media. Rothberg urges that we be aware of how it is represented—or mediated—in contemporary culture and of how we process the various kinds of representation.[167]

(4) Is it possible or ethically proper to identify closely with the experience of others, and in particular with the extreme experiences suffered by people in the camps?

Like Rothberg, Eaglestone is concerned with the problem of identification, albeit in a different way. His book resonates with an ethical injunction: you should not try to penetrate or possess another person's being or experience. This injunction, which is central to the work of the Emmanuel Levinas, has some roots in postmodernism and its responses to the Holocaust. In particular, there is the idea that certain destructive tendencies in Western culture, and especially in Western thought, helped to enable the Holocaust, and that these tendencies go right to the heart of our ways of being in the world, our very disposition towards the people and things we share the planet with. Eaglestone's term for this flawed attitude—which includes a habit of categorizing people and things, often in ranked order of supposed superiority and inferiority ('black' above 'white', 'gentile' above 'Jew')—is 'the metaphysics of comprehension'.[168] This means a sort of grasping, prying, classifying, controlling intrusiveness towards others. To the extent that it can be summarized, the opposite attitude would be one of profound reverence for others; a preparedness to cherish and respect them as other in relation to one's self. According to Eaglestone, among the dispositions inconsistent with such reverence is the act of identification whereby we implicitly claim that another person's reality—or story—is fundamentally like our own.

There are various possible objections to Eaglestone's position. For one thing, it is very hard to conceive of a viable form of moral life that does not involve some significant degree of identification with others. Moral behaviours often entail 'feeling with', 'putting yourself in the position of' another. Without such identification, which typically involves extrapolating from our own feelings and needs in order to 'read' the feelings and needs of others, we would not know how to tailor our well-meaning moral acts to their intended recipients' benefit. This does not of course mean that all forms of identification are morally good or psychologically desirable: the sort of over-identification with the other that can fuel irrational sexual jealousy, for example, is clearly dangerous. But, as Eaglestone seems to acknowledge late in his book, it does not follow from this that all forms of identification are undesirable. Conversely, to withhold the feelings of interest and connection that often accompany identificatory impulses can actually leave the other feeling abandoned.

Eaglestone also seeks to characterize the experience we do in fact usually have when we read Holocaust autobiography. He suggests that these texts 'lead to identification and away from it simultaneously. This stress between centrifugal and centripetal forces is played out, but not resolved, in the texts of testimonies and it is this that characterizes the genre of testimony.'[169] I think that is too prescriptive—testimony does not possess this kind or degree of distinctiveness from all other autobiographical genres—but it is a fair description of what many of us feel when we read much Holocaust autobiography, and it is a respect-worthy attempt to negotiate some of the ambiguities and challenges that the genre presents. There are some things in such texts with which we can identify; others seem almost impossible to comprehend. Notwithstanding his disclaimers, it seems to me that, finally, Eagelstone is committed to postmodern scepticism about representation, be it in Holocaust testimony or other sorts of text, and to an anti-realist notion of how such texts should be read.

(5) Does the fact that no two people see anything in exactly the same way mean that we cannot agree about the 'truth' of certain representations of the world?

Epistemology is the branch of philosophy which explores the kinds and degrees of knowledge that human beings can have of the world. Testimony—written or verbal accounts based on eyewitness reports—

raises many epistemological questions, including: How reliable is the evidence of our senses? Does memory fade or become distorted over time? What if—as is often the case—two or more witnesses of an event see it differently? Is there such a thing as a narrative report which can be proven 'true' beyond reasonable doubt, or beyond any doubt whatever? Is there such a thing as an indisputably 'true' interpretation of an event or a text?

One of the hallmarks of modern culture in the West—and not just among postmodernists—is the increasing tendency to question the existence of objective, verifiable 'truth'. Nietzsche's notion of 'perspectivism' has been highly influential in asserting that each individual can see the world only according to his or her own individual perspective, and that there can be no final and complete synthesis of points of view that will provide totally objective and exhaustive understanding. When James Young writes that 'Holocaust literary testimony is *also* interpretive',[170] he is in a sense denying that such testimonies can be objectively true. He's not suggesting—and here things become tricky—that certain 'facts' don't exist. He wouldn't, for example, doubt that specific Holocaust events occurred on the days identified by documentary evidence. His point is rather that there is no such thing as an interpretation-free fact: even where facts are 'certain', they must still be interpreted, and he lays great emphasis on the supposition that different people will interpret them differently. Hence his comment, quoted earlier, that the 'fictiveness in testimony does not involve disputes about facts, but the inevitable variance in perceiving and representing these facts, witness by witness, language by language, culture by culture'.

This view of testimony pictures individual people as experiencing specific events and interpreting them in fundamentally individual ways. In his *Testimony*, Coady designates the individual so conceived 'the epistemologically isolated self'[171]—a conception of the self, as it happens, to which postmodern theory is in some respects strongly opposed. In critiquing this conception of self, and against the highly individualistic notion of testimony with which it tends to be associated, Coady cautions against focusing too exclusively on discrete events when thinking about the powers and limitations of testimony. As I have noted, testimony isn't just a matter of bearing witness to exceptional events; on the contrary, a vast amount of what we take for granted about our familiar selves and our familiar world has been received via the testimony of others: things as basic as our date of birth, through to more complex matters like our understanding of right and wrong. We do not, and should not, take everything on trust, of course; but social life depends on there being significant areas of agreement between individuals who have taken 'on trust' various kinds of information about the world. Indeed language itself works in this way: we can communicate through words because they often have widely agreed domains of meaning which we have taken on trust from others. Where something seems untrustworthy, or scarcely credible, we may test it against the perceptions of others. Such testing, too, requires the existence of a community that is already engaged in dialogue, and assesses things within already familiar—though not necessarily finally fixed—parameters.

The picture of testimony I have just given would suggest that we should not assume that a survivor's description of a camp atrocity is unreliable simply because it is her description, or her interpretation of what she thinks she saw. The description may be unreliable for particular circumstantial reasons (there may for instance be no existing language that can adequately capture this sadistic extremity); but we should not disbelieve her simply because she is an individual who bears witness. To do so is to underestimate our reliance on testimony in general, our well-founded confidence in its capacity for trustworthy report; and to miss the extent to which dialogue, which includes weighing and comparing many thousands of individual testimonies, has enabled us to arrive at significant consensus not just about what 'happened' in the Holocaust but about what it 'meant'.

What it 'meant' goes way beyond the attribution of historical causes, personal motivations of key actors, and so on. What it 'meant' is also, and very centrally, a *moral* matter, and here in particular I think we need to be very careful about saying, as loose uses of Derridean theory sometimes do, that 'it's all a matter of interpretation'. Consider for example the sickening deportation of the children from the Lodz ghetto which started on 5 September 1942 and went on for about twelve days. There is no doubting the 'fact' that this happened: transcripts of the infamous speech in which Chaim Rumkowski, the Jewish puppet administrator of the ghetto, delivered the deportation edict are still in existence, and we have many eyewitness accounts of the horror that ensued. Some of these accounts are to be found in the memoirs of Australian Jews. Consider this passage from

David George Gilbert's *The Lights and Darkness of My Being*:

> First of all they checked the rooms in all houses to make sure no children had been hidden. We had been standing leaning against a wall, trembling with terror. Susan tried to hide behind us. When one of the soldiers passed, we thought he missed her. But when he came back, he noticed her. He grabbed Susan by her coat and pushed her to the truck. There she stood for a while under guard, looking in despair at us for help. On the look of her helpless face we could read what she was trying to say: 'Why are you just standing there? Is there nothing you can do for me?' I was stunned and speechless. I refused to believe this heartbreaking nightmare could be really true. Gisela broke down, bursting into tears, and when she tried to get near Susan, she was warned by a Jewish policeman not to move. Together with lots of other kids Susan disappeared in the open truck.
>
> Never in my life had I seen so much terror in children's eyes. [...]
>
> Do you know what it is like to write in the diary the memories of the loss of our brutally murdered innocent child? All this happened forty-three years ago, but the grief and very painful memories stay forever. In all those years, not one single day has passed without seeing in my mind Susan's helpless, distressed face when she was taken away from us.[172]

No doubt there were shades of difference in the way the people involved in this horror responded to it—some parents might have collapsed, others become hysterical; some children may have become catatonic, others screamed all the way to the gas chambers; some of the guards may have been disturbed or moved, others completely unfeeling; some parents may have been more inclined than others to believe Nazi assurances that the children we being taken to a safe haven. Such variations would not be surprising, but how significant are they? And how significant is it that Gilbert lacks the expressive finesse to make consummate art of this horror? Surely the general import of the scene is clear enough, both emotionally and morally. No one who has not been in such an atrocious situation will be able fully to identify with Gilbert's experience, but anyone with a modicum of sensitivity will be able to sympathize with the description.

What about varying interpretive perspectives that might result from cultural difference, as in Young's 'culture by culture'? Alas, Nazism was a culture of sorts, and no doubt most or all of those who mandated the deportation of the Lodz children saw the Jews through the lunatic lens of Nazi ideology. What then? Are we to say that this was just another perspective; that it was no more right or wrong than any other, but merely different? The notion that one cannot make moral assessments of other cultures because they are fundamentally dissimilar to one's own (so-called 'cultural relativism') runs deep in much postmodern literary and cultural theory. No respectable Holocaust scholar of any complexion would argue this line, and in his highly regarded exposition of Nietzsche's thought Alexander Nehamas insists that 'perspectivism... is not equivalent to relativism';[173] but it is fair to assert that cultural relativism is the logical consequence of naïve versions of perspectival theory.

(6) Is there such a thing as human nature?

Terrence Des Pres's *The Survivor: An anatomy of life in the death camps*,[174] a pioneering account of the concentrationary universe and the testimonies of those who survived, is one of the most moving and intelligent books in the field. The author's position differs sharply from many postmodern views in that he has a concept of human nature—a concept which, moreover, occupies a central place in his humanist orientation. On the whole, as I have noted, postmodern thought either is sceptical about concepts of human nature or rejects them outright. Two assumptions tend to be at work here. The first is that human beings are caused to be the way they are by their cultural environments, and not by characteristics that are 'hard-wired' into the species; thus there is no human nature as such. The second assumption links to the aforementioned scepticism about linguistic representation. It says that even if there is in some ultimate sense such a thing as 'human nature', our languages, which are already loaded with cultural presuppositions, could not penetrate to that nature's essence, could not provide an objective representation of it. Des Pres, on the other hand, spends the last twenty or so pages of his book outlining a view, heavily influenced by evolutionary theory and moral philosophy, of what human nature is like. He insists that we must learn from the Holocaust what it has to tell us about human nature—both its diabolical and its finer propensities. Yehuda Bauer agrees: 'What happened before can happen again. We are all possible victims, possible perpetrators, possible bystanders.'[175] In other words, these dire possibilities are always with and even within us, and can erupt given certain precipitating circumstances.

I do not know whether everyone is a potential torturer, but I do agree that the Holocaust must be understood, very centrally, as a reflection of human nature. Intellectual analyses of the Holocaust which in principle deny the concept of human nature are in my view disabled by that denial. This would apply to Derrida's deconstructive critique of the distinction between 'nature' and 'culture',[176] as it would to Adorno's thesis about modern capitalist culture's role in the catastrophe.

There is no denying that the concept of human nature is philosophically difficult and that it has given rise to various debates. One of these concerns the question whether human nature includes an inclination to act morally. The sadism of Holocaust perpetrators has profoundly challenged sanguine assessments of human nature. This is one reason why postmodernists came to doubt certain traditional humanist presuppositions about human beings and to see the human individual as fragmented rather than coherent, as fundamentally shaped by cultural factors; and why humanists like Todorov were moved to declare that evidence of ongoing moral life in the camps shows that 'moral reactions are spontaneous, omnipresent, and eradicable only with the greatest violence'.[177] Todorov believes that, like the capacity for evil, such 'reactions' are in some sense intrinsic to human nature: 'moral values and behaviours are a constitutive dimension of life'.[178]

Just as readings of Holocaust autobiography tend to vary according to whether the camp world is assumed to be continuous or discontinuous with the everyday world, so they tend to vary according to whether or not readers believe that human beings possess profound internal coherence and natural moral inclinations. In fact, many of these readings were motivated by a need to ask, after this confidence-shaking cataclysm, what human beings are really like.

Des Pres's position locates the sources of Nazi barbarity in human nature, but, like Todorov and Frankl, it also finds among camp populations evidence of quite widespread and apparently instinctive moral behaviour, behaviour suggestive of innate moral proclivities: 'Life in the camps was savage, and yet there was *also* a web of mutual aid and encouragement, to which all books by survivors testify.'[179]

Such affirmations should, I think, be seen not just as descriptions but as morally deliberate and powerful acts of resistance. Des Pres reports a survivor of Dachau saying:

> 'The SS guards took pleasure in telling us that we had no chance of coming out alive, a point they emphasized with particular relish by insisting that after the war the rest of the world would not believe what had happened; there would be rumours, speculations, but no clear evidence, and people would conclude that evil on such a scale just was not possible.'[180]

Holocaust autobiography, then, is an act of resistance to genocidal brutality but also to the attempt to inflict silence on victims; reading and writing about Holocaust narratives, witnessing their witnessing, is a continuation of that same act. Early on, Des Pres comments with respect to the camp experience: 'An agony so massive should not be, indeed cannot be, reduced to a bit of datum in a theory.'[181] The remark typifies a certain humanist attitude to theory. It does not deny the usefulness of theoretical paradigms and explanations, but it is wary of imposing abstract theoretical constructs on particulars of experience. Des Pres is typical of humanist scholarship in wanting to move back and forward between theoretical generalizations and empirical particulars.

In very broad terms, then, it helps in considering various approaches to Holocaust memoir to distinguish between humanist and postmodern ones. As will be apparent, my sympathies are principally with the former. But this is by no means to deny that certain affinities—certain humane commitments, for example—can exist between these two approaches. It is noteworthy that Eagelstone's closing remarks call for the development of a 'postmodern humanism'.[182]

I want to conclude this section with a discussion of Lawrence Langer's *Holocaust Testimonies*, a book that is exemplary in its openness to the ambiguity of much Holocaust experience and to various approaches to Holocaust narrative. At the outset Langer states his objection, based on the taped testimonies he has witnessed, to 'the principle of discontinuity which argues that an impassible chasm separates'[183] the camp world from the world in general. Yet on this point, as on many others, his view is complicated by his finding that Holocaust testimony, even sometimes that of a single individual, will comprise not one voice but an array of voices, not one but multiple registers of memory; as he puts it, 'several currents flow at differing depths in Holocaust testimonies'.[184] Langer quotes approvingly Blanchot's attempts to find a new form of expression that can capture something of the terrifying paradoxicality and perversity of Holocaust experience. But he is also drawn to the humanistic orientation of the Canadian contemporary moral philosopher Charles Taylor. Like Todorov, Taylor believes that moral behaviours and orientations are intrinsic to human life.[185] Langer would like to believe this too; he would like to be confident that what he terms 'heroic memory' is right to insist on a fundamental 'connection between agency and fate';[186] that is, between how we choose to live and what happens to us. But alas, these testimonies often bespeak what he calls 'unheroic memory'—a register of memory and experience which proclaims precisely the 'absence' of that link between agency and fate, and the demise of the very 'qualities of inwardness, freedom, and individuality'[187] which Taylor affirms as the defining characteristics of post-Enlightenment Western human identity. I have noted that oral testimony and written autobiography differ in certain important ways, and to this extent not all of Langer's findings will necessarily apply—or apply without qualification—to Australian Jewish autobiography. Nevertheless, his anguished concluding observations have very broad application. Holocaust testimony, both oral and written, confronts us with a historical trauma so massive that it can be very hard to know finally what to affirm, what to doubt and what to disavow.

(7) In what ways and to what degrees does the experience of trauma affect victims' capacity to reliably narrate events that caused or accompanied that trauma?

Scholars and therapists in the area now known as Trauma Studies sometimes distinguish between 'historical trauma', which is in some sense built into and therefore widely experienced in a given environment (say, the dread many feel living in an era of nuclear weapons), and 'structural trauma', which is somehow specific to the experience of a particular individual (for instance, if a light plane crashes into a nearby house, thereby traumatizing a child).[188] Holocaust trauma can be of both kinds. For many people there is something inherently—historically—traumatic about living 'after Auschwitz', even if they had no direct exposure to Holocaust events. A survivor of Auschwitz will presumably have this kind of trauma superimposed on emotions caused by particular horrors she experienced in the camp.

Some academic accounts tend to blur the line between historical and structural trauma in a way that fails adequately to acknowledge the difference between, for example, being tortured in Auschwitz and reading about such tortures without ever having endured or witnessed them. Cathy Caruth's influential book *Unclaimed Experience: Trauma, narrative, and history*[189] is arguably guilty of blurring the line, in part because her application of the theories of the French postmodern psychoanalytic theorist Jacques Lacan suggests that the experience of trauma is intrinsic to the human psyche, regardless of particular events in an individual's history or the structural features of a given historical moment.

Trauma Studies derives its core definition of trauma from Freud.[190] In fact Freud returned to the topic on several occasions and his thinking about it changed somewhat over time. But the core definition of trauma entails three points. First, trauma is an event for which the person who suffers it is not adequately prepared. Second, the shock of the experience is so great that the mind deflects it into the unconscious, where in ways obscure to the victim it takes on a sort of life of its own (as Dori Laub says, 'massive trauma precludes its registration'[191]). Third, this life of its own can cause various symptoms, the quintessential one being involuntary 'reruns' of the experience—like images of the planes ploughing into the Twin Towers which many New Yorkers have suffered since 11 September 2001.[192] This phenomenon of involuntary recall shows that traumatic experiences aren't always hidden in the unconscious. Some concentration-camp survivors will be haunted by memories of camp life which come crashing into consciousness unbidden; others will have more controlled access to such memories, in that they can choose whether or not to summon them up; others again will have 'black holes' in memory where horrific experiences have indeed been filed away in the unconscious, such that the person is unaware of them and cannot recall them without some sort of assistance; for instance, from a therapist or facilitating witness to Holocaust testimony. Trauma, then, can take various forms, some of which won't necessarily fit our theoretical constructs of it. When James E. Young writes that 'the horrible irony is that, as nearly all the diarists and many of the survivors remind us, their insights, interpretations, and eyewitness descriptions may even be less reliable in a factual sense *because* of their proximity to events', he seems to be asserting that victims of Holocaust trauma will necessarily be unable to give reliable reports of it because trauma necessarily distorts memory.

It doesn't appear to me that Australian Holocaust memoirists generally 'remind us' of this supposed limitation—a limitation that would indeed be a 'horrible irony' if true. On the contrary, the majority seem to believe that they can remember enough to convey with some authority what it was that happened to them in the camps and elsewhere. One of the experiences many report is a narrowing of emotional range, itself a survival response: 'The span of our emotions was limited, nearly as limited as our physical life', writes Abraham Wajnryb.[193] But these writers do not seem to assume that such narrowing at the time renders them flawed witnesses later on. It seems that in this narrowed state much was being filed away and that later acts of memory can provide a kind of retrospective coloration to what was experienced in grim monotone at the time.

James Young, I believe, is prone to a confusion that often bedevils postmodern work on Holocaust trauma, not least a confusion between the notion of 'trauma' or 'post-traumatic stress' as a particular diagnostic category (something like Laub's 'massive trauma') which has specific symptoms (reruns, black holes, etc.), and 'trauma' in the colloquial sense of the word, where it means something like 'a horrible and massively distressing experience'. Except in very unusual circumstances, a Jew in Auschwitz would inevitably experience trauma in the colloquial sense of the term. However, it does not follow from this that everyone who suffers traumatic experiences of this kind will manifest the clinical symptoms of trauma or post-traumatic stress as a psychiatric disorder. Young, Caruth and others do the survivors and those who want to hear their stories a disservice by giving the impression that anyone who has had a horrible and massively distressing experience will necessarily be unable to give a reliable account of that experience. Of course *some* Holocaust testimony will be unreliable for this reason and in this way; but it is quite unwarranted and, I would argue, *an ethical affront* to survivors and their families, to claim that *all* survivor narrative is necessarily thus disabled. Nor should we use the term 'survivor' too sweepingly. There are various kinds and degrees of Holocaust survival, from mere physical survival that is blighted by crippling psychological disturbance, all the way through to that of the many who emerged from the horror to lead remarkably rich and fulfilling lives.

Survival of this resilient kind seems often to occur in individuals who have achieved a viable sense of attunement between their history and their feelings. Sometimes this occurs with the help of a therapist—therapy being a profoundly narrative activity. The notion that trauma blasts certain events irredeemably out of context, beyond integration in a wider individual life-narrative, is, as Rothberg's notion of 'traumatic realism' suggests, too simple.

Dori Laub's discussion of these matters, a discussion informed by therapeutic experience, is particularly valuable. Laub does not deny the depth of the problem. Of being caught up in the Holocaust he writes:

> [It] was also the very circumstance of *being inside the event* that made unthinkable the very notion that a witness could exist, that is, someone who could step outside of the coercively totalitarian and dehumanizing frame of reference in which the event was taking place, and provide an independent frame of reference through which the event could be observed. One might say that there was, thus, historically no witness to the Holocaust, either from outside or from inside the event.
>
> What do I mean by the notion of a witness from inside? To understand it one has to conceive of the world of the Holocaust as a world in which the very imagination of the *Other* was no longer possible. There was no longer an other to which one could say 'Thou' in the hope of being heard, of being recognized as a subject, of being answered. The historical reality of the Holocaust became, thus, a reality which extinguished philosophically the very possibility of address, the possibility of appealing, or of turning to, another. But when one cannot turn to a 'you' one cannot say 'thou' even to oneself. The Holocaust created in this way a world in which one *could not bear witness to oneself*.[194]

This is confronting indeed and might seem consistent with James Young's pessimism about testimony. But what Laub is describing is a particular condition at the time; a condition that might persist for ever, or might be substantially alleviated later on. What is needed is a reinstitution of the 'Thou' (famously associated with Martin Buber's *I and Thou*[195]), because to be human is to be *in-relation-to*—not just to others but to one's own self. If I cannot take a view of my self, cannot have feelings about my self, cannot tell the story of my self, I cannot have proper human selfhood; and this of course is what the Nazis tried to smash out of Jews (and others). Laub works, then, not just as a witness to testimony but as one who, by reinstituting the presence of the 'Thou', by being there to listen, actually *makes the act of testimony, the witnessing, possible*. In doing this he aims to reinstate the I–Thou relation between survivor and other, and between survivor and self. The process also aims at a '*re-externalizing of the event*' that trauma has rendered almost incommunicable, and a 'reassertion of the hegemony of reality';[196] in other words, the survivor can (to some extent at least) be released from the mad hell of the camps and be freed to live more confidently in the post-Holocaust world. Making witnessing possible means making it possible to bear witness to individual trauma and to collective history as well. After all, history is experienced by individuals. Hence Laub's comment that in listening to a particular woman's testimony he 'came to understand not merely her subjective truth, but the very historicity of the event, in an entirely new dimension'.[197] This emerged not just through what she said, but through her silences and hesitations as well.

Holocaust autobiography, too, works to reinstate the I–Thou relation. In addressing a reader it invites us to bear witness and so provide that other-presence which makes witnessing possible. Though its modes and dynamics differ in some ways from those of oral testimony, many of the underlying structures of communication are the same. I think it is important for readers of such texts to remember this, and to understand the necessity in these processes of a shared trust in the possibility of reliable memory and representation. This in turn entails the possibility of profound identification and sharing between people whose experiences may seem radically dissimilar. There is an ethical need, and a genuine opportunity, to read in the spirit of realism, or of traumatic realism if the text so requires.

Let us see how such an approach might work with a particular text, Samuel Pisar's *Of Blood and Hope*. Here Pisar, who lived postwar in Australia between the ages of sixteen and twenty-four, describes his arrival in a cattle-train at Auschwitz as a boy of twelve:

On the railroad platform there was panic—blows, screams, and the gruff barking of the dogs. I held my suitcase up against my chest for protection as I stumbled over corpses. But I don't remember being particularly terrified. Despite all that had happened in the space of a very few days, I felt more sure of myself, more controlled, as if I had suddenly aged several years. What I remember clearly is being numb and yet so thirsty that I thought I would die if I did not have some water.

In the chaos, I walked up to a guard who stood on the other side of a line of barbed wire encircling the station. He pointed his submachine gun at me. I unlocked my suitcase and pulled out a package my mother had placed in it—my father's pocket watch, with its long gold chain. I opened the package and offered it to the German. What gave me the idea, I think, was the trade my father had made with the Nazi in Bialystok: my stamp collection for food.

The guard studied the package as if he could not believe his eyes.

'Tie it up, throw it to me.'

'*Wasser*,' I said. I had to have water.

'Throw it to me!'

'*Wasser*,' I repeated.

I knew, of course, that he could shoot me. But then he would not have his booty, because he was on the other side of the wire.

He left. After a few minutes he was back with a bottle. He pushed it through the wire and I threw my package over. I think now of that trade as the most fruitful I have ever engaged in. It probably saved my life.

I brought the bottle to my lips, took a long gulp, then another. Before my thirst could he slaked there was a clamor, and a dozen of the deportees descended on me from all sides. Judging by their wild cries and faces I thought they were going to kill me; I surrendered the bottle and jumped aside. As outstretched hands grasped at it, the bottle dropped and broke. The men fell to their knees to lick up the moisture with their parched tongues as it slowly seeped into the ground.

* * *

As I observe the world scramble, on its knees, one might say, for the last barrel of oil, I cannot help recalling a proposal put forward by two Americans, experts on the problem of overpopulation, William and Paul Paddock. Their idea was that in dealing with underdeveloped countries in dire need of Western aid, we proceed on the principle of 'triage'—although a plainer word, such as selection, would mean the same thing. In brief, the industrialized nations would decide which of the needy countries were to be helped along the road of development and which were to be left to their own devices. We would identify, on strictly utilitarian grounds, the countries that were better able to contribute to our own economic and strategic objectives.[198]

The above passage, whose details are very close to those of many other descriptions of arrival at Auschwitz, has several layers. First, there is the overwhelming immediacy with which it recalls this scene of squalor, sadism and degradation. Then there is the description of Pisar's state of mind at that moment, reconstructed through a form of retrospective intro- spection that occurs in much Holocaust autobiography. He remembers feeling 'numb', a feeling often associated with trauma, but the numbness does not seem to have blocked his experience in a way that would cause a hole in later memory. On the contrary, he seems to recall the scene in great detail and to be confident that his recollection is at least substantially accurate. Momentarily the description shifts to the present and to a tone of calm rational appraisal—'I think now of that trade as the most fruitful I have ever engaged in'—before descending again into the chaos of the scene with the water bottle. The pitiful image of men licking moisture as it seeps into the ground is followed by a section-break which signals a shift of voice and register. Now Pisar the political adviser speaks, but this is a counsel with 'feeling'—empathy—born of his own experience of suffering, and the effect of the orchestration of the passage is to pit 'feeling' against utilitarian political policies, here a debased form of utilitarianism rooted entirely in self-interest. Pisar wants compassion and emotional identification, not self-interested bureaucratic calculation, to motivate aid, and the weave of voices is movingly effective in simultaneously addressing the past, the present and the future. The passage records a traumatic and bizarre experience, but in a way that contextualizes it morally and historically. It also explicitly asserts continuities between Auschwitz and other times and places.

Pisar's narrative position here is interesting. Like all who commit Holocaust memory to narrative, he isn't just remembering: he's remembering *for*. For whom? Sometimes it's for one's self, as when Gilbert says that he stays at his typewriter recalling shocking memories 'with hope of finding relief by getting it out of my system'.[199] But as Gilbert makes clear elsewhere, he is not writing merely for himself; his Introduction, which refers to 'hope that we can learn from the past', shows that the book is addressed to a collective readership that needs to know about the Holocaust. The reader, then, is in receipt of a narrative—a narrative which he or she witnesses, thereby becoming a witness to witnessing—and is invited to see, believe, know and adopt an appropriate moral attitude to what has been reported.

Pisar went on to a distinguished career in the law. But many survivors did not prosper, and many have never written of their Holocaust experiences. Those who have done so are a small and in a sense self-selecting group. The very fact that they are inclined or able to write suggests a level of accommodation with the past—even when such accommodation comes late in life—which some others do not have. This study of Australian Jewish autobiography remembers those who perished, those who have chosen not to write, and those whose survival has been too anguished for them to do so—people like the man described by Jacob's Rosenberg's wife, Esther, in the second volume of his autobiography: a survivor 'who won't undress when he goes to bed at night, keeps a packed suitcase by his door, walks to work for fear of trains, and sees a swastika in every church cross'.[200]

Generational Shifts in post-Holocaust Australian Jewish Autobiography

Holocaust trauma, as we know, passes down the generations—to children, but also in subtle ways to grandchildren and even beyond. In Australia, as in other places, it is important to consider generational patterns and influences in Holocaust memoir writing, since they help to explain variations in what is a strikingly heterogeneous body of work.

Like Australian Jewish autobiography more generally, Australian Holocaust memoir is extremely variable in quality, kind and intent. These texts need therefore to be approached on a case-by-case basis. It is particularly important to consider their conditions of authorship, including:

- the author's culture of origin;
- the degree of assimilation or separateness of the Jewish community from which the author comes;

- the degree of the author's religious and/or cultural identification with Judaism prior to arrival in Australia;
- the nature of the Holocaust experience, if the author is a survivor or otherwise severely affected by the Holocaust;
- the author's personal life in Australia after the Holocaust;
- the manner of Jewish community reception, and the life the author finds in Australia;
- the degree of the author's assimilation, separateness, and Jewish observance in Australia;
- the author's reasons for writing;
- the intended audience for the narrative.

These texts, in common with so much Holocaust memoir, look back, but also forward; indeed they often have a particular rhythm of looking back in order to look forward. The writers are motivated by the desire to bear witness to the catastrophe, but also to reconstruct the family tree decimated by the war. The narratives stand as memorials to those who perished, and also as archives of lost family for later generations. The dedications to murdered relatives are a special and extraordinarily poignant feature of such autobiographical writing:

> *I dedicate this book to the memory of my parents and family*
> *who perished in the Holocaust.*
>
> *It is also dedicated to my late husband.*
>
> *But mostly, I have written this book for my children and grandchildren*
> *so that they will understand and remember their heritage.*
> *It is my legacy to them.*[201]

It is important to distinguish between first- and second-generation (and even third-generation) narratives, because the children of survivors, some of whom were child survivors who were embroiled as youngsters in the Holocaust, often aspire to a greater degree of aesthetic sophistication in their narratives than do their author-parents. For the second generation the testimonial impulse is not quite the same as for the first. The children are of course at a greater temporal remove from the horror; fewer images, if any, are imprinted on their memories. When they bear witness they often depend on testimonial 'transmission chains':[202] parental stories, Holocaust literature, scholarship and autobiography. Frequently, too, offspring write of the Holocaust's generational aftermath: silences in the home about the past, ambivalent feelings towards parents at whom children cannot express anger or voice certain other of the more scalding emotions of family life.[203] Second-generation writers are often moved to ponder the possible metaphysical implications of what their elders have been through. They need, if possible, to seek some meaning in and beyond the terrible events; and part of that aspiration is to make art, or at least to fashion sophisticated autobiographical narratives that evince a sense of creative and emotional mastery. In the wake of the destruction, they want to create a literature that can endure.

Second-generation writers are usually better equipped than their parents to realize such aspirations. It is important to bear this in mind because the fame of major Holocaust writers like Primo Levi, Charlotte Delbo and Elie Wiesel, all of whom were intellectuals, tends to give the misleading impression that Holocaust writers in general are intellectuals. In fact, the great majority are not. Most had their educations interrupted or wrecked by the war. Their children are generally more highly educated than they. Many of these parents arrived in Australia with little or nothing and had to work extraordinarily hard to become established and raise their families. This left scant time for speculation or reflection. Their offspring have enjoyed the luxury of reflective space and have been more inclined to imaginative indulgence than their seniors, for whom reflection is laced with the threat of traumatic recollection. This helps to explain another characteristic difference between first- and second-generation narratives: the latter tend to be far more introspective. While the children tend to be intensely self-aware, the earlier narratives typically revolve around events, political contexts and implications, and discussions of historical causation. In part this is because, however traumatic their experiences may have been, the parents arrived in Australia with their adult identities already largely established. As we have seen, these identities often crystallized in cultures not given to psychological introspection.

For the second generation, however, including the child survivors, the construction of personal identity is a more complex matter. They have had to face the sense of existential doubleness that can occur when early processes of identity-formation undergo revision, or take shape, in a new adoptive culture. Such existential complications place much of the onus of construction on the individual, since the surrounding culture tends to seem too new, ambiguous, threatening or remote from ancestral cultural worlds to function as the source of secure identity-formation. This effort of self-construction precipitates a high degree of introspection and, concomitantly, the impulse to write psychologically self-scrutinizing autobiography. Thus arises a generational shift from narrative modes that incline to memoir and the bearing of witness, towards full-blown autobiography. But the shift, though widespread, is not uniform. A first-generation writer like Jacob Rosenberg displays many of the characteristics I have associated with second-generation texts.

Post-Holocaust Australian Jewish autobiography is best thought of, then, in terms of a spectrum. At one end, there are the first-generation narratives like Joseph West's *Survival, Struggle & Success*—these books are self-published, historico-testimonial in impulse, written primarily about, for and in memory of the author's family, not markedly concerned with aesthetic attainment, seldom given to introspective psychological analysis, and somewhat limited in linguistic range. At the other end are second-generation writers like Lily Brett, Andrew Riemer, Susan Varga and Arnold Zable—writers with significant literary reputations and highly evolved narrative techniques. They write for a general reading public, both Jewish and non-Jewish, in registers that are often self-consciously literary, highly introspective (Zable is something of an exception here), and reflective.

Let us now consider in detail some of the most accomplished voices in Australian Jewish autobiography.

Part Two

Narrative Art, and the Art of Community Narrative

'Hush My Wounded Soul, Dance My Broken Heart'

Jacob Rosenberg's *East of Time* and *Sunrise West*

A people's interrupted song

Jacob Rosenberg is Australia's most accomplished Jewish autobiographer and a world-class figure in Holocaust literature. His two autobiographical volumes, *East of Time*[204] and *Sunrise West*,[205] span the three major phases of his life. *East of Time* narrates his prewar childhood and adolescence in Lodz, through to the liquidation of the ghetto and his family's deportation to Auschwitz. *Sunrise West* recounts his incarceration in Auschwitz, Wolfsburg and Ebensee, his liberation, followed by three and a half years as a displaced person in Italy, and the early period of his life in Australia. Many Australian Holocaust narratives halt the narrative at the end of the war; others allocate a brief coda to life in the Antipodes. Whether or not they deal with the Australian phase, they tend to exhibit considerable stylistic unevenness: often the prose is at its most lyrical in describing the prewar world but, understandably, more mechanical when recalling Holocaust experience; where Australia figures, the writing is frequently tentative in its efforts to capture the nuances of the adoptive culture. Of course this is to be expected. Prewar European life, Holocaust dislocation, and life Down Under can seem worlds apart.

It takes a special writer to narrate such dramatically disparate domains of experience with stylistic consistency. A few autobiographers, like Israel Kipen and Leo Cooper, neither of whom was actually incarcerated during the Holocaust, manage this difficult feat, but most such authors employ a quasi-documentary writing style which does not aspire to literary sophistication. Jacob Rosenberg is different. In the world of his prose a quiet place is one 'where silence listened to the wind' [*EOT*, 62]; someone has a 'voice like a spider's footfall' [*SW*, 77]; a woman about to enter the Lodz ghetto with her family and a cartload of possessions stands desolate, 'her face a tapestry of murdered dreams' [*EOT*, 114]. Rosenberg, author of three volumes of poetry and prose in Yiddish, another three books of poetry in English, and a collection of English short stories, writes autobiography in a unique mode of prose poetry—a mode which deftly spans and integrates the various chapters of his life.

Born to a working-class family in Lodz in 1922, Rosenberg grew up in a remarkably rich cultural milieu. His father, Gershon, was a leading member of the Lodz branch of the Bund, a Jewish socialist movement which espoused Yiddish and sought Jewish emancipation in the diaspora rather than a return to Palestine: 'Ideologically speaking, our school was Bundist, and distinctly non-Zionist. A return to the land of the prophets was not our dream, but rather to make prophetic the land of our present.' [*EOT*, 79] Gershon was much influenced by the British Fabian movement. The Fabians, some of whose works had been translated into Yiddish, argued for evolutionary rather than revolutionary political change. In matters of religious belief Gershon was a 'God-intoxicated agnostic' [211]; one who believed that there was no God but that 'one ought to live one's life as if there is' [13]. Gershon tells Jacob that 'Bundist theory became my Torah' [211], meaning that he and his ilk espoused socialism with the same passion that fired religious observance among Orthodox and ultra-Orthodox Jews. This intellectual dynamism, an almost messianic intensity in the life of the mind, suffuses the prewar cultural world that *East of Time* so lovingly describes. The intensity is there throughout Rosenberg's opus, but in a form inevitably moderated by tragic knowledge that includes the gassing of Gershon and most of his family at Auschwitz. Rosenberg's first volume of poems in English bears the title of a fine poem therein, 'My Father's Silence'. At one level, his work can be read as a response to that silence; a refusal to let his father's wisdom and the cultural world it so magnificently reflected perish at Auschwitz. The Gershon of *East of Time* is one of the great figures in Australian literature.

To live as if there were a God was to be a *mensch*, a good person whose deeds possess a beauty no less potent, no less beautiful than the beauties of art. On a freezing January day in 1942 Jacob makes one of his fortnightly visits to Miss Fela, his beloved former kindergarten teacher who now lives a parlous ghetto life with her goldfish, Rebecca, an adored emblem of better days:

The door stands surprisingly open. I dash in. Miss Fela is sitting on a low chair; as usual she is wearing her white dress-coat. But droplets of sweat prickle her cheerless face. Her thin white lips are like death, and her large eyes are brimming with tears; they direct my gaze to the aquarium. Red Rebecca, open-eyed, is lying on her side, virtually encased in ice.

With a small hammer I freed the little body from the solid matter, and as I took out the goldfish Miss Fela burst into uncontrollable weeping. Rebecca was the only living thing she had. But there was nothing we could do, there is no antidote to death. Lucky little Rebecca—at least she died in her own bed. What a great privilege, in those surreal days, to outwit the ashes.

I kissed my teacher and left, just as the first star appeared and lit up heaven's callousness. [*EOT*, 182]

Soon after, Miss Fela is deported and presumably gassed at Auschwitz. The young man's kiss is benedictory. The passage has several moral trajectories. It records a good deed done in extremity, though quite without moral self-congratulation. But there is a second good deed—the writing itself, which brings a fine woman back from the dead and honours her life of devoted community service. The writing's profoundly altruistic orientation is subtly reflected in the verb 'prickle', which tells us how the perspiring lady looked, but also tries, through an act of empathetic identification, to imagine how those beads of sweat felt to her as she sat freezing in her chair. This deep care for the other is a hallmark of Rosenberg's work. Like the Yiddish writers who so profoundly influenced him, his autobiographical art is above all about the fate of a community. In the Preface to *East of Time* he writes: 'The touchstone of these reminiscences—their informing spirit— is the desire and determination of an entire community to remain human, even at the last frontier of life.'

Yiddish, that ever-changing demotic language of eastern European Jewry, had existed for almost a millennium by the time the young Rosenberg encountered it in Lodz. A rich blend of Hebrew, German, Slavic and Romance languages, plus whatever other linguistic materials happened to be at hand, Yiddish possessed two of the essential qualities required for the formation of a vibrant literary tradition: cultural inclusiveness, which could range from folk tales to sophisticated modern literary forms, and a mix of nostalgic affection and irony—a combination that enabled writers to blend reverence for enduring cultural values with a critique of what they saw as antiquated, stifling and hieratical. Yiddish literature reached its peak from about 1870 to the first world war. The three giants of this 'classic' period were Mendele Mocher Sforim, Sholem Aleichem, and I. L. Peretz.[206] The last of these in particular had a massive influence on Jacob Rosenberg, who cherished Peretz's unflinching opposition to moribund cultural forms and his ability imaginatively to fuse the sentiments of religious piety and sceptical secular modernity.[207] Yiddish was also a carrier of culture from elsewhere; indeed it was the main conduit through which the Enlightenment reached the Jews of eastern Europe. This was especially important in moderating the age-old cultural isolation of the *shtetl*; but it was significant too in a large industrial city like Lodz where Rosenberg first read Shakespeare, the Russian and French novelists and other writers who were to have a major influence on him in Yiddish translation. Solomon Maimon's *An Autobiography* famously narrates an eastern European Jew's encounter with Enlightenment values.[208] Rosenberg did not read this text as a young man, but he did read Yiddish translations of the autobiographies of Rousseau, Goethe, Stefan Zweig and others.

Virtually any Yiddish-speaker spoke at least one other language. This bilingualism, the linguistic corollary of the Jews' adaptive cultural condition in exile, was conducive to a reflective awareness of language as the currency and shaper of social worlds. The Lodz of *East of Time*, a place where 'a penman was equal to a prince' [*EOT*, 34], throngs with writers and others who espouse Judaism's ancient devotion to the word in a form heightened by cultural displacement. Here as so often, Gershon speaks as a secular humanistic sage, a proletarian intellectual whose worldview is unclouded by scholasticism or sentimentality. As spiritual life battles strangulation in the increasingly grim ghetto, this reverent awareness of the word—the belief (as Gershon's friend Mechel puts it) that language is 'the physical manifestation of man's spirituality' [126]—encounters its lethal antithesis in Nazism's systematic use of language as a tool of demagoguery, deception and repression. Rosenberg sees Nazism as a dream sustained in a devilish circularity by the language it breeds: 'The dream had spawned its own language, and the language nourished the dream.' [149]

He writes: 'There are times when we desperately need imagination to pierce the darkest dark with a sliver of light.' [*SW*, 19] Art then is potentially the most profound power of resistance to barbarism—an inversion of Adorno's famous but misunderstood dictum that 'to write poetry after Auschwitz is barbaric'. Rosenberg offers this counsel in a short poem, 'To Adorno':

> Art
>
> transcends suffering
>
> watch out poet
>
> don't create
>
> by destroying
>
> Leave this to
>
> nature[209]

For this agnostic Jew, the Bible—which he reads as secular artistry at its greatest—epitomizes the beauty and profundity of human storytelling.

Rosenberg's aesthetic has four main tenets: language should aspire to the evocative condition of poetry; the writer should not preach, but rather dissolve abstraction into the living fabric of his language; writing should have deep roots in the culture's folk tradition, as only such roots can sustain the necessary daring of artistic innovation; and writing should be of and for a community, not the expression of a narcissistic Romantic ego. It is striking and typical that Rosenberg often delegates the espousal of these principles to others. A writer from childhood, he recounts how in his teens he sent a piece to a famous author. A meeting ensues during which the older man tells him that writing by one who does not have deep cultural roots 'will be as enduring as an epitaph written with one finger on the surface of a lake' [*EOT*, 34–5]. Yuda Reznik, who taught Jacob Yiddish literature, proffers another memorable piece of advice: 'a story without a shadow is a sad tale' [27]. Rosenberg's prose memorializes these doomed sages of the ghetto; but more than this, the work's very existence, and its author's ongoing passionate commitment to writing, confirms the continuing power of their counsel in the post-Holocaust world. This same humble sense of indebtedness, of creativity as a communal act, persists through the Australian sections of the autobiography. The aptly named Ivon Sage, an assimilated Anglo-Jew and close friend, first broaches with Jacob the possibility that he might write in English as well as in Yiddish.

Ivon's suggestion has a resonant, almost Shakespearean quality that occurs in many of Rosenberg's passages of dialogue. Ivon believes that writing in English will enable Jacob to reach a wider audience. He adds: 'Perhaps more importantly, it will enable you to keep singing, in the language of your adopted land, your people's interrupted song.' [*SW*, 178]

This perfectly encapsulates the diasporic Jewish writer's vocation—one that must continually adapt to new language worlds and must resume a narrative after periods of communal suffering and displacement. Thus, if the writer embarks on an autobiography in the adoptive language, he has to engage in a process of what Besemeres calls self-translation,[210] wherein both the pre-migration and the English-speaking self must be brought under the aegis of the English language with its particular ways of conceiving and narrating selfhood. Only highly accomplished autobiographical writers can move from the 'natural' to the adoptive language world without betraying a strong feeling of narrative 'interruption'—one that can mirror the interruptions of Jewish history. But the 'song', as Rosenberg conceives it, is first and foremost of the 'people'. The fact that Sage's wise counsel comes from a deeply acculturated Australian Anglo-Jew is critical: it reassures Jacob that even on these remote shores he can continue to tell his story and that of his people.

Memory, trauma and imagination

Rosenberg describes *East of Time* as a 'rendezvous of history and imagination' [*EOT*, 9]. In the preface to *Sunrise West* he writes: 'Like its predecessor, *Sunrise West* is imbued with pictures and visions of a bygone yet ever-living reality—it is a personal weave of autobiography, history and imagination.' [*SW*, xi]

This autobiography is not then simply a work of realism. Its major imaginative sources, which include Yiddish literature, the Bible, Shakespeare, and more recent influences from Kafka to Calvino, suggest that Rosenberg writes in—and has to some extent invented—a particular hybrid (I shall use the less technical term 'blended') genre of autobiography. As his prefatory comments and the books' constant concern with real-world politics show, this autobiography also sees itself as answerable to history and bound by a rigorous notion of historical 'truth'. Truth so conceived does not stand in opposition to 'fiction'; on the contrary, Rosenberg argues that creative fiction, with its capacity to select salient details and shape them into a nuanced narrative artifact that can be voiced by one human being to another, is indispensable to the writing of this kind of truth. In seeing narrative thus he is in good company. Nowadays most would concede that narrative cannot simply hold a mirror up to life: it must always select, must always reflect a given writer's voice, point of view, sense of audience. To say this is not to deny its potential 'truth', but rather to suggest that our best approximations to 'truth' occur when various people with a serious commitment to its disclosure draw upon the resources of narrative and participate in an ongoing conversation about what things, including human history, mean.

Rosenberg's two autobiographical titles allude obliquely to the relationship between history and imagination. The first sentence of the first volume—'I was born to the east of time'—conveys (among other things) a sense of history and time that shaped the imagination of many eastern European Jews. Particularly in the *shtetl*, but also in a place like Lodz, the sense of time that prevailed among Jews was often messianic rather than historical. The master narrative was that of the Chosen People. History was understood in terms of Jews' relationship with their God and the purportedly historical events that sprang from this relationship: the fall, dispersion and exile, the expectation of messianic redemption. In 'The Chosen', one of the 102 vignettes[211] that make up the book, Rosenberg writes that 'Jews are forever carrying on a love-affair with hope' [*EOT*, 136], meaning that messianic expectation would usually take precedence over current misfortune or misery. The sentiment of hope, which reverberates throughout Yiddish literature, was put to the ultimate test in the ghettos and the concentration camps. Remarkably, some survivors emerged with their faith in God and the future intact; others repudiated faith, though without necessarily abandoning hope of earthly redemption—a prospect that seemed most plausible in a far-flung haven like Australia. Rosenberg's sober but subtly vital art is in part an inquiry into the meaning and possibility of Jewish hope, before and after the Holocaust.

His descriptions of Lodz suggest that the anhistorical messianic sense of time coexisted there with what looks like its contrary: the secular historical doctrines of communism and in particular socialism. But in fact the two seem to have been entwined, since secular historical doctrine absorbed and indeed expressed the messianic fervour of Jewish redemptive narrative. To the extent that the mythic and the historical were interfused, Rosenberg's blended genre is both an outgrowth of and a singularly apt medium for the reconstruction of the cultural and narrative world he knew in Lodz. It also brings revealing narrative possibilities to the storying of Australian society, a place in which white settlement reflected Enlightenment commitments to rationality, and in which mythic time as understood by indigenous Australians was to be brutally subordinated by colonialism and its aftermath. One in Rosenberg's position, of course, will not be preoccupied, at least in the first instance, with the iniquities of British colonialism, notwithstanding his profound commitment to multiracial and multicultural social equality. Like virtually all Australian Holocaust survivors he feels a deep gratitude to this place, which struck him from the outset as 'an amazingly peaceful world' [*SW*, 124]—a world where policemen apologized for knocking mistakenly at one's door, and where early-morning revellers who availed themselves of a bottle of milk from one's doorstep left cash and a note of apology [135].

The second volume's title suggests various metaphorical resonances, including that of Australia as a new dawn in the antipodean West. To Jacob and his wife Esther, this was a land of history free of nightmare, where the Jews' 'everlasting Exodus' [120], their non-messianic historical destiny, could be pursued in a relatively tolerant Western democracy, remote from Europe.

Rosenberg's blended genre must also accommodate nightmare and trauma, and this presents a familiar problem. He agrees with Primo Levi and Elie Wiesel that 'There is, and will always remain, a gulf between Holocaust survivors and the rest of mankind—a separateness which no outsider can fathom' [154]. In a similar vein he argues that there can be no explanation of Auschwitz because Auschwitz, 'unstable as water, graveyard of human decency, had no meaning, no meaning at all' [14]. And yet he is not so sure: 'One *can* understand and feel with those who survived,' he tells one of his many interlocutors [155]. Like Levi and Wiesel, he finds that he must write these experiences—and that he can do so with some confidence that receptive readers will be able to identify, at least to some significant degree, with these harrowing descriptions. In *Sunrise West* he insists that it is in Holocaust poetry, not in 'dry scholarship', that 'the scream of our slaughtered people lives on' [159]. A Holocaust poet himself, in both poetry and prose, he believes that testimony is most powerful when it is most creatively eloquent.

> We arrived at Birkenau in the middle of August 1944, a summery morning like any other, yet not like any other at all. I can still see the troupe of unreal men in striped rags, lingering in a nearby field like an ensemble of resigned clowns on a condemned stage, raking grass. In my heart's innermost chamber, enveloped in tattered years, there still hang the pictures of my mother's terrified eyes, my father's bleak gesture of farewell, my sister Ida's numb paralysis, and the horror of my two little nieces, six and four, standing like adults in the queue with their arms up, awaiting Selection. And I cannot erase from my memory the sight of my sister Pola three days later, stretched out on the wires of the electric fence, her head shaved, her hands in supplication, her mouth kissing death... [*SW*, 13]

These excruciating images are imprinted on memory in a way that seems to guarantee their essential veracity; which is all that really matters. The skill of the writing—the clown-like appearance of the desolate rakers, the characteristic rage-free tone of understated mournful bewilderment—deepens the description as few witnesses to these outrages can. Those who believe that trauma necessarily distorts memory should note how closely the core details of Rosenberg's description resemble those in hundreds of other accounts of arrival at Auschwitz.

He reports another form of recollection thus:

> Like most survivors, I constantly had to reassure myself that I was living in a new reality. One Monday morning, as I turned from Eildon Road into Grey Street and walked towards St Kilda railway station, a thought flashed across my mind: I had abandoned my pickaxe, an offence punishable by death! *But I'm not in Ebensee*, I reminded myself. *But then, you never know*. Perhaps I ought to buy a replacement in a local hardware store, so that I wouldn't be accused of stealing.
>
> At the station I asked for a weekly ticket, and all at once everything grew misty. 'Are you all right?' asked the woman from behind her little window.
>
> 'Yes, sure. Would you like to see my identity card, my passport?'

'No, that's quite unnecessary. Not here, sir. Have a seat, there's no hurry, there's been a delay and the next train won't be arriving for a few more minutes.'

I thanked her, but immediately wondered if the delay had been caused by the late arrival of fresh human cargo. [*SW*, 151]

Here Holocaust trauma crashes in on the relative calm of Jacob's life in Australia. The memories come unbidden, momentarily paralysing the capacity to tell delusion from reality. Such involuntary reruns of past scenes are typical of post-traumatic memory 'disorders'. The will seems unable to intervene, either to stop the flow of memory or to insist on the restitution of one's customary postwar grasp of reality. Massive trauma has the effect of blasting occurrences out of narrative sequence and (so) out of explanatory context. However, in an instance such as this the disabling of the will and of normal discriminatory processes applies only to the delusional event itself. The act of autobiographical narration, which contains both the initial memory of Holocaust horror and its antipodean rerun of that memory, is not disabled. In this passage Rosenberg is able to restore the past to narrative sequence and understanding through the act of writing. The respectful kindliness of the woman behind the window suggests that restorative narration is not just temporal (seeing the original experience through two subsequent time-frames) but also cultural. Having this acutely painful disturbance happen in Australia, where bureaucratic efficiency is not usually associated with menace, helps Jacob to read reality back into the delusion. The recollective nuances at work here should alert us, once again, to the dangers of generalizing about the processes of memory, be they 'traumatic' or other. These nuances show, for instance, that an individual's disposition towards his Holocaust experience will in part depend on the character of his post-Holocaust life. If that life is fundamentally secure and productive, it may render Holocaust memory more manageable. This is not to say that such memories will then be distorted by rose-coloured filters, but rather that a secure postwar life may better enable a survivor to cope with the unvarnished memories of life in a ghetto or a concentration camp.

After the war Jacob tells Sergey Nutkiewicz, his former tutor in political economy, that 'the gods have endowed me with a long memory—which by the way is not always a blessing' [*EOT*, 98]. The comment is typically understated: the 'gods' have sent him enormous suffering and then, just for good measure, a memory that denies him the gift of forgetting. Condemned to remember, Rosenberg's autobiography constantly struggles with the dualities of consciousness. There is the two-sidedness of memory: memory is a blessing insofar as it enables him and others to reconstruct the wrecked world of eastern European Jewry and to summon the historical record in cautioning against other catastrophes; it is a curse in that it threatens to imprison the self in an intolerable past. There is also a two-sidedness about the imagination: at its beneficent best imagination can fly the prison of the past, opening out new vistas of vision and feeling; but for the writer, especially one of Rosenberg's literary sophistication, imagination must necessarily return to that prison because it is constantly enlisted in the effort to deepen testimony by transmuting it into the terrible revelatory power of art. And there is this further twist: the line between creative imagination and delusion is fine at the best of times. These two imaginative forms seem to draw on contiguous, sometimes common sources of energy and inspiration.

How then can we distinguish art from delusion? Rosenberg's principal response to this question is that art asks what it might or should mean to be human; how we should understand 'human dignity' [*SW*, 103]. Its terms of inquiry are in this Aristotelian sense ethical. Here 'inquiry' has a certain force: it refers to a form of questioning which is to some extent guided by an individual's conscious intention. Delusion, by contrast, springs from the unconscious as if by some unknown force and is not under conscious control. Delusion, like the involuntary reruns of traumatic experience, can imprison the self in a terrible past. Creative inquiry into that dreadful history can put the individual into a different and more productive relationship with the past. It can furnish a 'usable past'[212]—one which can produce insight, a degree of healing accommodation, and even autobiographical narrative, including accomplished art like Jacob Rosenberg's.

To say that the past is usable is to suggest that it can be *put* to use; that one can go to work on it in a way that is directed by a kind of will—and also, if the enterprise is to be successful, by research, imagination and inspiration. It implies that one can (within reason) choose a relationship to the past. We recall that Viktor Frankl argues that a certain 'spiritual freedom' was possible even in the camps; that 'Fundamentally, therefore, any man can, even under such circumstances, decide what shall become of him—mentally and spiritually'. One would like to accord this bracing claim a full-blooded endorsement. For those (such as myself) who have not suffered major trauma, it is hard to know what human depths and capacities can survive such experiences. Even a survivor like Jacob Rosenberg seems uncertain about this. In one exchange he says: 'what outsiders cannot grasp is that sense of *inner* destruction felt by survivors. Once you've been tortured, you're forever tortured.' [*SW*, 155] Yet *East of Time* contains a vignette which concludes with Gershon proclaiming the need to maintain 'our inner sense of freedom' [*EOT*, 148] even in extremity, a sentiment echoed by Aron Wolman, another sagacious citizen of the ghetto [188]. It would seem reasonable to resist sweeping generalizations here. Some no doubt had their 'inner freedom' destroyed by the Nazis. Such people would probably be unlikely to write autobiographical accounts of their experience later on. Others, like Jacob Rosenberg, seem to have returned damaged but still remarkably human, and able to practise destruction's converse—creativity.

Raymond, another priestly mentor figure whom Jacob meets in Auschwitz, is perhaps the most important commentator in these volumes on the issue of the past. His initial advice to Jacob is: 'Don't, friend! Don't even try to think of the past. You can cry later, much later. Start now, and soon there'll be one voice less to testify to what we've witnessed.' [*SW*, 29–30] Jacob heeds this advice; so much so that, looking back, he is surprised at how seldom he and other displaced persons after the war thought or talked about the past. As we know, many survivors opted not to speak of it long after, even to their own children, the 'children of the shadows', some of whom were haunted by this silence.[213] But there is a great difference between never looking back, never speaking, and choosing when one will allow oneself these dangerous luxuries. Raymond's advice in effect involves adopting a series of attitudes to the past: don't look back while your mind must focus all its energy on survival; later, when it is safer to do so, you can recollect, you can 'cry'. If, like a Jacob Rosenberg, you were a writer before the war, and if the inner freedom needed to write has not been destroyed by trauma, writing may assist, may give voice to, the looking back that is done later. Mendl Blicblau, another friend of Jacob's in Australia, remarks:

'Our past walks ahead of us.' [142] The Holocaust autobiographer, like any survivor, will encounter the past in the future, in one way or another. Writing it will entail capturing the presentness of the past, now and forever. In Rosenberg's work time is often visceral, anthropomorphized, as if it has a mind of its own. Sometimes that mind is wilful, wayward, one of history's instruments of Jewish demise: 'Time had embarked on a precipitous, irreversible journey, roller-coasting along the brink of a fathomless abyss.' [*EOT*, 92] Sometimes it is governed by trauma's compulsive circling back to the scenes of horror: 'I cannot erase from my memory...' Elsewhere it gives rise to a liminal life of the imagination in visions and dreams, as when, in one of several brilliant passages of hallucinatory writing, Jacob imagines encountering his mother after the war:

> I found myself walking beside my mother as she pushed a cart through the night. The cart swayed like a drunkard on our cobbled street.
>
> 'Son,' she said, 'the last moments in the gas chamber were beyond the most horrible imaginings. I don't know if I have the right to tell you how it was, but on the other hand you ought to know. You're entitled to know about your family's end, even though your father always said, *Leave the dead alone and they'll leave you alone.* [*SW*, 109]

In another vision, this time at a ballroom in Melbourne, he dances with his sister Ida. As the waltz ends, 'Ida began to dissolve into my arms. "Don't ever forget us, my brother," she murmured. "Ever... ever... ever."' [138] Such moments gild mourning with a subdued enchantment—as in 'The Waltz of Survival', a fine Rosenberg poem dedicated to Esther and based on a Yiddish melody. Rosenberg's beautiful concluding line is: 'Hush my wounded soul, dance my broken heart.'[214] Enchantment occurs frequently in his work, but generally it is tinged with melancholy, regret, insatiable feelings of loss.

A powerful example is 'Nemesis' in *East of Time*, where a young woman, Reizl, refuses the marriage that her parents have arranged to prevent her from marrying her sweetheart, Motl. On the morning of the wedding Reizl disappears. After three days her mother approaches a seer in desperation. He directs her to a lake: 'Sit by the lake and wait until the moon comes out. You will hear the song your daughter heard, and you will know.' She obeys, and presently hears a beautiful voice:

> I am Rusalka, the lake-fairy,
> Abandoned alone,
> Come to me, Reizl, my sweetheart,
> Make my bed your home. [*EOT*, 50]

The tale ends with a soldier whom we know to be Motl standing 'like a stone statue' after the funeral in pouring rain until 'the sky was about to swallow the last morsel of light' [51]. As Rosenberg explains it,[215] the story accurately states that Reizl and her parents occupied the ground floor of the tenement in which his family lived. It is also accurate in reporting that Jacob carried messages between the two lovers. But he has melded these non-fictional elements with a famous Slavic folk tale in which the lake fairy sings her valedictory song. The resultant fusion of artistic modes is perhaps best described as a form of magic realism in which imagination circles back from the painful ghetto actualities of the present to a mythic and enchanted past. This active imaginative response recalls the title of Bruno Bettelheim's famous study of fairytales, *The Uses of Enchantment*.[216] The enchantment, however, is moderated by melancholy and woe, so its effect is complex. The circling back is in one sense a release from an increasingly hellish present; it is also a creative counter to trauma's compulsive revisitings of horror. But folk legend does not here function as a myth of consolation: Reizl still dies. Legend in this narrative serves two of Rosenberg's deepest artistic impulses—to narrate tragedy, but also to reassert the possibility of post-Holocaust re-enchantment. The curiously consoling qualities of strange-ness emerge hauntingly in another of Rosenberg's musings, this time an imagined return visit to Lodz where a distraught prostitute sits alone in a bordello after everyone else there has been murdered. Jacob asks why she stays. She replies: 'I'm waiting for you to forget me.' [*EOT*, 77]

Narrative craft

'Nemesis' is a beautifully crafted, self-contained narrative which is stylis-tically continuous with, but structurally distinct from, the stories that surround it. Set before the ghetto is sealed off, it is more concerned with life in Jewish Lodz than with its annihilation by the Nazis, though that later fate of course casts a retrospective pall over all the mini-stories' events, infusing individual tragedies with the knowledge of impending communal doom. The tale itself is about Orthodox Jewish life—Chana's father, Reb Nachman, is a kosher slaughterer—but it is told by the agnostic Jacob who also peripherally participates in the events. His main role however is a narrative one: to make accessible to a general reader the feelings associated with this culturally specific set of events—indeed to imply that though the events are particular, the feelings they occasion are universal. Of Chana's flight from the family home Rosenberg writes: 'It is a task beyond the best of pens, therefore, to describe their pain and desolation when, at daybreak on the appointed morning, they found Reizl's bed empty.' [*EOT*, 50] Though this voice is technically Rosenberg's own, its tone resembles that of a fable. In this sense the narrative is already pointedly aestheticized, already a work of magic realism, before the uncanny events foreshadowed by the seer occur. Rosenberg's autobiographical writing, particularly in *East of Time*, frequently evinces this productive tension between realist writing and the more ethereal impulses of fable and magic realism.

The ethereal quality owes much to Calvino's *Invisible Cities*, from which Rosenberg principally derives his vignette technique, whereby the larger narrative is constructed out of short, partially self-contained narratives. Rosenberg, however, uses this method to convey a social and historical specificity largely absent from Calvino's book. 'Nemesis' occupies less than three pages. It is longer than average among *East of Time*'s 102 vignettes. Some are less than a page in length. *Sunrise West* contains 63 such pieces, their average length being slightly greater than that of the pieces in its predecessor volume. This compositional structure, which is very unusual in autobiography, is loosely chronological, in a way that allows for associative ruminations and imaginative digressions. The vignettes are written in a poetic prose whose rhythms and phrasing require the sort of close readerly attention generally reserved for verse. The narrative trajectory is not identical in the two volumes. The vignettes that comprise *East of Time* recall a city frozen in time, terror and poverty. There is limited change or momentum in this shrinking island of Jewish survival, save for progressive deterioration in conditions as German policy tightens its screws on a powerless population. The journey at book's end is on cattle-trains to Auschwitz after the liquidation of the ghetto. *Sunrise West*, after the grim early descriptions of life in the camps, narrates a journey into freedom—to a place where the Rosenbergs can be largely free to script their lives, to envisage and realize a future. If the vignette technique is marginally more effective in the first volume, it is because vignettes are by their very nature better adapted to the representation of stasis than to movement, even when they are chronologically framed. Vignettes are essentially discrete word-pictures. Conventional realist narrative by contrast works through stricter temporal sequence, causal and other explanatory linkages, and a sense that the clock is ticking unerringly in the background.

The art lies not just in the vignettes themselves but in their sequencing, and in the 'white space' that separates them. Each piece has a title, and the range among these reflects the blended generic character of the book. Some, like 'My Father', 'My Mother', are matters of familial fact and could occur in any autobiography. Others, such as 'Bible and Bund', convey specific cultural information about the community. Still others—'The Philosopher', 'The Improviser', 'The Melamed'—refer to personality types or stock characters from Yiddish literature or, like 'Karinka', to particular people whose obituaries appear in these pages. Others again, such as 'Dialogue' in *Sunrise West*, contain intellectual exchanges of a kind that Rosenberg encountered particularly in Russian fiction. Another group of titles suggest a fable-like strangeness—a strangeness often indistinguishable from the madness of Nazi policy—which transcends historical time: 'Legends', 'Riddles', 'The Absence', 'Enigmas'. The countervailing tendency to narrative progression and chronology is provided by titles like 'As the Days Darkened', 'The Last Summer', 'Final Departure'. Such chronological markers become more common in *Sunrise West*—'Italy', 'Melbourne'—as do sociological references to immigrants, democracy and the adoptive culture. Here the out-of-time vignettes tend to announce hallucinatory visions of mother, sister, the world of the past. Throughout, Rosenberg's love of people registers in titles that bear the names of family, friends and mentors. The foregoing is merely a selective account of the titles, but it indicates how various and rich are the pieces that comprise this narrative mosaic.

Yet it is more than a mosaic because the pieces are separated by white space: a gap between each vignette and the title of the next, and then a smaller gap between that title and the piece it introduces. White space is important in many forms of writing, most obviously in poetry where so much can 'go on'—in the poem, in the reader's mind—between stanzas.

White space gives the reader 'room to move', to let the imagination go to work on what has just been said, to fashion possible links between this and what comes before and after. Here are two examples from Rosenberg's autobiography.

In *East of Time* the vignette entitled 'The Pyramid' describes the often corrupt bureaucratic structure that existed under Chaim Rumkowski, the Nazi-appointed Jewish puppet administrator, or 'Eldest of the Jews', of the Lodz ghetto. To this day survivors and historians debate Rumkowski's moral flaws. Was this man who was ordered to organize the deportation of the city's Jewish children a power-crazed monster intent on currying self-interested favour with the Nazis, or was he an individual trapped by history and trying to do his best in response to impossible circumstantial pressures? The second of Rosenberg's detailed references to Rumkowski is less damning than the first. It concludes with this question:

> And in the end, who knows how many times, during sleepless nights, this man who projected such strength and confidence shrank back in horror at the echo of his own fateful words: 'Mothers, give me your children!'? [*EOT*, 156]

The disinclination finally to judge a given individual is typical of these books, yet we don't get the full measure of this moment of hesitating assessment until we pass to the next vignette, 'Mercy', a Job-like account of one Fishl Binko, who curses his God after the deportation of his young daughter and the murder of his distraught wife. Here again legend enters the story, in the form of an angel who tells Binko that God repents of his sins against him and offers him a new wife and three new daughters as reparation. Binko pronounces himself 'overburdened with His mercies' and is determined to commit suicide, thereby defying Jewish law but joining the other ghetto suicides, whose 'faces are shining'. The narrator comments that 'most of our legends are so rooted in reality that sometimes it's hard to tell which is which' [158–9]. Having read these harrowing paragraphs the reader's mind circles back to Rumkowski. The white space between vignettes becomes a place of redoubled moral reflection. Well might he have been tortured in the night by his edict that the children had to be deported. But now, having read of the plight of Binko and his family, one is perhaps inclined to say: Nothing, absolutely nothing, can justify such an edict. *Anything*, and certainly Rumkowski's own suicide, would have been better than *that*.

'Dialogue' in *Sunrise West* contains a discussion at a restaurant between Jacob and an academic named Aaron Feldman concerning poetry's role in reporting the Holocaust, the limitations of academic Holocaust scholarship in this task, and, in closing, the sense in which the Book of Job quintessentially expresses the Jews' 'unbroken faith in the future, despite betrayal by their God'—a faith in turn epitomized by the 'postwar behaviour of many survivors'. Throughout, Jacob has made reference to his father Gershon's views. As they leave the restaurant Feldman offers Jacob a lift home. He declines, explaining to the reader, in deft and beautiful phrasing: 'I needed to be alone, with dad.' [SW, 160] That qualifying comma before 'with dad' provides a grammatical separation between the Australian present and the Lodz past. Jacob needs to be alone in order to revisit the past.

The next vignette, 'Linguistic Feuds', plunges us again into the post-Holocaust present: 'At the peak of Australia's postwar immigration tide, considerable numbers of Jews landed on these peaceful shores. They had been liberated from the camps or were running from the antisemitism they still encountered in their land even after the war.' [160–61] Then follows a scene in which one Morris Blattmann—a long-settled, university-educated, practising Anglo-Jew—urges an audience of migrants to abandon Yiddish and embrace Australia's mother tongue. In effect Blattmann is asking these people to shed their cultural pasts. Understandably he encounters angry opposition, because such migrants' 'faith in the future' can be realized only if they can acculturate in Australia in a way that enables them to maintain their cultural roots even as they start to put down new roots here. In this way 'Dialogue' informs our reading of 'Linguistic Feuds': the white space between them becomes a place where we can more deeply ponder what Jewish faith in the future actually entails, and see that it requires preserving aspects of the past in the new land, asserting continuity in the face of the massive rupture occasioned by the Holocaust. It is part of these migrants' pressing need to create a 'Republic of Memory' [143].

The obese but intellectually vibrant figure of Feldman is well drawn, as are most of Rosenberg's characters. His art, we might say, rests on three main pillars: imagery and metaphor (the wonderful suggestiveness of the finger writing on the lake, the voice like a spider's footfall, word-pictures that so powerfully evoke Lodz), ideas (as in 'Dialogue'), and characterization. Memorably, he suggests that 'Every story has a life of its own, and every life has its own story'.[217] Early in *East of Time*, Rosenberg avows that 'I'm no psychologist' [*EOT*, 13], and in terms of modern fictional and autobiographical techniques this is true. In his work, human inwardness resembles the interiority we find in Yiddish literature more than it does the Freudian innerscapes of contemporary American or second-generation Australian Jewish writing. The hallmarks of Rosenberg's psychology are its profoundly moral gaze (Freud, one might say, displaces focus from the moral to the psychological), and its communal orientation: mind only makes sense here as a manifestation and component of community. Even the feeling of solitude that haunts many survivors [*SW*, 58–9] is echoed but also moderated by the collective experience of exile. Ezro the Spaniard, another Lodz sage, says: 'A man who *has* nowhere in his heart cannot *go* there. How can he be in something, when that very something is in him?' [*EOT*, 99] To have a place in the heart is to retain and rebuild inner freedom. If you have *that*, and if you have it in community, you are never completely in exile.

The Holocaust autobiographer must convey one of the defining psychological states of many who endure, and many who perpetrate, horror: compartmentalization. This phenomenon, so brilliantly anatomized by the deracinated Jewish intellectual and autobiographer Arthur Koestler,[218] involves various forms of psychic partitioning and discontinuity, such that one can 'cut off' from what one is having to endure, or from one's wrecked past, or from one's normally sentient mode of selfhood; or can cordon off one's conscience so that a Nazi can blow a young Jewish girl's brains out in a forest and then come home and cradle his young daughter on his knee while reading her Grimm's tales. Nazi representations of Jews as vermin, bugs and other subhuman creatures were in part designed to facilitate such compartmentalization: what better way to becalm conscience than to imagine that the live baby you are throwing onto the flames is but an insect you might tip off a cake-plate into the fireplace?

For Rosenberg, compartmentalization sets in almost from the moment of his arrival at Birkenau: 'Within the blink of an eye I became bestially free, a lone caged animal on the prowl. Was this a prerequisite for survival? I am not trying to explain, there is nothing to elucidate.' [*SW*, 14] In fact, the subsequent camp descriptions do not entirely corroborate this asserted suspension of conscience and customary personhood, what Langer calls 'the Impromptu Self'.[219] Certainly he performs mind-numbing chores, like loading corpses onto trucks, and there are times when he experiences a deep apathy, as if he were a living corpse himself; but most of the horror vignettes focus on compartmentalization in the guards and in the Jewish *kapos* who served them. Jacob and his friends, especially Raymond, maintain something of the moral life that Todorov, Des Pres, Frankl and others insist survived to significant degrees in the ghettos and the camps. Always reflective, Rosenberg wonders how this can be, and his answer, which recalls Pascal, takes not just the id and the superego into account, but also that more spiritual presence, the soul: 'From my camp experience I could perhaps venture to say, with Pascal, that the mind has a soul of its own, and the soul has a mind of its own, and they protect each other.' [*SW*, 63] While the soul is intact, so too is some degree of 'inner freedom'. This sort of compartmentalization is fundamentally different from the kind that enables a man to engage in child-murder and affectionate parenting within a span of hours. That form freezes or kills off the soul. Rosenberg's kind enables the soul to maintain, however fragilely, a coordinating and edifying presence in the person. It enables one to *remain a person*, an imaginatively and morally engaged being, and not merely a 'caged animal on the prowl'.

We might distinguish three broad registers of selfhood in Rosenberg's autobiography. There is the incarcerated self, as just described; the post-Holocaust liberated self, about which more presently; and articulating these is the narrating self, a present self who stories the past and brings it, at the end, into close proximity with the present. One of the narrating self's most important functions, especially but not exclusively in *East of Time*, is to honour the dead. Having inherited his father's agnosticism, and witnessed God's apparent absence during the war, Jacob Rosenberg does not choose to say a traditional *Kaddish* for his family or for the other Lodz Jews who perished in the Holocaust. However, art has its own spiritual resources, its own powers of consolation and commemoration; and one of the finest things about these immensely moving books is the way in which the writing brings the people of Lodz back from the dead, placing them vividly, lovingly, sometimes bemusedly before us, then saying a kind of agnostic poetic *Kaddish* for them before consigning them again to the grave. Here are some excerpts from the opening of 'Lipek's Irony':

> Lipman Biderman, whom his friends called Lipek, was a remarkable young man. I had known him from childhood...
>
> Lipek was a well-built youngster with straight shoulders, a pitch-black mane that topped an elongated face, and a few freckles around his shapely nose. Two dark rings under his lower lids emphasized the slightly melancholic look in his stark black eyes.
>
> There was a rare harmony between Lipek's mind and tongue, and he had an extraordinary way of expressing himself. His favourite mode was irony. [*EOT*, 140]

And then the concluding paragraph:

> One winter evening, as my friend's temperature rose, two uniformed men entered Lipek's apartment. His mother pleaded with them to let her son remain at home. They dragged him out of bed and handed him over to the thugs to whom they swore allegiance. At the break of dawn, while the gods were still snoring under their sky-blue eiderdowns, Lipek, renowned paragon of our youth, was marched off to a desolate place and shot. [*EOT*, 141][220]

These shattering moments convey a tragically compromised enchantment: the prose that would recapture the beauty murdered in the ghettos and camps must now be shadowed by that murder, torn between a will to re-enchantment which defies genocide and a sense that enchantment after such horror is a travesty, or an impossibility.

In one obvious sense the post-Holocaust self is present throughout the two volumes of this autobiography, since the entire narrative is told by the survivor-author, now in his eighties and writing from his home in suburban Melbourne. But in other respects the post- and pre-Holocaust selves seem decidedly distinct. One is shaped by Polish and Yiddish language and culture; the other by antipodean English and its world. The two selves are separated by the massive—but not absolute—rupture that was the Holocaust. The current self is elderly (in years, but certainly not in energy); the Jacob of *East of Time* was young. And yet the experience of reading these volumes is not disjunctive; indeed, as I have suggested, they possess an unusual degree of aesthetic integration. One reason for this is simply Jacob Rosenberg's special talent as a writer. Another is that in many ways the narrating post-Holocaust self is not so different after all from the Lodz one. Jacob lived long enough in Lodz for the contours of his identity to settle, and it was here that he learnt to write. This continuity is apparent both in the way the self maintains connection with the past through memory and autobiographical reconstruction, and in the nature of the self we meet in the second volume. This later self has a profound inwardness and privacy; a vital if haunted inner life. But it is not introspective in the way, or at least to the extent, that second-generation Australian Jewish autobiographers like Mark Baker, Susan Varga or Doris Brett are introspective. Before he is transported by the vision of dancing with his sister Ida, Jacob is content to be left to his own ruminations when Esther is invited to dance by another man:

> I was pleased to be left alone. I had come here only because of Esther; she needed this, I knew it would be good for her. But for me there was little appeal in the swinging firmament of Maison de Luxe, and since this was not yet the time when a woman invited a man to a frolic on the dance floor, my solitude was pretty secure. For a while at least, I was free to let my mind embark—as it often did in such situations—on an excursion into my inner self, the realm of visions, imaginings and other forbidden realities. [SW, 136–7]

Whatever the 'forbidden realities' might be, they are not gone into. It's the 'realm of visions' that matters most and is most characteristic here. He recalls a conversation earlier that day with a fellow Auschwitz deportee: 'I have no right to be alive,' the man had said [137], and this now inclines Jacob's thoughts towards ethical issues. And then—Ida's ghost touches him on the shoulder, and he is off in the 'realm of visions', delighted and desolated by this ghostly re-encounter with his sister. The 'inner self' is here an ethically focused journeyer through memory, not a denizen of 'forbidden realities' of a Freudian kind.

In 'The Voice', Jacob again embarks on inner meanderings, this time at a Jewish wedding where most of the guests are survivors. The 'voice' that comes in his reverie is bitter, sardonic, utterly cynical: 'Mere illusions, hallucinations, mirages (the voice argued). Surely everything must be clear by now! Life is like a chameleon ...' [190] It preaches a fatalism that runs counter to the way he lives: '*your* fate was planned, down to the last detail. Not even God's own Adversary could emulate such infamy.' [192] Jacob tries to fend the voice off, pleading the festive nature of the occasion. Esther, noticing his troubled abstraction, solicits his attention.

> 'You haven't said a word to anyone.' Esther bent closer and tenderly took hold of my hand. 'Wake up,' she smiled. 'Listen ... You're going to become a father!'
>
> I came to with a start. And there and then, in front of our table companions, I embraced and kissed my wife. [*SW*, 193]

Now it is his wife with whom he dances. Incredibly, their murdered family has a future after all. If the interior dialogue perhaps seems slightly stilted, this vignette again shows that inwardness in this writer is generally outward and communal in its trajectory.

Ethics: post-biblical, post-Holocaust

The vignette 'Beginning' quickly becomes self-explanatory:

> And the black magician said, 'Let there be darkness,' and there was darkness, and he saw that the darkness was good ...
>
> And on the second day he decreed that no Jew be allowed to walk on the footpath, or in the middle of the road. No Jew should be permitted to have a dog, cat, bird, money, gold, fur coat, piano, violin, mandolin, guitar, gramophone, or to breathe Aryan air. All Yiddish books and all writers who wrote in Yiddish were to be burned ...
>
> And then he said, 'Let all the Jews be herded into one precinct,' and they were herded in, and he saw that the herding was good ... [*EOT*, 107–8]

Jacob Rosenberg is anything but a bitter writer, and yet—it would be hard to imagine a more calculated affront to scriptural authority, or to the canonical Jewish notion of the Chosen People, than the substitution of Hitler for God in this inversion of Genesis. Something similar, though less confronting, occurs in *Sunrise West*, where Hitler becomes the new

Pharaoh, precipitating another Exodus—at least for those who aren't slaughtered. The last vestiges of his father's 'God-intoxicated' agnosticism seem to have been swept away by the Holocaust. What then is left? How might we characterize the Jewishness that Rosenberg still so clearly espouses?

Mendel Singer, another wise friend whom he meets in a displaced persons' camp after the war, offers the following definition of a Jew:

> '... not every Jew is necessarily Jewish. A Jew is a physical being, whereas Jewishness is a spiritual thing. This means, my friend, that an individual Jew can become an antisemite, a Fascist, even a Nazi, but Jewishness—as a living ideal of universal brotherhood—is in eternal conflict with anything life-denying.' [*SW*, 89]

This formulation, with its repudiation of genetic notions of Jewishness, appears to represent Rosenberg's considered view. Jewishness so conceived requires no God, but rather a commitment to a universalistic ethics and a sentiment of piety: a prayerful attitude without a deity. This impulse to see the divine as imagined by and therefore potentially characteristic of the human, to promulgate a reverent ethics not premised on supernatural authority or solicitude, is the quintessential gesture of humanism. He writes in the poem 'Redemption' of 'the Messiah's plea to man':

> To release Him from His bond,
> Man's eternal dream,
> And bring Him among the living—
> For the living to redeem...[221]

Rosenberg's image of an 'authentic' person [*SW*, 117] is not of one who has been chosen, but one who *would* be chosen if there were a God. This is a matter of being a good person, a *mensch*, regardless of creed. *East of Time* and *Sunrise West* are the poetic autobiographies of a humanist who had little religious faith to lose, but managed to retain a measure of faith in humanity despite staggering odds. Since there is no divine plan— 'Topography shapes a river's character. Chance is a man's topography.' [*SW*, 79]—and no heavenly accounting of our deeds, there is only ethical responsibility: to others, and to the self whose ethical calling it is to take responsibility for others.

The *mensch* on this understanding is not one who slavishly follows moral rules, but rather one who makes flexible and empathetic moral assessments in particular situations and seeks actively to do well by others. Evil can take various forms, one of which, systematically practised in the camps, involved techniques of degradation that destroyed the 'inner freedom' upon which ethical selfhood depends. While marching to Ebensee concentration camp, famished prisoners are astonished to find a cauldron of hot soup awaiting them. Their guard watches as the men surge towards it; he turns away, then back, capsizing the cauldron with a kick. Rosenberg continues:

> He stood there waiting to see our reaction, but to his disappointment none of us moved: everyone remained frozen to the spot. At the time I didn't really know why this was so—was it his gun we feared? Only much later did I come to understand that somehow, from deep within ourselves, we had unanimously chosen to refuse to validate his delusions—the conviction that his *Herrenvolk*, his Master Race, had succeeded in completely dehumanizing the children of the Hebrew Bible. [*SW*, 40]

The choice not to respond is an active gesture of moral resistance. It is unanimous and seems almost instinctive. Only with the passage of time does Rosenberg come to see the full meaning of this collective act, and to see how deeply physical survival can depend upon the survival of the soul, and how wise even the judgment of the wretched can be. This vignette is entitled 'Pyrrhic Victors'. The one that follows, 'The Prophetic Flame', recalls a deed as noble as the guard's is debased. After many days of starvation the prisoners cry out for bread and water as their cattle-train pulls into a station in western Bohemia:

> I recall a little woman running towards our wagon with two huge loaves of bread, and a guard warning her: 'One more step and I'll shoot.' When she pointed to the wedding-ring on her finger, he told her to come forward. But she just took off the ring and placed it on a stone lying on the ground where she stood. 'Come and get it,' she shouted, 'while I deliver the bread.' [*SW*, 41]

This is the Righteous Gentile, a figure who appears in a significant number of Holocaust autobiographies. In this black world a deed such as this is luminous and carries inestimable weight. It has a beauty akin to that of art, and perhaps only art can do it justice. To refuse to be an accomplice to degradation is to refuse to surrender one's inner freedom. It is to keep alight what Rosenberg calls 'the eternal flame of human decency'.[222]

As I have agued elsewhere,[223] decency is a central but often undervalued moral virtue. It is less spectacular than the so-called 'heroic' virtues like courage; less intense than the romantic passions. But it has the mildness and dependability of what Hume called 'the calm passions',[224] and it has a special kind of impersonality. This is not impersonality in the sense of uncaring detachment; rather, a decent person will extend to all others the assumption that they warrant and will reciprocate respect. It is what is sometimes termed a 'civic virtue'.[225] Jacob Rosenberg is a passionate man who writes passionate books; yet their after-effect is a surprising calm. When he writes that 'my friend Mendl and his siblings had already managed to replant, in remotest Melbourne, the warmth and decency of their parents' home' [*SW*, 123], he pays tribute to the ideal of decency that runs so deep in Australian culture, and to its equivalent in the eastern European Jewish world of his childhood. To be decent is to be a *mensch*, to practise what the Nazis tried to annihilate in Auschwitz, that 'graveyard of human decency'.

These books seem so deeply to care—for those who perished, for those who survived, and for readers who have inherited the post-Holocaust world. We owe this quality to Rosenberg's subdued but affectionate tone and to the moral perspective from which he speaks. It also springs, I think, from his profound belief in the light, and in art's capacity to find its way out of darkness. The memoirist in his eighties is heir to the youth who, decades earlier, 'in a dark ghetto basement', felt a mysterious stirring of hope as he beheld 'a green plant climbing a wet wall towards a tenuous crevice of sun.' [*EOT*, 30]

'Queer Passion'

David Martin's *My Strange Friend*

The curse of the species

Impassioned and often heterodox, David Martin was never one to shirk controversy. In his autobiography, *My Strange Friend*, he writes:

> To the grave with tribalism! It is the curse of the species. It will destroy us if we don't take care, for all its poetry, for all its art and beauty, for all its heroines and heroes. Adolf Hitler, who taught me I was a Jew, also taught me that there is no nationalism which does not become fanaticism. The Jewish as well? Naturally, why not?[226]

These are confronting sentiments from a Jewish writer, especially a former Zionist socialist who had lived in Palestine before the war. Though Martin escaped the Holocaust and makes only occasional references to it in this book, the denunciation of 'tribalism' reflects a Holocaust-haunted consciousness. He is one of a significant number of reflective Jews who believed that future genocides could be averted only if tribalism gave way to new forms of social inclusiveness.

In what sense did Hitler 'teach' him that he was a Jew? Not in the sense that, like Andrew Riemer, he had little Jewish awareness before the war. Born Ludwig Destinyi, to an upper-class family in Budapest in 1915, Martin grew up observing both Jewish and Christian festivals. The Destinyis were acculturated but not fully assimilated. Ludwig knew he was a Jew all right. What Hitler did was to bring home to him, and to many like him, the parlousness, the inescapable historicity, the enormity of the Jewish fate.

Personal identity is a many-faceted phenomenon. Construals of identity which are assumed or imposed from the 'outside' are one thing; my own sense of who I am can be quite another. In a tolerant society general perceptions of what a Jew is can sit fairly comfortably with how it actually feels to be a Jew. Under such circumstances personal identity can be relatively unproblematic. But, unless I am a 'self-hating Jew' who has internalized antisemitic attitudes, the presence of antisemitism, even when virulent and clearly pathological, opens up a vast gulf between how I am seen from the outside and how I perceive myself. Now personal identity becomes a matter of self-defence as well as of self-definition; the question 'Who am I?' is laced with anxiety and complication. David Martin is among the most self-conscious of all Australian Jewish autobiographers. For him the identity question—'Who was I?' [45]—was bound to be complex, what-ever turn the history of the Jews had taken during his lifetime. His book's restless, impassioned quality bespeaks 'an individualist of the purest water' [143]—one whose sense of self was never going to accord comfortably with social categories. For such people personal identity is almost as fluid as water. Their autobiographical narratives report on a self that is constantly in process; indeed narrative becomes a way of seeking and fashioning a self, of discerning new possibilities of selfhood and bringing them, however transiently, into being.

Martin arrived in Australia at the age of thirty-four after living in Germany, Holland, Hungary, Palestine, Britain and India. A communist from the 1930s through to the late 1950s, and later in life an 'old counter-revolutionary' [324], he served as a medical orderly during the Spanish Civil War. In Australia he was to become a journalist, an editor and a writer in several genres. Early on, he edited the Sydney edition of the *Australian Jewish News*, and he was to make a distinguished contribution to Australian letters. But was he an Australian Jewish writer? His answer to this, another identity question, was nothing if not equivocal:

> The description fits me only if it is stretched to make a convenient ethnic label. I don't think I am protesting too much, though of course any disclaimer will be taken as a sign of Jewish self-hatred. To be an Australian Jewish writer, with or without a hyphen, Australianness and Jewishness would have to be of broadly equal importance, as they seem to be in Hertz Bergner, Morris Lurie and Serge Liberman. But not in me. I am not religious, and to me to be a Jew is not like having a nationality… If E. O. Schlunke is a German Australian writer

and Miles Franklin a German or Irish Australian writer, and Henry Lawson a Scandinavian Australian one, then I, in my small way and to please my friends in the Jewish community, confess myself an Australian Jewish writer. [225]

This must be among the most hedged-about passages ever penned by a man of passion, but it is consistent with his distaste for the tribal, and it is certainly true that his writing has less 'ethnic' inflection than that of (say) Judah Waten, a writer with whom Martin was often bracketed, rather to his displeasure [224–5].

His unease about Waten, who had been a valued friend in the early days, was in essence political. Unlike Waten, who refused to denounce Stalinism, Martin went through a 'deconversion'[227] from Marxism. This divergence had aesthetic consequences. Martin suspected that Waten remained committed to socialist realism; whereas he, Martin, meant to write '*socialist* realism' [238]—a mode, deeply committed to realism, that expressed socialist ideals but without aesthetic prescription from any party, constituency or political regime. Here too he saw himself as 'an individualist of the purest water', a left-leaning humanist who could not repose faith in either of the two great thought systems with which he had engaged, Marxism and Judaism:

Marxism? No, as a guide to action; yes, as a means of understanding and interpreting the main drives of history.

And:

Not for me a belief in the will of the Father whose eternal law delivers the lawless herd from pitching into the crater. But I would so conduct myself as if that law applied to me. Without faith in a last judgement I would live as if I expected to be judged, which would not be so desperately difficult if I were more consistent. [322–3]

To 'live as if I expected to be judged'—this is precisely the ethics of Jewish agnosticism which permeates the writings of Serge Liberman, Jacob Rosenberg and many other authors in this study. Martin, an accomplished and widely published poet, writes:

Great, boundlessly great is the soul of man in his mortality
That creates the idea of God, an immortal creator.
How beautiful is the limited that creates the limitless! [254]

Unappeasable yearning: the Rousseauvian Romantic

The 'strange friend' of Martin's title is none other than himself. Among
Australian Jewish autobiographers Martin most embodies the mood and
values of Rousseauvian autobiography. Published posthumously in 1782,
Rousseau's *Confessions* is the quintessential autobiographical testament of
the tortured modern consciousness. This consciousness, which does not
feel adequately defined by theological or social categories, and cannot abide
the perceived constraints of Enlightenment rationality, must attempt a
titanic act of self-definition from within.

Rousseau's autobiographical mode was confessional in a new sense. The
template for confessional religious autobiography had most influentially been
set by Saint Augustine in his *Confessions* (AD 397).[228] Augustine confessed to
his God and was in effect overheard by his human reader. Rousseau's confessions are directed principally to his fellow man. In fact, much of his book is
devoted to self-vindication in the face of real and imagined detractors; but
where he does concede personal frailty he often ascribes it to what he calls
'my natural perversity'.[229] 'Perversity' here means unpredictable action without rational motivation. This perverse and bemusing self was Rousseau's
constant companion—a figure through whom he lived, but also one at whom
he gazed in puzzlement, as if at someone else.

Until death do us part, or perhaps unless mystical experience trans-
forms our sense of personhood, most of us move through life as an odd
couple: there is the 'me' that corresponds to the 'I am' feeling, and the 'me'
who is the subject of the stories I tell about myself, whether over coffee, in
an email to a friend, or in an autobiography. There are aspects of my self
that feel unproblematically like 'me', but others (perhaps occasionally
glimpsed in rage, passion or distress) that seem oddly remote from who 'I
am', as when Martin writes: 'Over the distance of years I am trying to touch
the thin fellow who is standing on that square in Morata...' [110] That
'fellow' is an earlier instalment of himself.

The self, *any* self, is to some extent heterogeneous. Postmodernists tend to see such heterogeneity as radical and insurmountable. Humanists generally retain some faith in our capacity actively to integrate the various facets of personhood, be it at a given moment or through the synthesizing process of autobiographical retrospection. David Martin's autobiographical tone can be anguished—as when he recalls a difficult period during which 'I was screaming for an unattainable fecundity of body and ... what?' [230]—but more often it is puzzled, and streaked with accepting amusement. Rousseau claimed to have 'bared my secret soul' so uncompromisingly that his autobiography had 'no precedent'.[230] In writing his autobiography David Martin was determined 'not to expatiate on my soul' [228]. But, as he concedes, he fails dismally in this self-effacing endeavour. *My Strange Friend* is very much—though not exclusively—a chronicle of the soul.

Rousseau was scandalously frank about his sexuality. As a boy he boards with a pastor, M. Lambercier, and his wife. Though affectionate, the good lady had sometimes to administer discipline. These occasions proved momentous for Jean-Jacques, then and in later life:

> But when in the end I was beaten I found the experience less dreadful in fact than in anticipation; and the very strange thing was that this punishment increased my affection for the inflicter. It required all the strength of my devotion and all my natural gentleness to prevent my deliberately earning another beating; I had discovered in the shame and pain of the punishment an admixture of sensuality which had left me rather eager than otherwise for a repetition by the same hand.[231]

David Martin recalls seeing a boy in his class in Berlin being caned by their teacher:

> The boy howled. When he had doled him out his portion the man laid the stick aside, sucked in his mouth and looked at the boy in a very strange way, as if he had just tried a new dish and was savouring the after-taste. I have frequently observed this expression on the faces of people like him, women included. Doris, our energetic Fräulein [a governess], displayed it at suitable times. It also appears on my face, no doubt.

Oswald and the caned boy: a scene from vanished childhood. I still learned easily, I was still cock of the walk. But if it was a thing of slight importance, would I not have driven it away long ago?

When does a proclivity become fixed and a tendency established? Is it gradual, one step at a time, or like a hidden spring which suddenly gushes forth? The young sado-masochist does not know what is happening to him: as soon ask a kitten why it chases a ball. To what branch is this voluptuous fruit grafted? [24]

Like Rousseau, Martin is puzzled by but finally accepting of his sexuality: 'No special pleading! I am conscious of damage sustained but also of happiness gained.' [26] He perceives this aspect of self as perverse, but not sexually so: its sexual proclivities, like its other dimensions, are 'strange', mercurial, but not deviant. Indeed he suggests that they have roots in universal, primordial human needs and drives. They spring from the craving to abolish personal singularity, to merge with the Other: 'The flagellator's thrill derives from pain shared in imagination. The beater is the beaten, the beaten the beater: each a glutton for punishment. This is the unappeasable yearning to draw the other into the self, restoring what was before the biological one became the biological two.' [26] He wonders: 'if sadism is not our common-or-garden power lust, what kind of lust is it?' [25–6]

This is no idle speculation. As Martin well knew, harrowing sexual sadism occurred in concentration camps; and even where extreme physical cruelty does not assume an explicitly sexual character we know that it often has origins in tortured unconscious erotic sources. No Jew writing after the Holocaust can be oblivious to such matters and Martin's autobiography makes clear, often in subtle ways, that he was well aware of them: seeing a ZR3 airship over Berlin, the young Ludwig senses for the first time 'how beautiful power can be' [29]. There is an erotics of power that runs all the way from sex to politics and often involves opaquely ornate interrelations between the two. During his early years in Berlin he was bullied at school, and in the holidays by *Lumpenproletariat* boys. He formulated a response which involved absorbing blows until he bled, then suddenly retaliating, often to good effect. He doesn't tell 'grown-ups' about these encounters but had they asked he would have been able to assure them in good faith that 'life was not treating me badly', because:

There was a second spring bubbling inside me from which splashed jets of pride and a queer passion.

Justice! I was about twelve when justice took me by the scruff and shook me. [32–3]

What is this 'queer passion'? It 'splashes', rather as sado-masochistic impulses 'gush' from 'a hidden spring'. Presumably, there was pleasure in being beaten before hitting back. It might also be (and the two possibilities are not mutually exclusive) that the 'queer passion' is another name for a passion for 'justice'—a sentiment we also associate with Rousseau, especially the author of *The Social Contract* and other political writings. It is impossible finally to know what Martin intended by the break between paragraphs that separates 'passion' and 'Justice', but the passage as it stands on the page perhaps suggests subterranean connections between power, the erotic, and the civic virtues which would set limits to the bullying omnivorousness of what Nietzsche called 'the will to power'. When Martin quotes that phrase [182] he means to caution against the dangers of transformative political aspiration.

The Gods that failed

In the early 1950s Martin's communist faith is collapsing. Looking back on this period is like being subjected to an 'ink-blot test': in recollection the 'personal and the political flow together and flow apart, a hopeless untidiness' [247]. Such uncertainty about the relationship between the 'private' and the 'public', the 'personal' and the 'political', became extraordinarily widespread in the West once the true horrors of totalitarianism—of both left and right—had become known. Richard Crossman edited a famous collection of essays by recanted Marxists entitled *The God that Failed: Six studies in communism*.[232] Contributors included Arthur Koestler, whom Martin greatly admired, and the English poet-autobiographer Stephen Spender, whose fine autobiography, *World within World*,[233] explored the relations between private and public worlds through the metaphor of concentric circles, and through narratives in which politics and personal relationships mutually impinge. Like David Martin, Spender is a confessional Romantic autobiographer. In this as in some other respects,

My Strange Friend lies squarely within what I have elsewhere called the tradition of 'post-totalitarian autobiography'.[234]

In *The God that Failed*, Koestler writes brilliantly about the experience of conversion. This had been a staple of religious autobiography in the West from autobiography's inception in religious confessional narrative. Here again Augustine's *Confessions* was the towering early example. In narratives of this kind the self undergoes an experience of transformative enlightenment, a turning-point, which occasions a sort of ninety-degree turn: the sinner, now filled with God's grace and forgiveness, mends his ways and embarks on a new life-trajectory. As Koestler shows, this narrative template was an ideal medium for recounting conversions to particular political ideologies, in this case Marxism. Its mirror image was the 'deconversion' narrative, which traces emergence from bewitchment by an ideological system—the repudiation of 'the God that failed'. David Martin reports 'notes of acrimony' [246] as he begins to fall out with ACP colleagues over Stalin and comes to fear the 'great collective noun, the People' [227]; but *My Strange Friend* does not feature any major conversion or deconversion sequences. It does however exhibit a fascination with turning-points, both authentic and false; it is particularly interested in the distinction between authentic and false 'revelation', and in how enlightenment or disenchantment in private life might impinge upon one's politics. Here again he is very much a follower of Rousseau, whose great rambling narrative abandoned Augustine's conversion structure for one in which various turning-points, some authentic, some not, occur along life's way; in which one's progress can involve backsliding as well as forward movement.

Martin's turning-points are occasioned by various registers of experience. There are moments of aesthetic bliss, as in the 'happy shocks' [64] he feels when he views two Rembrandt paintings in Holland. There are moments of surpassing spiritual calm such as he felt in Palestine—but not, as he might have expected, at the Wailing Wall. It is while looking out over Lake Tiberias that he experiences 'the peace that passeth understanding' [90]. And there is this, during a breakdown occasioned by an extramarital affair in the 1950s:

> I was dragging myself along Albion Street one mild, blowy morning under a
> wall topped by small, white, sweet-scented flowers. There I had a revelation. It

was like a sudden conversion, a leap from darkness into day. My soiled rags fell from me, the weight lifted: it does not matter what clichés are used. The goodness of the real touched me. [253]

The clichés do not matter because the 'revelation' proves to be bogus. This was not a moment of transformation: he was 'undergoing a perfectly commonplace middle-aged crisis'. The retrospectively amused Jew inquires: 'Great jumping Hasid, is that all there is to revelation?' [253]

Retrospection discerns 'sadism and masochism' [251] in his tangled love-life at the time and the reader is left wondering precisely what this means. Martin's long-suffering wife, Richenda, figures quite frequently, but always via Martin's ebullient, occasionally tortured narcissism. What did *she* make of all of this? Not just of his sexuality but his infidelities, and the relationship with June, which apparently triggered his breakdown in the 1950s? The book is dedicated to 'my anchor, my rudder and my sail'. The reference, as we discover during the breakdown narrative, is to Richenda:

> I loved Richenda. Or still better: she was my anchor, my rudder and my sail. *Every line that I have written all these long years through / Does bear your name even as it bears mine: / I write no poem but you write it too.* I slept with my arms about her and struck her in my bad dreams. After sixteen years together we still had sport. And a problem. She wanted to be courted even when I was racked by pure lust. [250]

This is one of the few moments in the narrative that attempt to represent Richenda's point of view. 'Love', he argues in familiar power-inflected terms, 'has no symmetry' [148]. Certainly his narrative account of love is asymmetrical, even by the standard of that most self-engrossed of genres, male autobiography. In the end, it's hard to know what he wants us to understand about the damage sustained, the happiness gained by his 'queer passion'. Perhaps he could not say more without doing more 'damage' than he already feared he had done. But it is also hard to know what he wants finally to say about the relationship between the personal and the political. The closing pages of the book feature some typically fine lyrical prose, particularly where Martin's characteristic stylistic dynamism seems to will itself to subside, to embrace intimations of mortality: 'One moment there is life, the next there is not ... I try to feel it. There is, vast beyond grasping and describing, the weight, the substance, the mass of matter: air, water, rock, clouds: layer upon layer of what fills and what is the cosmos.' [320] Most of these pages are taken up with a paean to Beechworth, the Victorian country town in which the Martins settled late in life. Many Romantic autobiographies conclude thus, departing the fraught world of metropolitan culture for such resolution as the pastoral can afford. Martin, to his credit, does not lay claim to a final calm. Even here he remains haunted by the Holocaust ('I cannot forgive them'); troubled by the life not lived ('I have not loved enough women', 'I have not seen enough of the world', 'I have not done the work I meant to do, not achieved what I hoped I would'). And although he writes 'I have lost my faith in the brotherhood of man', he is able to add: 'I still have some hope for man's cousinhood.' [323–4]

What does this 'hope' amount to? In what is it vested? 'There are no values on which to stand as upon a rock, for there is no "rock". Only the relative is absolute...' After all, 'nature abhors a monolith as it abhors a vacuum' [227]. Here again the Romantic eschewal of prescriptive rationality; the post-totalitarian horror of monolithic ideology. These attitudes in their turn express a form of postwar liberal humanism that knows itself, finally, to be without a synthesizing theory yet lives acceptingly with that knowledge, given the genocidal outcomes that certain theories had recently wrought. In the end, what an autobiographer of this kind—be it Koestler, Spender or David Martin—offers is not a synthetic worldview, but rather a self: the author's own, in all its complexity, contradiction, its fraught determination to transcend its own narcissism and to make generous contact with the bewildering plurality of the world. Such a self is driven but also riven by all manner of passions. Perhaps David Martin's 'queer passion' was both tortured and just. If so, he seems to say, he can accept it; and like Rousseau, he bids the reader to accept him too.

Deracination and Self-fashioning

Andrew Riemer's Multi-volume Autobiography

Always and already an illusion?

Deracination is literally the condition of being torn up by the roots. It can refer to physical displacement, especially from one's 'home', but also to cultural, spiritual and intellectual dislocation and estrangement. Deracination has been a feature of the Jews' history of exile and physical displacement for well over two millennia. The past two centuries, and particularly the post-Holocaust period, during which traditional forms of Judaism have been challenged by secularization, have seen the rise of a now familiar figure: the secular Jewish intellectual whose passion for ideas reflects the intensity of earlier forms of Jewish intellectuality, but whose intellectual orientation stands in tense, even refusing relation to traditions of Jewish belief. Andrew Riemer, a Hungarian Jew by birth, is a deracinated Jew *par excellence*, a man for whom Jewishness, and the Jewish fate more generally, occasions a kind of obsessive but alienated puzzlement and preoccupation.[235] In this as in some other respects he resembles another Hungarian Jew to whom he sometimes refers: the intellectual autobiographer and novelist, Arthur Koestler.[236]

An academic in the English Department at the University of Sydney from 1963 to 1994, in recent years Riemer has published no fewer than four works of autobiography: *Inside Outside* (1992), *The Habsburg Café* (1993), *America with Subtitles* (1995), and *Sandstone Gothic* (1998). A fifth first-person volume, *Between the Fish and the Mudcake* (1999), comprises a series of vignette-like autobiographical essays; its form inclines to memoir rather than full-blown autobiography. In 1996 he published *The Demidenko Debate*, a book that offers a qualified defence of Helen Demidenko/Darville's Holocaust novel, *The Hand that Signed the Paper*, and of those who bestowed literary awards upon it.

Riemer's autobiographical volumes constitute a large, strikingly cohesive and generally impressive body of work.[237] They capture with particular power the condition of a Jew whose family paid dearly for a faith they did not espouse. Given his personal history it is by no means a criticism to see him as a culturally estranged and largely disenchanted writer, a man who discerns in himself something bordering on 'deracinated cynicism'.[238] This cynicism, an all too familiar feature of post-Holocaust and postmodern culture, is reflected in the fear that everything that promises lasting value in human affairs is always and already an illusion. We might in some sense survive a disaster like the Holocaust, but redemption after such an event—if by that we mean the reinstatement of some supposedly lost condition of wholeness, innocence and security—is a very different matter. Riemer's 'project of self-fashioning'[239] is a memorable instance of the post-Holocaust and postmodern quest for personal and spiritual consolation—a quest that is both driven and blighted by doubt.

Chronicles of disenchantment

Riemer's family roots lie in Budapest. His parents were highly assimilated, non-practising, bourgeois Jews. His father, a textile manufacturer, and his mother shared a fascination with opera, cinema, various aspects of modern—and especially American—culture, and a love of the cosmopolitan café society of prewar Budapest and Vienna. Having survived the war in Budapest (though his father, who had been periodically separated from the family while doing forced labour, was shot and seriously ill at the end of the war), the family left for America, and made eventually for Australia in 1946. They arrived in Sydney in February 1947, days before Andrew's eleventh birthday. Most of his extended family had perished in the Holocaust. He and his parents settled in Sydney, Andrew going on to do an honours degree at Sydney University, then a PhD on the Elizabethan playwright James Shirley, at the University of London. Thereafter he joined the staff of the English Department at Sydney.

Riemer's autobiographical books are organized around a series of tropes, most of which reflect an outlook whose defining attitude is one of disenchantment. The volumes' arresting titles indicate the ways in which he thematizes and narrates his life-story. *Inside Outside*, a fine-grained inquiry into the exilic state, explores the migrant's feeling—so characteristic of diasporic experience more generally—of never being quite at home; of being almost inward with one's adoptive culture, but always, ultimately, external to it and to the ways it shapes and expresses selfhood. He writes of being 'neither inside nor outside, dwelling in a no-man's-land between the alien and the accepted' [*IO*, 109], a condition in which 'your otherness cannot be expunged' [5]. This volume, which deals predominantly with Riemer's life in Australia, and with a return visit to Hungary in 1990, makes relatively little reference to his Jewishness and declines, albeit in an oddly dismissive way, to detail the immediate family's brush with the Holocaust: 'It would serve little purpose to recount the tale of our survival, or to tell how we were reunited in a devastated Budapest in the spring of 1945.' [56]

Inside Outside ponders two aspects of the exilic condition that are central to Riemer's autobiographical oeuvre. One is the activity of 'refashioning' [104] the self, which many exiles and migrants engage in as they seek to adapt to a new culture and to reorient themselves in relation to their pasts. The second is an inner landscape of yearning and idealization he calls 'the other country of the mind' [2]. This 'country' is composed of highly charged and condensed images, recollections and fabrications of the actual country the exile has departed; but—and this is one reason why these books are so resonant, so rich in wider psychological and existential implication—it is not only exiles and migrants who harbour such internal landscapes. Such yearning idealization is fundamental to the very structures of human consciousness, to what Hegel and Sartre call our 'negativity': our drive and capacity to imagine ourselves as other than we are. In *The Habsburg Café*, Riemer puts it thus: 'We all carry in the secret recesses of our imagination a myth world—a place, a house, a landscape, a time—which often speaks to us most eloquently precisely because it is remote, perhaps forgotten, a very particular symbol of our longings and dreams.' [*HC*, 264] The imaginary café of Riemer's title is one such mythic symbol. In an early passage he describes a recurrent but not unpleasant haunting whereby the past revisits him in the form of a vision of a quintessential café of the Habsburg era:

> In my imagination, this café of the Habsburg world—in some unknown city or town of my early childhood when that Empire and realm, though no longer a political reality, still exerted an influence throughout its former territories—has

assumed a position of undisputed centrality. It has become a distillation, a compact, fleeting yet powerful image of a world irrecoverably lost, a world compromised by hatred and brutality, a world which must be approached with the armour of irony fully in place, and yet a world of irresistible allure. And it provides, no matter how tenuously, or how contingently, some signs of the survival of that world in dreams, in the imagination or in visions imprinted on my memory many years ago, a time when all experiences and sensations were new, fresh and shiningly clear. [*HC*, 19]

This passage exhibits some of Riemer's special talents as an autobiographer. It is delicately balanced between disenchantment and a kind of yearning for finer possibilities, an 'irresistible allure' in which the narrator seems not quite to have ceased to believe. There's a sense, reminiscent of Proust, of the way consciousness is composed and composes itself out of a weave of time, memory, yearning, dread, and the imperious drive to self-fashioning. The mode of consciousness revealed is highly symbolic, working through intense 'distillations' of image, other forms of sense memory, and association; it is also guardedly ironic, self-defensively distanced, as it confronts the horrors of the recent past. The café is an image of a vanished world, and yet, if only in memory, the world is not quite gone; it survives, however 'tenuously', 'contingently', in that 'country of the mind', where it exerts tremendous power, occupying a position of 'undisputed centrality' in the autobiographical consciousness.[240] Tantalizingly, the prose seems to hark back to an era when the world was young and did not stand in need of redemption. But was the world ever thus, or is this just the child's recollection of 'a time when all experiences and sensations were new, fresh and shiningly clear'—a recollection which adult awareness and the realities of history have shown to be pathetically naïve? The great café city of Budapest, after all, is 'the city where most of my family were killed, or else where they started their journey to death' [*HC*, 141]; and he knows that such cafés 'overheard terrible sentiments and hatreds expressed over cups of thick rich coffee' [178]. Elsewhere in the same volume he writes that the Holocaust has made the café world, the world in general, 'incapable of redemption' [148].

Such comments reflect a profoundly tragic view of the world. There are various notions of the tragic, some of which claim that human beings learn from tragedy and are therefore less likely to reproduce it. Riemer, who admits to having 'what is probably an excessively pessimistic temperament' [*IO*, 199], is not so sanguine. In *America with Subtitles* he argues: 'Humanity is, by its very nature, imperfect—there is no need for a doctrine of original sin to account for that. We do not profit from adversity, nor do we look into our own hearts when we endure the cruelty and contempt of others.'[241] The Holocaust and other such events—he insists that there is no qualitative difference between the Holocaust and other genocides[242]—show that there is tremendous evil in the world and that human beings are powerless to curb it. Of course, if Riemer meant such sentiments without qualification his entire autobiographical project, which he describes as the chronicling of 'the emotional, cultural and spiritual quandary of people like myself... before they recede from communal memory' [*IO*, 162], would be called into question. Why bother chronicling anything if there is nothing to be learnt from it? In fact his outlook, though tragic, is not quite as despairing as some of his more apocalyptic pronouncements might suggest. His autobiographical volumes indicate that one can be profoundly disenchanted without entirely losing faith in the possibilities of human betterment, or of personal and spiritual accommodation.

America with Subtitles is another autobiographical study in disenchantment and undeception, much of it focused on his parents' experience during a few disorienting weeks in New York in late 1946 and early 1947, prior to the family's arrival in Sydney. Like the first two volumes, this one has a 'palindromic' [*HC*, 6] structure wherein the narrative is precipitated by, and centrally concerned with, the impact of Riemer's return visits to the places of his childhood five decades later. The 'subtitles' of the title refer to the fact that in New York his parents, who had become enamoured of American modernity in Budapest principally through American movies, were rudely confronted by a city that afforded no running translation of itself. They were also to find that translation is in any case a woefully approximate source of cultural understanding; that their cherished dream image of America—their 'country of the mind' [*AS*, 24]—had been derived from Hungarian subtitles that rendered the essential alienness of American culture in deceivingly familiar Hungarian terms. It is in New York that 'powerful illusions' are 'shattered' [160], as the mecca of modernity is revealed to be 'a disappointing and banal world' [287].

On his return in 1996 Riemer manages to recapture important aspects of that first visit—in particular, to find a hotel that had been the scene of an embarrassing and revealing incident in which his mother had shied away from physical contact with a black woman in an elevator [305]. The return is not without its pleasures and consolations, but the book's emphasis again falls on the sense of disenchantment: the New York that is fabled and misrepresented in subtitles proves to be, like so much of Riemer's own experience, a bathetic disappointment.

Something similar occurs in *Sandstone Gothic*, whose title refers to the Sydney University campus, and also presumably to some of the traumatic events that occurred during the split in the English Department in the 1960s: the campus looks like the real—European—thing, but is in fact an imitation, a mini-landscape that flatters to deceive. So too does the English Department, which in this volume at times stands as a symbol of the moral tawdriness of academic life more generally, though the book does affirm some of the ideals that characterized the department before and after its internal upheaval. Much of the second half of the narrative is taken up with the split, and with an utterly damning account of S. L. Goldberg, the Challis Professor of English from 1963 to 1966 and one of Australia's foremost literary scholars.[243] *Sandstone Gothic* has a shrillness of tone, an indicting rancour towards others, an air of ungenerous self-justification, that are not present in the earlier volumes. The veracity and ferocity of Riemer's attack on Goldberg have been questioned by some former Sydney colleagues.[244] What can be said with certainty is that the salvo does not reflect sentiments such as the following in *America with Subtitles*: 'our secular world might benefit from the essentially religious spirit that urges the forgiveness of sins irrespective of the merits of the individual' [332]. Riemer is utterly unforgiving of Goldberg, and claims—perhaps revealingly, given that they were both deracinated Ashkenazic Australian Jews—that 'Goldberg and I had almost nothing in common' [*SG*, 113].

The 'bad Jew' as 'self-fashioner'

Riemer's claim about himself and Goldberg does make some sense insofar as neither man sets much store—culturally, and certainly in religious terms—by his Jewishness. Both are highly assimilated, secular men, more given to seek spiritual sustenance in English literature than in Jewish tradition. Indeed throughout his autobiographical writings Riemer disclaims positive identification with Jewishness. In *The Demidenko Debate* he pronounces himself a 'bad Jew' because he cannot see the Holocaust as qualitatively different from other genocidal events: 'For that reason, no doubt, I am a bad Jew, even perhaps a self-hating one as some have suggested'.[245] Whether he is self-hating, I cannot and do not wish to judge. What is clear from Riemer's autobiographical narratives is that his Jewishness does not adequately ground, or provide an organizing structure for, his sense of self, of personal identity. This doesn't, at least in my view, make him 'a bad Jew', but it does mean that he is confronted with a much greater need to fashion a self than would be the case for someone able to derive the parameters and stuff of selfhood from an already-given set of cultural materials, be they Jewish or other. Riemer is a deracinated Jewish autobiographer—his Jewishness is an element but not the key determinant of his complex and shifting sense of personal identity. His autobiographical writing thus recalls and partakes of what he terms a 'long and perplexing process of self-fashioning' [*SG*, 3].

But there is more to be said, in this case, about the relationship between Jewishness and self-fashioning. Riemer, a fine autobiographer of migrant experience, attributes most of his need to self-fashion to his exilic status. He says of himself as a boy at school in Sydney: 'I attempted to invent a personality for myself based on what I understood to be the most desirable characteristics of Australian boyhood' [*IO*, 105]. Yet—and this is where the Holocaust, and so his Jewishness, re-enters the picture—that exilic condition was caused by the Holocaust, by the fact that his family, though secular and thoroughly assimilated, happened to be Jews. His situation is the familiar one in which, by a grotesque but somehow fitting historical irony, the Holocaust—the event intended, at least in its later stages, to liquidate European Jewry—engenders in many hitherto highly assimilated Jews a degree of engagement with the Jewish fate that would probably not otherwise have occurred.

The Holocaust marks Riemer's autobiographical writings in three principal ways: it more than anything shapes his deeply tragic worldview; it functions as a contingent and indirect cause of the condition with which he as an autobiographer is most concerned, that of the exile who is never quite at home; and it precipitates a puzzled and troubled engagement with what in general terms can be called the Jewish fate. For this deracinated Jew, that fate cannot yield much by way of conventional religious belief or consolation. But this does not mean that Riemer is merely a secular, 'cynical' rationalist. On the contrary, his autobiographies include an attenuated version of the spiritual quest that runs deep in the history of the genre of autobiography. He writes of a state he calls 'spiritual desiccation' [*IO*, 164]. He often uses the term to describe the condition of first-generation migrants like his parents; but he also applies it to white Australian society at large —'We are all strangers in the land. We have all been cut off from forces that are necessary for our psychic or spiritual survival.' [163]—and to the general condition of secular late modernity. He himself is a victim of that condition, and the autobiographical volumes, with their palindromic quest structures, are in part attempts to find and narrate forms of personal and spiritual accommodation that will help redress the sense of spiritual nullity he bemoans.

The books present the 'project of self-fashioning' and the quest for spiritual accommodation as intimately related, even mutually sustaining processes. Like all sophisticated liberal-humanists [*AS*, 330], Riemer is interested in the part that culture plays in shaping self, and the sense of self. In *Inside Outside* he writes of 'the intimate, deeply-ingrained, essentially mysterious core of the personality which seems to be implanted very early in life' [*IO*, 4–5] by one's culture, and which the migrant carries into his or her adoptive cultural world. Riemer often seems torn between the idea that human consciousness is intrinsically exilic (in other words, naturally splintered and given to feelings of estrangement), and the contrasting belief that there is something uniquely divided, inauthentic about the consciousness of exiles. On the second of these views, the exile can never redress the gap that arises from his or her consciousness having been shaped in a different culture. Yet it is exactly here, in the drive to redress this situation, to make one's self an authentic instance of the adopted culture's modes of selfhood, that the 'project of self-fashioning' or 'refashioning' has its inception.

The great danger of this project is that it could lead to deeply inauthentic modes of selfhood. In Riemer's autobiographies, inauthenticity is associated with a number of terms that pertain to simulation and fabrication: 'imitation' and 'pastiche' [*SG*, 149], 'ventriloquism' [28], 'nostalgia' [20], 'parodic mimicry' [29], invention of identity [*IO*, 105]; it is also associated with a kind of willed amnesia—he writes of the 'all-encompassing voluntary amnesia' [104] that he had practised during his school days in Sydney—which seeks to dodge the difficulties of reconciling present and past by annulling earlier phases of one's life. The typical characteristic of inauthentic self-fashioning is a brittle and ultimately hollow simulation of models of selfhood that circulate in the adoptive culture. In *Inside Outside*, Riemer writes: 'I had learnt to mimic with some efficiency the superficial characteristics of Australian adolescence, but it was no more than mimicry, representing nothing fundamental or intrinsic, merely a thin veneer pasted over emptiness.' [146]

Here, as in some other respects—his deracinated Hungarian Jewish condition, his horror of totalitarianism, his tragic outlook, his yearning for the numinous—Riemer's autobiographies resemble those of Arthur Koestler. In Koestler's classic second volume of extended autobiography, *The Invisible Writing*, he describes himself as a young man whose 'smirk' and 'brilliantine' concealed a 'gaping emptiness: the void of the nineteenth century's scientific materialism'.[246] Like Koestler, Riemer seeks a dimension of meaning beyond the mechanistic, rationalistic, secular spirit of modernity. Koestler sought this in the New Physics, parapsychology, and explorations of his own 'oceanic'[247] mystical experiences. Riemer, a sceptic about the possibility of visionary experience, at least in the modern era,[248] nevertheless has his moments. In *Sandstone Gothic*, recalling a church service on Christmas Day in Hertfordshire, he writes: 'it was hard not to be moved by some sense of the numinous and the miraculous, no matter how much a rational or cynical self might have mocked that improbable tale of a virgin birth' [*SG*, 103]. The 'numinous' is the very antithesis of imitation, pastiche, simulation. It offers access to a dimension that transcends the frailties and falsehoods of human culture. Its existence suggests that, after all, everything is not always and already an illusion; that there is some form of transcendent 'truth' in—or rather beyond—the world. It is typical of Riemer the assimilated Jew that the experience he reports in this instance should occur in a church and not a synagogue; yet there are related instances that have quite specific Jewish content. There's a complex moment in *The Habsburg Café* when he visits a synagogue in Szeged, a town whose Jewish population was almost totally liquidated during the

Holocaust. One of the few surviving members of the community gives an account of the synagogue—an account which is heavily 'fiscal' in emphasis. Riemer finds himself feeling deeply ambivalent about the man, even to the point of starting to 'entertain disturbing suspicions about racial stereotypes'. But then:

> His voice is unsteady and cracked, yet for all its imperfections, his chant pulses with echoes of a world none of us has experienced—a world of worship, belief, a sense of community with a people in its joys as well as in its sufferings, a world richer and perhaps more satisfying than our humdrum existence. And I begin to sense that despite the shabbiness of this old man, despite his unattractive singsong accounts of vast sums of money, his life may be fuller, more worthwhile and certainly closer to God than mine. [*HC*, 173]

There lurks in this passage a tone of muted condescension that occasionally shadows Riemer's autobiographical writing; nevertheless, one does not doubt his fundamental sincerity. What is perhaps most important about this incident is not its Jewish content, which is after all largely a moment of wistful nostalgia for a lived Judaism that Riemer's family shed generations ago, but rather the way autobiography here attempts, through the narration of a physical return to the world of childhood, to provide such forms of spiritual possibility and solace as are available to this deracinated, sceptical man.

The Habsburg Café climaxes and approaches its conclusion with another such moment. It occurs in the Hungarian town of Sopron, where his parents had lived at the time of their meeting and courtship. (The fact that his mother was educated by Ursuline nuns in Sopron is one of many indicators of just how assimilated the families had become.) During his palindromic visit of 1991 Riemer returns to Sopron, having failed to do so a year earlier. Sopron holds a special place in his memory as an embodiment of the world of his youth. It is the 'centre, focus or perhaps shrine of an eccentric mythology' [*HC*, 272], a mythology whose landscape is that 'country of the mind' which has haunted his consciousness all these years. His mother had taken him on visits to the town before the war. His first impressions on returning to it are underwhelming; he does not even seem to have been particularly moved by seeing the flat where his mother and family had lived. The one clear memory he has of the town is of its watch-tower. After walking for some time he finds this edifice, 'just as I remember it, at its base a squat, rough-hewn construction but rising to a graceful baroque steeple' [274]. He describes this vindication of memory, this moment of achieved reconnection with the past, as 'the moment of integration, the re-entry into mythology' [275]. It is no small matter for an autobiographer so riven by internal and circumstantial disjunction to use a word like 'integration'. As is shown by the beautifully understated description that follows, something of real consequence has happened:

> I experience an entirely irrational sense that somehow or other I belong here, in a way that I do not quite belong in Budapest, that city of terrible memories, or Vienna, despite its allure, or even Sydney, the familiar place I now fondly call my home. [*HC*, 275]

For this moment, at least, the exile has come home; more importantly, he *feels* at home, and is thereby released, however provisionally or fleetingly, from the cycle of need, yearning and unfulfilment that has marked the last half-century of his life. He continues:

> There is no illumination, no sense of a peace passing all understanding as this goal is achieved. There is, however, a mildly pleasant sense of satisfaction— despite aching eyes, running nose and fiery throat—that the myth world which has coloured so much of my imagination in the course of my life does have at least some foundation, that it is not entirely the product of misplaced longings and dissatisfaction. [*HC*, 275]

The vindication of memory that comes with recognizing the tower has several dimensions. It suggests that memory in general may have a fair degree of reliability and that, therefore, the world which resides in memory is to some significant degree 'real', and thus assimilable to the more readily verifiable 'reality' that is the present. Vindication also has powerful implications for self-esteem, since it suggests that the 'country of the mind' is not simply the product of inconsolable yearning, regret and neurosis. The 'country' is *there*, at least in part; and what is really important is that—in this instant—yearning, memory, past, present and future all somehow fuse.

At such moments 'self-fashioning', or 'refashioning', attains a mysterious efficacy that belies Riemer's more apocalyptic pronouncements. Fusion and 'integration' are the very antithesis of the 'all-encompassing voluntary amnesia' he had sought in that earlier and inauthentic phase of self-fashioning. They signal the emergence of a self that, to some extent at least, can now live the continuities of past, present and future, and can thus more fully *be* a self than hitherto.

The vision of the watchtower may be mysterious but it is not mystical. Riemer takes pains not to overstate the drama of what has occurred. The phrasing pointedly eschews the prose of mystical—in this case Christian—revelation: there is 'no sense of a peace passing all understanding'. There is no euphoria, no blinding light, just 'a mildly pleasant sense of satisfaction'. This, then, is a moment of psychological and spiritual accommodation, one that assists in the lifelong search for what he calls 'cultural salvation' [*IO*, 210]; but is not a moment of redemption. It suggests that, after all, everything is not already an illusion; that some of what we see, remember, cherish and believe in *is* real. But there is no radical affirmation of the world, nor of the possibilities of salvation or meaning. Much that made Sopron and other places of his childhood seem worth cherishing was obliterated by the Holocaust and the war. The moment by the watchtower cannot restore a world that was for ever 'poisoned' [*HC*, 141] by these harrowing and faith-destroying events.

It is striking that Riemer here reports feeling more at home in Sopron than in Sydney, the city he now 'fondly' calls 'my home'. Here as elsewhere, Australia occupies an ambivalent and shifting place in his consciousness. In *Inside Outside* he had written: 'I am nevertheless more Australian than anything else.' [*IO*, 207] Like so many Australian Jewish autobiographers, he is grateful for the security Australia has offered [22], and for what he sees as 'the essential health of Australian society' [23]. Yet his strongest sense of 'home' still lies in the world of his childhood. In part, this is because the 'mysterious core' of his personality was formed there; in part, too, because all white Australians are 'strangers' in their own land, bereft of the 'forces that are necessary for our psychic or spiritual survival'. In fact, for Riemer even Australia, apparently the very embodiment of solidity, has the transience and tragic vulnerability to evil that he thinks characteristic of human affairs in general. His autobiographies reflect the mind's intermittent and often unavailing struggle to wrest substance, solidity, decency, verifiability, continuity, from a world that all too often seems a landscape of travesty and illusion.

'In the Land of pre-Memory'

Relational Life-writing in Susan Varga's *Heddy and Me*

With the Other in the territory of fear

In August 1990, Susan Varga, an Australian Jewish writer of Hungarian extraction, meets up with her mother, Heddy, and her stepfather, Gyuszi, in the mother's native city of Budapest. The family, which includes an older sister, had migrated to Australia in 1948. Susan's father had died in a labour camp in early 1944; Gyuszi's wife and two sons were killed at Auschwitz.

During this return trip in 1990, Susan and Heddy visit the flat in which Heddy had lived, with various interruptions, between 1938 and 1948. In *Heddy and Me*,[249] a book that skilfully combines autobiography, biography and testimony, Varga writes:

> Mother is telling me where everything was, how it was, but I really don't take much in. I am content just to be here. I feel comfortable, familiar. I could sit down in a corner and read, or go to sleep. Aah, I am in the land of pre-memory again—I *feel* this territory. I can feel myself, at three or four, watching from the balcony as the bogey man comes down the street. [277]

This moment of apparently reassuring restitution isn't altogether misleading. Such experiences occur in other second-generation post-Holocaust Australian Jewish autobiographies. These books often record a return journey to Jewish ancestral places wrecked by the Holocaust. In *The Habsburg Café*, Andrew Riemer describes experiencing a 'moment of integration'[250] in the Hungarian town of Sopron. Visiting Bialystok for the first time, Arnold Zable finds 'Romance and terror, light and shadow… Yet, somehow, never have I felt so much at peace.'[251] But such episodes tend to be fleeting: soon it emerges that the wife of the couple who now occupy Heddy's old flat is an Auschwitz survivor and that, in reality, Varga is back in that world she calls 'my territory of fear' [61].

On another day, when they visit the town of Pécs, an information sheet they are given at the door of the old synagogue says that the quotation engraved on the ark reads: 'Those who trust in the Lord will not be disappointed.' Varga writes: 'Bullshit, I think, look what happened to the trusting and the Godless alike.' [254] This, then, is secular post-Holocaust Australian Jewish autobiography; a form that bears witness, at this antipodean remove from Europe, to the 'territory of fear' that is the European past.

Susan Varga's case is complex, for she is not in any simple sense the child of a survivor. Indeed this is one of the book's central findings. It is also complex in narrative terms. Like most Australian Jewish autobiographies, *Heddy and Me* is essentially realist in its narrative mode. However, the book's structure is somewhat unusual in that the Holocaust story is focused through the mother–daughter relationship itself: Heddy and Susan. This is one of many examples in Australian Jewish autobiography [252] of 'relational life-writing'. [253] The defining characteristic of such narratives, at least as I understand it, is that the authorial self comes in some fundamental way to define itself through its relationship with an important Other—in Varga's case, a parent. Of course we all come to such understandings via the Other (I capitalize the word as is sometimes done in philosophical and related discussions); but autobiographers of this kind take the process further than most: they explore it in their narratives. Often the act of writing itself deepens, extends and redirects the process. Like many relational life-narratives, *Heddy and Me* arises out of a collaboration between author and significant Other.

Not properly her mother's life-story

Heddy and Me involves a literal auto/biographical 'pact' between mother and daughter. In this it resembles an important work of indigenous life-writing published in the same year (1994): *Auntie Rita* [254] is Rita and Jackie Huggins's attempt to penetrate 'a double fold of silence' [255] wrought by colonialism and the older generation's diffidence about bespeaking the horrors of the past. Susan Varga has been reluctant to probe her European past, but finds to her surprise in early 1990 that, in fact, Heddy wants to talk about it; indeed she has been 'waiting for Susan' [5] to help her do so— to talk not only about her life in hiding with the children during the Holocaust, but also about being raped by Russian soldiers, and much else.

Susan begins recording Heddy's recollections in March 1990. At this point she is forty-seven; Heddy is seventy-three. These sessions last for six months, after which the two meet, together with Gyuszi (and Susan's partner Anne), in Hungary. The narrative interleaves four principal time-perspectives: first, the period from Heddy's birth in 1916 to 1960, where the story ends, bringing Heddy to age forty-four and Susan to seventeen; second, the present of the recorded interviews, the account of which includes commentary about the two women's experience of the narrating situation and the way it impinges on their already complex relationship; third, the post-interview return to Hungary, with its many memory probes back into life before, during and just after the war; fourth, the writing present, which renders the interview phase and the return to Hungary as part of the relational past, and provides a vantage-point from which the various pasts, together with the evolution of the torn but fond mother–daughter relationship, can be accorded a kind of provisional summation. As Susan's early warning to Heddy makes clear, this is no simple story of the mother-as-survivor's life:

> I've told her it won't be her life story, not properly. It will be filtered through my reactions and thoughts, my second generation eyes. [5]

Acts of restitution

These 'second generation eyes' belong to one for whom being a daughter involves a kind of existential doubleness: she's a daughter who seems to ascribe enormous causal power to the mother–daughter bond; but she's also a particular kind of daughter. She is the progeny both of a Holocaust survivor and of a migrant. It is this convergence of factors—Holocaust and migrant—and the interaction between them which define Susan's position as 'daughter' in the narrative. Like Andrew Riemer, also a Hungarian migrant, Susan feels 'really different, and alienated' [208]. Later she feels 'my Australian and my other self synthesising' [208]; but still the need for emotional separation from Heddy requires that Susan become 'her antith-esis' [226], that she define herself in opposition to Heddy. What she wants to be is 'a proper New Australian—forward-looking, polyglot; and a new kind of Jew—proud of who I was, but cosmopolitan' [225]. Individuation through separation from the parent is a very widely occurring need; in some cultures it amounts to a kind of individual right. But for the children of survivors this elemental pattern can encounter complicated, even tortured forms of resistance. So massively has the mother–daughter relation been shaped and mediated by the Holocaust that Susan cannot focus on the one without also confronting the other.

The same is true, at least in part, for the critic of the text; but what critical perspective could accommodate such complexity? Feminist readings, especially those informed by psychoanalytic approaches, will address some of the more familiar, or so-to-speak generic, mother–daughter issues involved here. But the Holocaust dimension seems to require forms of discussion that reach beyond 'normal' developmental processes. The psychiatrist Melanie Klein famously writes of what the resentful baby experiences as the 'bad' breast.[256] Children born during the Holocaust fed at some of the least soothing breasts imaginable. Looking back on herself as a baby, dangerously ill with dysentery, her mother in terror and hiding, Varga writes of 'that child who drank in anxiety and terror with her mother's milk' [135]. One thinks of the refrain from Paul Celan's great Holocaust poem, 'Deathfugue':

> Black milk of daybreak we drink you at night
> we drink you at morning and midday we drink you at evening
> we drink and we drink ...[257]

In March 1944, when the Germans arrive, Heddy's milk literally dries up. This form of deprivation has been a major source of discussion in a field of psychology known as attachment theory.[258] *Heddy and Me* tries to retrace a story of catastrophic disruption in early life, and to identify and address its consequences in later years. In a passage from which I've already quoted, Varga writes of the interview process:

> It occurs to me, too, that maybe I am not just searching for him [her biological father], but also for a small child who didn't die. I am beginning to wonder about her, that child who drank in anxiety and terror with her mother's milk and who hovered apathetic between life and death for months. Until now she has been no more than an object. Heddy's baby, not me.

I inch a little closer to her. She may be nearer than I know, deep within me, still alive. Waiting. [135]

There's a sense in which autobiographical writing (and autobiographical consciousness more generally) inevitably 'others' the self, rendering the written-about self as Other, an object, for the writing self. In this somewhat paradoxical sense autobiographical writing is indeed constitutively relational. In the above passage, Susan's infant self appears as 'object', opaque to her adult consciousness. With Heddy's assistance, however, she can begin to reconstruct that infant's world and so, tentatively, to match certain persistent feelings with the circumstantial recollections Heddy provides. This matching resembles what the child psychologist Daniel Stern calls the 'working heuristic' through which patient and therapist seek a 'narrative point of origin'[259] for emotional disturbances that seem to have their inception in very early interpersonal disjunction between carer and child. Whether the feelings and the developmental occurrences do in fact match can never finally be known, any more than such things can ultimately be known in psychotherapy. But in either case, it is the conviction that they do which holds out the possibility of healing. In a sense, the processes of interviewing and writing recapitulate in more sustaining form the inaugural mother–daughter relation: Heddy's gift of story helps compensate Susan for the deprivation she suffered as a Holocaust baby.

In the book's Epilogue, there is a final and decisive twist. Susan tells of attending a conference called 'Child Survivors of the Holocaust', and of its transformational impact on her: 'I went as a member of the second generation. I come home a member of the first. I was there.' [300] She is not just the child of a survivor, but a survivor herself; a child survivor. This puts her in a dramatically revised relation to herself, and to Heddy. Of that baby again, she says:

I know who she is now. She is a child who survived the War, at the outer edges of the Holocaust. I can trace her through who I am now. She is my fears, my sense of displacement, my omnipresent sense of threat. She is also my resilience and accommodation, my will to find meaning and to make things work. [301]

The emphases on will, agency and capacity for accommodation are fundamental in *Heddy and Me*. Varga's 'will to find meaning and to make things work', reminiscent of Viktor Frankl's notion of the 'the will to meaning',[260] animates a narrative that has the power, partially at least, to release the self from the most destructive aspects of the past that it narrates. We are reminded that in many instances relational developments don't just happen: they are sought, cultivated, elaborated—sometimes, as in the case of Rita and Jackie Huggins, through the writer's agential role in collaborative life-writing. Of course most lives will contain a network of relations with important others, and changes in any given dimension of a life will often interact with patterns in other dimensions. Susan's decision to leave her marriage and enter a relationship with another woman [229] is an extraordinarily important moment in her own journey; but inevitably, in the short term it complicates relations between mother and daughter.

A profound change in the relationship begins during the interview phase. Finding that her hostile attitude to Heddy's preoccupation with possessions is beginning to moderate, Susan writes: 'Only recently have I started to think of Heddy and myself as part of something bigger.' [225] That something, of course, is the Holocaust. Towards the end of the return trip to Hungary, Susan senses 'a new ease, born of something shared, between Mother and me' [288]. During the interviews, and subsequently during the writing, Susan has had to confront Heddy's stories of terror, rape and loss. Having done so, and having come to know herself, too, as a survivor, as one who shares her mother's historical fate more intimately than she had ever imagined, Susan establishes a new sense of self-in-relation-to Heddy; a kind of other-directedness, an *alterity*, that befits their particular shared history. There is nothing normative about this: Varga offers no prescriptions that might hold beyond this horrific and anomalous history. But there is a strong sense that a unifying existential thread—something relating to her status as child survivor—has come to light, first in the talking, then in the telling. The book's title is *Heddy and Me*, but the new-found sense of internal coherence, and the commonality that has emerged through narrative collaboration, occasion a change in Susan's use of the first-person pronoun. The book's last line is: 'We have things in common, Heddy and I.' [302]

Because her mode of relation to Heddy, and the relations between hitherto disparate aspects of her own life, seem so much clearer now, Susan can stand more confidently, more givingly, alone. *Heddy and Me* suggests that the richest kinds of singularity are sustained by relation.

'What For Do I Have to Remember This?'

Artistry and Family Angst in Mark Baker's *The Fiftieth Gate*

Beyond realism

The Fiftieth Gate[261] begins with a poem by the author:

> *There is a palace of hidden treasures.*
> *In this palace there are forty-nine gates that separate*
>   *good from evil, the blessing from the curse.*
> *Beyond them is a fiftieth gate larger than the entire world.*
> *It is a hidden gate.*
> *On this gate there is a lock, which has a narrow place*
>   *where the key may be inserted.*
> *Come and see.*
> *Through this gate all other gates may be seen.*
> *Whoever enters the fiftieth gate sees through God's eyes*
>   *from one end of the world to the other.*
> *The darkness or the light.*
> *Come and see.*
> *The key is the broken heart, the yearning for prayer,*
>   *the memory of death*
> *The key is the forgotten heart, the murdered prayer,*
>   *the death of memory.*
> *It opens the blessing or the curse.*
> *Come and see.*

Some of the poem's many implications emerge as this rich and complex text unfolds, but even then readers not deeply learned in Jewish theology will need help from the explanatory notes that conclude the book. Here Baker provides some of the sources for the figure of the gate, which include the Bible, Talmudic literature and Jewish mysticism. A particularly important source is the Midrash, a body of writings in which Jewish sages offer interpretations, some of them highly creative, of scriptural passages. Thus the book's short twelfth chapter recounts a passage according to which four rabbis, including the legendary Rabbi Akiva, 'entered a field, past a gate guarded by an angel brandishing a sword made of fire'. Only Rabbi Akiva emerges from this field, which is like 'the Garden whose fruits reveal the secrets of the world'. Baker's text continues:

> My parents taught:
>> Rabbi Akiva entered the field,
>> through the gate,
>> past the fiery sword.
>
> He does not exit. [61]

The parental Holocaust narrative here functions as a text which sits in dynamic and ironic relation to the Midrash narrative. The age-old act of Jewish textual interpretation now incorporates the Holocaust, insisting that Jewish tradition take account of the Annihilation and asserting the right of this son of survivors to fashion interpretations of his own. Given the traumatic perplexities of Holocaust memory, the search for a new interpretive synthesis will sometimes take strange, associative, even mystical forms. Baker's narrative suggests that however inventive, his interpretations are just that—interpretations. It seldom implies that there is a final bedrock of 'truth' that can be reached.

The poem is also reminiscent of a modern source: T. S. Eliot's *Four Quartets*, the first of which, 'Burnt Norton', contains the lines:

> Other echoes
> Inhabit the garden. Shall we follow?
> Quick, said the bird, find them, find them,
> Round the corner. Through the first gate,
> Into our first world, shall we follow
> The deception of the thrush?…[262]

Eliot's High Anglican outlook is—to say the least—at a great remove from Baker's worldview, and one would not want to overstate the stylistic similarities between the two poems. Nevertheless there are affinities: each has a tone of ironically understated prophetic solicitation, and each alludes to gates that open into mysteriously salient worlds of moral-spiritual experience. Baker's literary manner, with its amalgam of Jewish learning and hints of poetic High Modernism, says much about his book. *The Fiftieth Gate* is Holocaust memoir of high literary aspiration and complexity. Indeed it is the most accomplished example of an Australian Jewish autobiography that eschews the realism characterizing most such texts and embraces modernist narrative experimentation: not just poetry, but inventive techniques of narrative juxtaposition and transition, interleaved historical documents, innovative engagements with sociological generalizations about survivors and the experience of their children.

The experimental impulse, however, does not express an angry or transgressive attitude towards mainstream Australian culture and its ethos of literary realism. Australia figures in the book largely as an antipodean haven from horror, albeit one so removed from the scene of the tragedy that the Holocaust cannot be negotiated without return journeys to Europe. Baker's experimentation is an attempt to gain greater imaginative penetration of the Holocaust and its aftermath than realist techniques might enable him to achieve. But the sophistication of the approach has another and less intended outcome. In this, as in so many second-generation Australian Jewish autobiographies, the author has much greater formal education, and a far more secure grasp of English, than the parents. The greater his sophistication, the greater the potential intellectual and expressive gulf between the generations. Here, as in many other instances, the second generation's superior intellectual attainments have not only narrative but also emotional implications: this itself is a major factor in family relations, which can become tense, complex, even explosive when the child undertakes to reconstruct family history, including the survivor-parents' Holocaust experience.

When Mark and his mother, Genia, return with his father, Yossl, to Birkenau, where he had been incarcerated, Yossl displays a range of responses: anxious, flippant, denying, admitting, angry. As he seeks familiar places in the camp his feet scuff water from lush grass into the air. The son of the survivor walks quite literally in his wake: 'I walk behind, dodging the spray that follows his movements.' [163] They come to a door—another gate—but it is locked. Yossl tries several doors before finding one that admits them into the barrack where he had slept. As the visit concludes, the

father demands of the son: 'What for do I have to remember this?' [165–6].
In its intent, as in its Polish inflection, the question is reminiscent of
another second-generation narrative, Art Spiegelman's *Maus*, where the
father, Vladek, finally pleads of his inquiring son: 'So… let's stop, please,
your tape recorder …' [263] Yossl's question stings, because as Mark so repeatedly and self-accusingly tells us, this narrative project springs from an
'uncontrollable urge' on his part to ask questions, to discover everything he
can about the Holocaust's impact on his family—not least on himself and
his identity. His father's accented Polish-Australian way of posing the
question strikingly highlights the gap in expressive sophistication between
the two men. As survivor and survivor's son they have much in common,
yet a vast generational and experiential disparity divides them.

This is painfully, but also in its way beautifully, apparent in Mark's
narrative reconstruction of the death of Hinda, Yossl's mother. The account
must be imagined because Hinda was deported to Auschwitz and gassed,
and thus unable, like millions of others, to tell her own story. Here again
Baker calls upon the deeper resonances of poetry for assistance, in this case
six short lines by Dan Pagis, a Romanian-born survivor who emigrated to
Israel. Baker quotes in full Pagis's best-known poem, 'Written in Pencil in
the Sealed Railway-Car' [14]:

> here in this carload
> i am eve
> with abel my son
> if you see my other son
> cain son of man
> tell him that i

Holocaust writing, of whatever kind, is an attempt to complete the poem of
the life that was silenced, whether in death or in the pain of survival. In a
magnificent extended passage late in the book, Baker inserts Hinda's name
into the Pagis poem—

> here in the carload
> i am Hinda
> tell him that i … [261]

—then imaginatively completes her story, right to the moment of her death in the gas chamber.

> Two eyes watch from glassy cavities behind the sealed door. What do they see?
>
> Letters dancing, etched on broken tablets soaring up to angel arms tapping on the gate to God's palace.
>
> *Aleph, beit.* Holy letters blue and bloated, befouled with filth and excrement.
>
> *Gimmel, daleth.* Rivers of blood gushing through gates from crowns of wounded scrolls. Letters with eyes, holes wide open, tangled in words carved on arms strapped in leather.
>
> *Heh, vav* spewed from twisted tongues and mouths. Seraphs dancing for God, banging at His gate.
>
> *Zayin, het.* Bulging eyes peering through keyholes broader than Wierzbnik. Stone letters turning locks; limp bodies lying in a room larger than the world.
>
> *Tet, yod.* The point of light, pouring through the fiftieth gate.

>> tell him
>> tell Him that i [274–5]

The words in italics are letters of the Hebrew alphabet. The fact that *yod* is the tenth letter suggests that this might be a reference to the kabbalistic notion of the ten Divine Attributes of God, attributes which represent His radical transcendence. Only a privileged few experience the disclosure of these attributes. The dying Hinda is among them. Her vision takes her to the Fiftieth Gate, the place associated with the highest perception and sanctification of the Divine. Few reach this gate. Scripture has it that Moses did so on the last day of his life. In her death agony Hinda becomes a visionary Jewish martyr whose final utterance, which arcs prophetically forward to Pagis's poem and back to the Prophets, affirms her faith: the first-person pronoun is in the lower case befitting Jewish humility before God; the divine pronoun 'Him' is capitalized.

The perspectives in Baker's passage are complex and even confronting. The two eyes that watch are those of the camp guards who monitor the death throes of those in the chambers. But the sealed door behind which they peer does not wholly separate the ghastly detachment of their perspective from Hinda's vision. Her vision—of barbarity, filth and revelation—gathers those 'bulging eyes' into its torrent of agonized transcendence. The eyes become entangled with that which they are murdering (Hebrew letters 'with eyes'). The poetic prose seems to suggest that transcendence always bears the memory of that which it transcends, and that the murderers who monitor their victims' death must also witness their visions, the immortal traces of their humanity.

It is hard to say how affirmative this passage finally is. One concern might be that it involves a sort of 'negative sublimity or displaced sacralization'[264] which seeks consolation through myths of martyrdom and redemption, or which implies that the act of the murderer in some sense weds him, as in Levinas's notion of the 'logical absurdity of hatred',[265] to his victim. Whatever one concludes about such complexities, there is no doubting the creative power of the writing, nor its capacity imaginatively to revivify Hinda in her last hours in a way that would be quite beyond her survivor son, Yossl. Several questions arise here. Whose psychological needs are being met—or perhaps even discounted—when Mark retrieves Hinda from the gas chambers in this way? Does the son here function as an extension of parental vision, or as one who is in some sense usurping the parental prerogative of memory, and the father's entitlement not to pursue certain imaginative lines of inquiry?

Narrative trajectories

The narrative is segmented into fifty chapters, each announced with roman numerals flanked by a sketched gate icon on either side. The icon is standard throughout and the chapters move numerically through from I to L. This, together with the book's subtitle, *A journey though memory*, might suggest a structure that is fundamentally teleological—that drives towards an end-point. In some respects this is the case, but in others it is not. One of the most striking things about *The Fiftieth Gate* is the way it renders historical chaos through deliberate narrative disorientation. More conventional Holocaust memoir tends to strive for maximum narrative orderliness: events are recounted chronologically, as are the emotions and reflections associated with them. Baker's book, like some other notable examples,[266] seeks narrative forms that will accommodate the often atemporal meanderings of memory and the resultant interplay between historical and psychological time; between the order in which things 'actually happened' and the order in which memory revisits them. The point is not of course that memory is *dis*orderly, but rather that it often works by an order of its own which entails patterns of association that are sparked by current emotional needs and states, chance connections, echoes and the like. Such patterns can be teleological in their own way. They drive not (necessarily) towards a destination in time but towards a yearned-for inner state: a sense of resolution, for instance, or confidence about who one is, or about the meaning and implications of the past. Like so many Holocaust memoirs, *The Fiftieth Gate* is strongly teleological in this latter sense: it is an attempt to *make* sense, to arrive at a position from which life in a Holocaust-haunted family becomes more manageable.

In *The Fiftieth Gate*, as in the other volumes that contain the narrative of a return visit to Europe, historical time subdivides: there is the earlier life-history of the survivors and their offspring, and the narrative of the return journey. A certain disorientation effect derives in part from the fact that these two time-sequences are sometimes hard to differentiate. The 'now' of the narrative is situated largely in the family's journey to Poland in 1995 where they revisit Holocaust and other locations. Interspersed with these scenes, however, are often extended passages from the parents' testimonies (given in italics), recorded by the author in 1994. Then there are flashbacks to life in Australia, to Mark's life in Israel and his research quest there and elsewhere. Beyond this, further narrative variations: poems, scraps of traditional Jewish learning and prophecy, fictional reconstructions of events for which there is no extant evidence, and more. At times it is actually hard to know whether something—say, a conversation between Mark and a parent—is occurring in Poland or Melbourne. Such uncertainty can have powerful effects for the reader: it creates a kind of narrative vertigo, as if one quite literally does not know where one stands; and it serves as a constant reminder of how, for survivors and their children alike, the Holocaust constantly impinges upon, threads its way through, the present. The psychic teleology of Holocaust memoir is frequently driven by a craving for a state in which this impingement ceases to happen: where knowing what one can know, feeling what one can feel, about the dreadful events releases one to live in the present—at least at times—without the past's unrelenting power of haunting encroachment. '*I just can't disconnect my past,*' laments Genia [107–8]; '*I wish I could forget what I remember.*' [18] The god-like view from the fiftieth gate doesn't promise complete release from the past, but—perhaps—a degree of separation between 'the darkness or the light', 'the blessing or the curse'.

At its best Baker's narrative technique can make almost seamless associative transitions between then and now, parental perspectives and his own. 'They shaved us in this room,' Yossl recalls as they tour Birkenau. The narrative now shifts to family life in Melbourne, as seen by Mark:

> My poor father. His hair is a perennial source of concern, an object of cunning manipulation and strategic arrangements. It's called making the best of a situation, and this, as with everything else in my father's life, inspires new schemes and inventive techniques. He has grown the surviving remnants of hair that extend from the side of his head so that two hippyish bands of hair, like tangled balls of string, can be folded diagonally across his head into a woven tapestry. It is resistant to everything, except the wind, and so my father applies a daily dose of hairspray to the juncture where the two strands meet. 'It is for my wife,' he tells the chemist. [168]

The transition to Yossl's postwar coiffure regimen feels and is entirely plausible: we sense that there probably is more to it than wishing to please Genia—that it might very well connect with the camp experience, and also with a certain touching vanity. But Baker wants more than this from the passage. The word 'surviving' alerts the reader to the fact that the passage isn't just about a survivor—it's about the psychic mechanisms that are associated with survival: the ability to make the best of situations, the adaptive 'schemes and inventive techniques', the 'cunning', the determination, the eccentricity that can help people to endure bizarre experiential extremes. The cues are pretty clear but arguably without the heavy-handedness that occasionally mars the writing elsewhere. Throughout, however, the book reminds us that those very survival mechanisms, whether deeply embedded before the war or precipitated by horror, have an inevitable and often powerful psychological aftermath within the family, a unit which now carries an enormous weight of responsibility: it has to replenish and reconstruct the decimated family tree, and to make a safe haven for life's ordinary intimacies. Perhaps the most confronting feature of *The Fiftieth Gate* is Baker's open declaration and creative exploration of the emotional ambivalence he feels towards his survivor-parents. Often they anger or puzzle him. Sometimes, as when during the family's Birkenau visit Yossl urinates into the same toilet he had used in the camp, the son seems incredulous at his parents' responses to the world: '*Shtinkt du, vey iz mir,*' says Yossl. '*Drek.* The same shit.'

> A minute later he emerges, mumbling 'phooy, phooy', over and over again, as he triumphantly kicks one leg sideways, and blindly leads his fingers to the zipper of his trousers. [173]

Family narrative, family angst

Running through *The Fiftieth Gate* is a contrast between intuitive knowledge, the kind that comes in visions and through acts of empathetic imagination, and the ominous orderliness of the inventory. The oft-quoted Nazi inventories of course embody scientistic rationality gone psychopathic. Postwar registers of survivors are the bureaucratic counter to genocidal checklists. Sometimes, however, Baker turns cataloguing techniques back on himself and his family. He itemizes aspects of his family's behaviour under headings derived from a 'survivor index'; and, like some other Jewish autobiographers,[267] he provides a list of factors that occasioned parental—in this instance paternal—anxiety:

> Other sources of panic include dogs, spiders ('Mummy,' he will call to his wife who picks up these hairy things with her fingers), all forms of transportation, balconies, bare feet, strenuous exercise, and the suburbs which spill off Map 58 of Melway's Street Directory; but nothing seems to set the alarm bells ringing as much as public demonstrations of Jewishness. [5]

Like Morris Lurie, Serge Liberman and many other second-generation Australian Jewish autobiographers, Baker seeks to convey the pre-eminent place that anxiety had, and has, in these survivor-family milieus. This is not really a matter of 'reactive anxiety'—the kind we all quite appropriately experience in response to actual threat—but a more diffused orientation towards the world in general. In these families worry is the very currency of one's encounters with reality, as in the Jewish joke about a Jewish telegram: 'Start worrying. Details follow.' Many of these second-generation texts are in part motivated by the need to write beyond irrational anxiety: to fix the past in a narrative that approximates as closely as possible to *how it was*, so that one can live one's own life relatively free of unwarranted worry. As bearers of irrational worry, however, survivor-parents, no matter how much loved and pitied, no matter how protective their children may feel towards them, are themselves a threat—a threat to the child's psychic equilibrium. Mark Baker is courageous in confessing to the rage that this kind of psychic threat can engender.

Baker is an academic historian, one who deals in 'facts'—or '*fecks*', as his father somewhat derisively calls them [35]. Not just facts, of course, but historical interpretation as well; the kind that sees 'facts' in historical con-text and tries to understand their deeper implications. Mark is driven by a ferocious and overwhelming need to gather all the facts he can of his lost family, his parents' Holocaust experience, and of the Holocaust in general. In this sense *The Fiftieth Gate* is both an archival and a personal journey. The same parents whose experiences and anxiety help create the need for clarity of understanding are also the bearers of much of the narrative information the son needs in order to get the past into a relatively stable condition, a state of at least partial intelligibility. Sometimes they feel like sharing their memories, and each has provided a testimony for the book; but sometimes they prefer the comforts of silence. '*I wish I could forget what I remember*,' says his mother, who elsewhere shouts at her son, 'Don't steal my memory' [221].

For his part, the guilt-ridden but obsessive son is all too ready to see himself as a thief of familial memory [211]. So much so that he likens his investigative self to the Holocaust denier David Irving: 'It was an uncon-trollable urge, this repeated questioning of her, this interrogation, as if I was David Irving and not her son pointing the video camera at her.' [190] This, the most brutal of self-accusations, signals how urgent is the book's inquiry into the ethical complexities of seeking, hearing and appropriately recounting the stories of others. At one point Mark feels that he has crossed what should be an inviolate ethical 'line' [198] in interrogating his mother; but how does one draw such lines? How does one weigh one's own needs against those of one's parents? We might surmise that even the most empathetic witness to Holocaust witnessing derives some form of psychological fulfilment from this immensely painful experience. Even if not a relative, the listener will gain some additional understanding of the collective history that the two share as Jews. But the child's needs are often more imperious because parents' stories are their children's as well. Without knowledge of parental stories it is hard to assume an adult identity. Echoing the famous dictum of Descartes ('I think, therefore I am') Mark says of his father: 'He remembers, therefore I am.' [128]

The Fiftieth Gate shows in sometimes agonizing detail just how tortured these family dynamics can be. One of its great strengths is its fearless exploration of the relationship between a post-Holocaust mother and son. Genia is a loving and committed mother, but only a damaged woman would say to her son, 'my children are my revenge' [13]. We know of course what she means—that to procreate is to deny the Annihilation—but still, such an attitude must betoken profound emotional complexities for the child. So too must the parent's ambivalent attitude to her past. Yossl and Genia both in one sense want their son to be a family historian—'And I was his memory.' [130] But they also want him *not* to be this. Genia's Holocaust experience is of a vexing kind in that she was not in a camp. She does not have a number on her arm, does not appear in Nazi records, and has little family history to draw upon for her sense of self. *'Because I don't have a number means I didn't survive?'* [194] she demands defensively; but she is also moved, by the paucity of historical evidence about the fate of the population of her *shtetl*, to muse: 'Maybe I am someone else?' [239] Her historian son can make good some crucial gaps in the record, but not without pushing relentlessly for information. She needs him in order to be more fully herself—one of several inversions of parent–child relations in this book. Thus parental love, so often and misleadingly fabled as pure and unconditional, is in fact streaked with ambivalence. Knowing this makes the child even more ambivalent towards his parents than children generally are. And so the cycle goes on. The Holocaust past unites them in their fears, their need for memory, their co-dependency; but it also instigates that profound generational divide: 'you don't understand, you weren't there' [183]. This is a narrative divide; and Baker's, like much second-generation Holocaust autobiography, is a narrative attempt to moderate its magnitude and its effects.

The book's cover bears the name Mark Raphael Baker. The author explains that he inserted 'Raphael' into his own name in order to restore branches of the family tree that were occluded by the New Testament names, Mark and John, which his fearful parents had given their sons [254]. (Baker is the 'circumcised form' of the Polish name Bekiermaszyn [235].) This typifies the complex autobiographical strand that threads its way though a generational narrative which is part history, part biography, and part poetic meditation. It is a painful, often tortured but also often beautiful book in which the son of survivors seeks, through writing, a measure of freedom from precisely that which his sophisticated narrative art aims to fix ineluctably in memory. Given the history, such freedom, while richly worth the effort, must necessarily be a form of spiritual accommodation and compromise: 'Freedom is not a happy ending. It is a flame that dances in remembrance, inside the blackness.' [314]

Narrative Pacts and the Problem of 'Truth'

Doris and Lily Brett

The meanings of survival

'What did it mean to survive?'[268] writes Lily Brett. Survival can mean many things and take many forms. Doris Brett's *Eating the Underworld: A memoir in three voices*[269] is partly about surviving ovarian cancer. The book's three voices are those of autobiographical prose, poetry and fairytale. It's an innovative and moving autobiographical configuration, distinguished particularly by its haunting poetry of illness, dread and enlightenment. In this book survival also concerns the Holocaust. The Brett sisters' parents survived Auschwitz and were reunited after the war, emigrating to Australia in 1948.

Eating the Underworld sparked extensive discussion when it appeared in 2001. Much of the discussion—too much of it—focused on scuttlebutt surrounding Doris's and Lily's divergent accounts of their mother, Rose, who died in 1985. In essence, the sisters disagree about the kind of Holocaust survivor their mother was. Did she, as Lily claims, often wake in the night screaming? Was she, as Lily also suggests, chronically depressed and haunted?

> Under this elegant exterior was an undercurrent of anxiety, anger, bitterness, agony and anguish. My mother did the normal things that other mothers did—she cooked meals, cleaned the house, shopped, and made school lunches—but there was an edge to everything.[270]

Was she given at times to unwitting emotional cruelty towards Lily?[271] Or was Rose—the 'real' Rose—the superbly generous and self-possessed woman of Doris's recollection, 'A woman of immense compassion, love and courage and one of the most inspiring human beings I have known'

[*ETU*, v]? Doris, a psychotherapist who reflects on the psychological and ethical phenomenon of conflicting family memories, notes: 'Psychologists have known for years that fantasy, unconscious needs and re-interpretation of events all affect our memories of past and even recent events. It is confusing, disorienting. And yet in this profusion of difference, our own experience is all that we have.' [*ETU*, 251] Lily writes often of an eerie sensation of becoming her mother, as in the poem 'I Wear Your Face':

> I wear the glare
> you froze me
> with
> [...]
> I wear your face
> and mother
> the green witch howls behind it.[272]

The autobiographical *In Full View* admits to an 'inability to separate my life from my parents' life. Particularly from my mother's life.'[273] This is a difficulty from which she claims years of psychoanalysis have released her.[274]

Eating the Underworld doesn't simply enter a plea for 'difference' among family recollections. It suggests that 'fantasy, unconscious needs' and the like can cause some people to represent family history in ways that are simply untrue. Doris is saying that in certain crucially important respects Lily has got Rose wrong. Her phrasing also leaves open the possibility that a degree of conscious choice is implicated in Lily's misconstruction of Rose: 'In this [Lily's] memory, my mother wears a face that is unrecognisable to me. It is clearly the way Lily has chosen to interpret her experience...' [*ETU*, 16] In offering her pained counter-narrative Doris is implicitly appealing to the possibility of dispassionate adjudication, even on matters as subjective as contrasting recollections of parents. Hence her reference to 'Lily's propensity for fabrication' [249]—a propensity Lily herself sometimes acknowledges.

Eating the Underworld is also about sibling relations and about surviving what amounts to sibling abuse. 'I have been shaped by being a sister' [*ETU*, 247], Doris declares, and the Lily we meet in these pages is often narcissistic, jealous, cruel and destructive. 'I lived my life in a peculiar juxtaposition of undiluted love from my parents and the opposite from my sister.' [13–14] Object-relations psychologists and others have drawn attention to the importance of sibling relationships for identity formation and psychological development generally, so this is fertile and appropriate ground for life-writing. One purpose of Doris's 'weaving together' [ix] of the three voices is to show that the various modes of survival with which the narrative deals are interwoven. Crudely summarized, she suggests that had her parents not been Holocaust survivors they might have been better able to moderate Lily's jealous and destructive behaviour towards her; that surviving such behaviour has given her a kind of strength, but only after long labour on her damaged self-esteem; and that surviving cancer has emboldened her to set the record straight about her mother and other aspects of Lily's account of the family: 'the experience of facing death also forces you to face life' [16].

I am in no position to adjudicate between the Brett sisters' versions of Rose. Rather than try to decide between the two accounts, I want to ask what such disagreements might reveal about various forms of narrative pact, and about the part that such narrative pacts play—or might play—in our ethical lives, particularly after the Holocaust.

Autobiographical pacts

The French theorist of autobiography, Philippe Lejeune, has proposed what he calls 'the autobiographical pact' as one of the defining generic characteristics of autobiography. This pact is an agreement or contract between writer and reader which specifies the genre of the text and genre-appropriate ways in which it should be read. Such pacts are of a particular, heavily implicit kind, since unlike most they don't spring from actual dialogue between participants. The author's inaugurating intention to write true-to-life might be signalled by something as minor as a phrase on the dust-jacket, or by something more definitive like the subtitle *An autobiography*, or a Preface where the author undertakes to be as truthful as possible about his or her life. According to Lejeune, autobiography aspires—and is understood to aspire—to referential reliability; that is, to accurate reporting of the self and the world. Writing an autobiography is like taking an oath: 'The formula for it [would be] "I swear to tell the truth, the whole truth, and nothing but the truth."'[275] This formulation, which invites philosophical elucidation and inquiry,[276] puts the main emphasis on the *communicative aspiration* that informs the pact. The autobiographer writes under a kind of oath, and readers, if they commit to the pact, undertake to read on the assumption that the author really is trying to be truthful. As I noted in Part One, Lejeune has subsequently revised this account of the pact in order to render the concept more flexible and less prone to unduly literal notions of 'truth'. Some other scholars of autobiography have followed suit.[277]

Two further points about pact-making. First, it is important to distinguish between the value of certain undertakings and their prospects of total success. Most of us would concede that it's impossible to report—say, in an autobiography—on anything of even moderate complexity in a way that is 'one hundred percent accurate'. But this does not invalidate the attempt to report as accurately as one can; nor does it annul the ethical significance of the commitment to do so—a commitment fundamental not just to autobiography but to many aspects of social life. Second, most autobiographers appeal for *trust*. Without trust there can be no effective practice of pact-making. Trust of course can be misplaced, and it can overlook the workings of that great trust-deceiver, ideology. But as Coady has argued in his study of testimony, 'our trust in the word of others is fundamental to the very idea of serious cognitive activity'.[278] Without it—without what might be termed discerning trust—social life could not function. Part of what we acquire when we acquire language is the ability to recognize and participate in a range of cultural practices. Pact-making is one such practice; and in learning about pacts and how they are entered into, we learn, with language's assistance, what trust is and when it is warranted. We learn to trust discerningly. Reading autobiography is one among many contexts in which such learning can occur.

Lily's pacts

A more finely calibrated discussion of these matters would need to allow for examples in which the autobiographer admits to vagueness about circumstantial details but still claims veracity for the core aspects of the narrative. It would also need to consider different—often implicit—'truth' claims that operate in various genres of writing; that is, the kinds and degrees of truth to which various narrative genres lay claim.

Lily Brett writes poetry, fiction and autobiography. Her main prose works are two books of short stories (*Things Could Be Worse* and *What God Wants*); three novels (*Just Like That*, *Too Many Men* and *You Gotta Have Balls*); and three books that invite reading of an autobiographical kind (*In Full View*,[279] *New York* and *Between Mexico and Poland*[280]). All of these texts, and the poetry as well, are massively preoccupied with the Holocaust. So much so that Lily Brett's reputation rests principally on her assumed authority as a chronicler of life among post-Holocaust Australian Jews.

Brett is good—sometimes very good—at many things. She has a distinctive and compelling narrative voice: self-absorbed yet intrigued by the world, confronting yet vulnerable, anguished yet funny. At its best the prose is sharp, suggestive, often powerful. She has fine comic touch and a particular gift for dialogue. She writes powerfully of the Holocaust-haunted consciousness that many Jews live with. It's a consciousness that constantly circles back to images of the horror, frequently by ingenious but involuntary patterns of association. Brett's writing shows how psychologically and ethically complex such hauntings can be. If at one level they simply reflect the traumatic impact that such images are bound to have for many people, at another level they can, among Jews especially, be implicated in self-involved and self-destructive patterns which actually compound the psychological and ethical disarray that the Holocaust and other atrocities leave in their wake. Many of Brett's second-generation characters use Holocaust haunting as the medium for a kind of sadism towards the self. In some cases this happens because they are stricken by 'survivor guilt'; others, whose internal conflicts may have little to do with the Holocaust, nevertheless find in the catastrophe a suitably vicious tool for self-flagellation. These patterns often involve acute self-punitive anxiety and a deep resistance to happiness. At one point in *Just Like That*, Esther catches herself starting to feel good, to feel that she has the capacity to be happy. Immediately the old resistance kicks in:

This morning, she had caught a glimpse of a soaring sort of happiness which was somewhere inside her. She knew she had a lot to be happy about... The thought of that happiness scared her.

No matter how miserable her anxiety made her, it also comforted her. The thought of a huge happiness scares the shit out of me, she'd thought to herself this morning.[281]

There's so much pain and psychic encapsulation in a Brett novel that it's easy to overlook the emotional range of which she is capable and to forget that amidst all the self-indulgence and sadistic rumination there is a search for transcendence going on, as in the scene in which Esther experiences the 'dense silence' of the Rothko Chapel in Houston.[282] That search is as much of body as of spirit. Brett writes brilliantly about the body—its libidinous and gustatory demands, its discomforts, fluids, disorders, its searing registration of psychic pain, its treacherous entanglements with women's self-images, but also its capacity for self-transcendence and pleasure.

Yet the treatment of sex is troubling in the overall scheme of Brett's work. So too are the pacts her works invite, because she's the sort of writer whose ostensibly non-fictional works are often almost indistinguishable in style and content from the fictional ones.[283] The passages I've just quoted from her fiction closely resemble passages in her autobiographical writing. The novels often use real Brett family names. Significantly, the mothers of both Esther (*Just Like That*) and Ruth (*Too Many Men*) are called Rooshka— a transliteration of Rose Brett's Polish name. 'Real-life' episodes (hair-cuts, battles over food and weight), patterns (the mother's waking in the night screaming) and perceptions are transposed to the fiction with little alteration.

So the question arises: what sort of pact are we being invited to join in a Lily Brett text? Should her autobiographical writings be read as if written under oath? One answer might be: 'What does it matter? The line between fact and fiction is always hazy anyway: all autobiographers resort to some fictionalizing and most novels have substantial autobiographical content. Lily Brett writes faction. Faction mixes fact and fiction. Most writers do.' But this view erroneously supposes that a text which contains some fictive elements must therefore be fictive through and through. It also mistakenly assumes that because total referential reliability cannot be achieved it is not a worthwhile authorial aspiration. This is seriously to underestimate the ethical importance of the will to truth in narrative. Faction—writing that deliberately mixes fiction and fact—is open to the same criticism, except where it differentiates for the reader between what it takes to be fact and what it knows to be invention. Even then, a given text needs to inspire trust in the reader; needs to convince that its aspiration to 'truthfulness', and its demarcations between 'truth' and 'fiction', are dependable and given in good faith. Lily Brett's writings do not inspire this sort of trust. There is consequently a serious problem with the kind of 'authority' that is often imputed to her as a chronicler of post-Holocaust Jewry.

Let me give another example. In the pointedly titled *In Full View*, Lily Brett writes:

> Having children has meant that there are more of us Bretts. We were so diminished in number. Hundreds of us were murdered. I wanted there to be more Bretts. I felt so outnumbered when I was young. Outnumbered by dead Bretts. Outnumbered by normal Australian families. Families with grandparents, aunts, uncles, cousins.[284]

This is a familiar lament in Lily's writings and one would like to be able to read such passages with the deepest sympathy. But there is a catch. Lily Brett has a sister—Doris—and Doris is almost totally airbrushed from Lily's supposedly non-fictional writing. Doris is quite literally hidden from view. There are very few references to Doris in the autobiographical *In Full View*, *New York* or *Between Mexico and Poland*, and she is never mentioned by name. Lily reports that a brother and sister who babysat the girls forced her to watch as they had incestuous sex on the couch in the Brett parents' bedroom. All this is said to have happened 'While my sister slept'.[285] More occluded still is Lily's explanation in *New York* that her GP advises her to have an ovarian scan because of 'a family history of ovarian cancer'.[286] Doris doesn't rate a mention, notwithstanding that the illness in question nearly killed her.

What are we to make of this? Is Doris's existence somehow irrelevant to the precarious ongoingness of the Bretts and the Jewish tribe more generally? Some life-writers report that it is harder to write about siblings than about parents, lovers and children. Perhaps Lily Brett is one such life-writer. But if this were so, and if she wants us to commit to an autobiographical pact predicated on the 'full view', something would have to be said about Doris's absence from the narrative. The airbrushing technique devastates narrative trust and calls into question Lily's bona fides as a reliable chronicler of family and of post-Holocaust Jewry.

'Morbid' or 'sordid'?: *shtooping a shikse*

The other theme upon which Lily Brett's reputation largely rests is sex. Sex as self-transcendence, but also sex as ruminative and often unwelcome obsession, as in an early story, 'You Will Be Going Back to Your Roots':

> The thought of her father's penis made Lola feel nauseous. If she thought about her father in sexual terms, she would have to think about him fucking her mother. She tried to blink that thought out of her head.[287]

We rightly admire James Joyce's revelation of the anarchic and often 'perverse' inner life of sexual fantasy; so in principle this could be another source of strength in Lily Brett's writing. In her case, though, there is a deep contextual complication in that a ubiquitous preoccupation with sex accompanies and continually pervades the books' obsession with the Holocaust. A reader of *Things Could Be Worse* and *What God Wants* could be forgiven for thinking that adultery, along with the gossip and moral dilemmas it generates, has been one of the principal activities of the post-Holocaust Melbourne Jewish community. One outraged Jewish wife paints a sign outside the family home in Caulfield: 'My husband is shtooping a shikse'[288]—Yiddish for fucking a non-Jewish woman. All the books, fiction and non-fiction, continually entwine or juxtapose sex and the Holocaust. Esther in *Just Like That* provides a window into this obsessional dynamic when she reflects that she'd 'much rather be morbid than sordid'.[289] In *Things Could Be Worse*, Lola gets laid then goes straight to hell—in this instance a dream about the Lodz ghetto:

> Lola had a long orgasm. She felt as though she'd been away. In another dimension. In another time. She fell asleep.

> Lola was in Lodz. She was in the loungeroom of the apartment. Everything was exactly as her father had described it. The rounded couch and chairs, the white-tiled heater. All that was missing was the family. Her father's parents, his three brothers and sister.[290]

In a sense, one can see a point here. No doubt at the very bottom of the Id-pit, where the most horrible things happen, sex and sadism are often mutually implicated. We need nuanced novelistic treatments of this horrific conjunction. But what about this?

> Edek Zepler used to fuck Polish girls. They were mostly maids, and he fucked them, standing up, in the hallways of the buildings in which they worked.[291]

These are the opening lines of *Just Like That*. Edek is an Auschwitz survivor. It's hard to imagine the kindly and emotionally sensitive Edek we meet in the book behaving thus as a younger man, and Brett hasn't done the necessary novelistic work to make it seem plausible. Later, Edek's sex-life, and his private life more generally, become the focus of some fine comic and not-so-comic writing. But those first few lines leave a kind of unease. Why would a chronicler of the aftermath of the Holocaust begin a novel in this way?

In another novel, Auschwitz survivor Edek Rothwax and his daughter Ruth visit Lodz, Warsaw, Auschwitz and other places. The book is entitled *Too Many Men*.[292] Suspicions that the old cocktail of sex and Holocaust might be present in alarming measure are not unfounded. After visiting Auschwitz, Edek and Ruth return to their hotel, whereupon two ageing Polish ladies, Zofia and Walentyna, whom they had met briefly days before, minister to Edek's presumed emotional distress. That night Edek beds Zofia, and the novel ends with Ruth's mortified realization that Edek plans to pursue the relationship.

So the mature, sensitive, if not overly sophisticated, Holocaust survivor *shtoops* an ageing Polish *shikse* the night he gets back from visiting the site of his harrowing past. No doubt funnier things have happened; but perhaps not *much* funnier. Did it in fact happen, we wonder. We know from Lily Brett's autobiographical writings that she and her father did visit Poland together. At least we think we know that. But then what can we know, given the promiscuous fluidity with which her narrative pacts operate? The deeper point, though, is this: whether it 'happened' or not, the novel, which contains some fine things, fails to justify its bizarre amalgam of sex and Holocaust. The connection is not adequately explored. These limitations are at once artistic, psychological and ethical.

Post-Holocaust pacts

One could think of any number of instances in which little or no harm is done when writers play fast and loose with narrative pacts. Faction's impact will depend upon context. However, tragic events put special kinds and degrees of pressure on our narrative conventions; they pose hard questions about the nature and implications of our commitments to those conventions. I suggest that faction which intersperses fact and invention without explanation—or without some disambiguating generic cues—is an inadequate narrative mode for writing about the Holocaust. The emotional, intellectual and ethical stakes are just too high. When reading about this and other catastrophic events, we need to be as clear as we can about the nature of the author's narrative aspiration. If it is to write some sort of fiction, then we know what pact we are in and can read accordingly; if autobiography, the same thing applies. Real-life tragedies and the representational imperatives they entail show that we need distinctions among narrative conventions, however finely calibrated or even hazy they might sometimes be. We need them so that we can be as clear as possible about what has happened and what it means, but also because these conventions must be practised and emulated if future communities are to orient themselves in ethical and historical space.

'The Bonds of Civility Cut Asunder'

Arnold Zable and the Multicultural Imagination

Civility overboard

In August 2001 a Norwegian boat, MV *Tampa*, rescued 433 asylum-seekers from an Indonesian vessel in international waters. The *Tampa*'s captain decided on humanitarian grounds to ferry these souls into Australian territorial waters, the plan being for them to disembark on Christmas Island. The conservative (Liberal) Australian government of the day refused to permit disembarkation on Australian territory. Eventually, after legal appeals and counter-appeals, and a devastating period of uncertainty for the asylum-seekers, some of the latter were taken to New Zealand and others to the Pacific island of Nauru. The Howard government, which was looking shaky in the polls not far out from an election, made a great play of being 'strong on border protection'. It was even implied that, notwithstanding the wealth of the major terrorist networks, some of the people on leaky, squalid and dangerous crafts, like the one from which the *Tampa* had rescued its human cargo, might be terrorists. This demonizing of the Other peaked with the now discredited prime ministerial claim that parents aboard another boat carrying asylum-seekers had thrown small children overboard in an attempt to pressure Australian authorities to take them in. It was—and continues to be—a moment of profound crisis for multicultural Australia.

For some of Australia's large community of Holocaust survivors and their families the '*Tampa* crisis' hit hard. Such folk generally feel enormous loyalty to Australia, where they have been able to live without persecution in climes blessedly remote, both attitudinally and geographically, from Europe. The word 'gratitude' reverberates through the 300 or so volumes of autobiography written by Australian Jews. But what does a Holocaust survivor feel when this beloved adoptive country, under the stewardship of a conservative prime minister who cynically but persuasively styles himself as the embodiment of traditional Australian 'decency',[293] the egalitarian 'fair go', behaves thus towards the victims of poverty, persecution, displacement? The government's demonization of the Other focused with particular spite on the 'people-smugglers' who in return for sometimes sizeable sums of money arrange perilous voyages like the one undertaken by those rescued by the *Tampa*. But as a Polish Australian Jewish man in his eighties—a writer and a graduate of Auschwitz—remarked at the time: 'What can you do? When things get desperate for Jews the first thing you do is go to a people-smuggler.' His gratitude and loyalty to Australia were being sorely tested. This haven for Jews seemed to be reneging on its moral responsibilities to the international community.

Arnold Zable is the son of Polish Jews who got out of Europe before the war. In this sense they escaped the Holocaust; yet such people, who (as in this case) lost almost their entire families in that catastrophe, are quite properly referred to as 'survivors'. In his first book, *Jewels and Ashes*, a memoir of his journey through ancestral Europe in 1986, Zable describes the predicament of the second generation—the survivors' children born in Australia:

> We were born in the wake of the Annihilation. We were children of dreams and shadows, yet raised in the vast spaces of the New World. We roamed the streets of our migrant neighbourhoods freely. We lived on coastlines and played under open horizons. Our world was far removed from the sinister events that had engulfed our elders. Yet there had always been undercurrents that could sweep us back to the echoes of childhood, to the sudden torrents of rage and sorrow that could, at any time, disturb the surface calm: 'You cannot imagine what it was like,' our elders insisted. 'You were not there.' Their messages were always ambiguous, tinged with menace, double-edged: 'You cannot understand, yet you must. You should not delve too deeply, yet you should. But even if you do, my child, you will never understand. You were not there.'
>
> Inevitably, we were drawn into their universe—the regrets, the nagging grief, the wariness and suspicion, and the many ghosts they fought to keep at bay as they struggled to rebuild their lives. And given the tale I seem compelled to tell to the end, could we have expected it to be otherwise?[294]

Could we indeed? And there is no Australian writer more devoted, more passionately committed to the power of story than Arnold Zable. The relationship between storytelling and the Holocaust is central to his work, in part because the Annihilation was such a viciously and mercilessly efficient attack on cultural memory. To hear and retell the stories of survivors is to reconstruct parts of a vanished world and the families who peopled it. As Martin, the narrator of Zable's post-Holocaust novel *Cafe Scheherazade* says, to ignore those stories would be a 'tragic betrayal'.[295] Yet to record them is a daunting, often devastating task, this reconstruction of narrative from 'fragments' among the ruins. Zable is what George Eliot in *Middlemarch* calls a 'belated historian',[296] one who arrives too late and must make do with insufficiency. In Zable's work, story does many kinds of emotional and imaginative work: the grim work of chronicling racism and genocide, but also (as in the writings of Jacob Rosenberg) the loving labour of re-enchantment, of returning elation, compassion, intimations of holiness to the post-Holocaust world.

Born in New Zealand in 1947 but raised in Carlton, an ethnically diverse inner suburb of Melbourne, Zable has published five books. An activist deeply committed to indigenous rights and the reform of Australia's immigration and mandatory-detention laws, he also writes journalism and occasional essays.[297] His home life was deeply steeped in the world of *Yiddishkeit*—his father wrote Yiddish poetry, his mother was a fine amateur performer of Yiddish song, but they were not strictly observant Jews. In fact they were prewar members of the Bund, a Jewish socialist movement that exalted Yiddish as a language of the people, opposed Zionism, and sought full emancipation for the Jews of the diaspora. Zable's Jewishness is that of a 'cultural Jew', albeit one of a deeply humanistic and spiritual kind.

The books are *Jewels and Ashes* (1991), which is told largely in the first-person but works through a weave of perspectives and voices (especially those of his parents); *Wanderers and Dreamers* (1998), a narrative history of Yiddish theatre in Melbourne; *Cafe Scheherazade* (2001), survivor tales as retold by a young journalist; *The Fig Tree* (2003), a first-person work which brings together the world of Arnold's Jewish past and that of his Greek-Australian wife, Dora; and *Scraps of Heaven* (2004), a novel that does for Carlton something of what Joyce does for Dublin. Told from the perspective of an affectionate but impersonal synoptic narrator, it roams the streets, houses and public places of Carlton, tracing the individual and collective lives of its inhabitants, Jewish, Italian, Greek, Irish and other.

In *Jewels and Ashes*, Zable writes of Polish Jews on the run in 1942, unavailingly approaching Polish peasants and acquaintances to plead for refuge: 'This was the season of hunter and hunted; the bonds of civility had been cut asunder and left to rot in the summer of 1942.' [*JA*, 93] Later, in one of the book's many time-shifts, he reconstructs from his mother's letters her experience at the hands of Australian immigration authorities in 1934. Hoddes had come from her beloved Bialystok to New Zealand, thence to Melbourne where she was working in a factory. Her fiancé and later husband, Meier, was still in Poland. Unfairly accused of falsifying her entry-visa papers, Hoddes is forced back to New Zealand. In a letter home to her family she writes: 'I have become a mere straw tossed around on wild seas, from earth to the skies, from the skies back to earth.' [193] In his doctoral thesis, titled 'Imagining the Immigrant Experience',[298] Zable records interviews he did with Amal Hassan Basry, an Iraqi asylum-seeker who died while resident in Melbourne in 2006. Amal's narrative—of life under Saddam Hussein, of being rescued after the boat she had boarded in Indonesia sank, of her complex feelings about family and home—reminds Zable of Hoddes's story:

> Amal's mixture of strength and fragility was all too familiar. This state of fragility and strength was an enduring presence in my childhood. My mother Hadassah was also traumatised by loss of family. She too was a woman in transition, a displaced person trying to find a renewed sense of belonging and security. She too was trying to cope with the horrors of a ruptured past.[299]

He notes 'striking parallels between the immigrant communities of previous generations, and the communities of recently arrived immigrants and refugees from the Middle East'.[300]

In *The Fig Tree*, Zable tells of Bishop Chrysostomos who refused to hand over the 283 Jews of Zakynthos to the Nazis. The passage becomes a paean to *filoxenia*,[301] the Greek word for the love of strangers; and the book, like most of his writing, a dialogue between the history of the Jews and the halting emergence of Australian multiculturalism in an increasingly globalized world.

The verb 'to move'

Zable's art is fundamentally realist in mode, if not always in inspiration. Its speech rhythms draw heavily on the Yiddish he learnt as a child and then honed in his impassioned reading of Yiddish literature. The oeuvre is very much a work in progress. Significant technical developments are in train: always an intensely visual and imagistic writer, Zable's technique in *Scraps of Heaven* makes pervasive use of metaphor's conciseness and power to surprise. The management of narrative viewpoint is also undergoing change as Zable's art evolves.

A striking feature of his writing is the use of the verb 'to move'. What looks like an insignificant detail is in fact very important as a stylistic device and as a bearer of various registers of pain and inspiration. It is also something of a barometer of aesthetic achievement in Zable's post-Holocaust, multicultural project.

In *The Fig Tree* he speaks glowingly of Martin Buber's famous collection, *Tales of the Hasidim*, which he read with rapture as a child: 'The Hasidic *rebbes* were master storytellers. They used their parables to help lift their people out of gloom.' [*FT*, 5] The work of this agnostic latter-day Australian cultural Jew is deeply indebted to the charged, mystical and often ecstatic world of the Hasidic tales, with their charmed anecdotes of exemplary, superhuman rabbinic deeds and declarations, their devout chronicling of devotional life, 'the way of fervor'.[302] The tales evoke a world, but also a way of going, a way of being in that world, a profoundly communal ethos. This way of going does not refuse the body—on the contrary, as Rabbi Shmelke teaches in one of the tales, 'the soul shall not abhor the body'[303]—yet many of the stories evoke a state of being that is otherworldly, a kind of out-of-body experience. 'For three years Zusya and Elimelekh journeyed through the land, for they wanted to share the lot of the Divine Presence in exile, and convert to it erring mankind.'[304] The word 'journeyed' gives, albeit in translation, a sense of the body moving through a landscape with its powers of attention absorbed in the Divine Presence rather than in the physical world or its own sensations. Something similar occurs when the great *rebbes* are deep in prayer, as in this charming moment: 'When Rabbi Elimelekh said the Prayer of Sanctification on the Sabbath, he occasionally took out his watch and looked at it. For in that hour, his soul threatened to dissolve in bliss, and so he looked at his watch in order to steady himself in Time and the world.'[305] As explained by a latter-day Hasidic rabbi, such experiences are instances of *avodah*, which translates roughly as the soul's 'cleaving' to God.[306] The cleaving soul leaves the body to be with, and be illuminated by, its divine source, thereafter to return to the body and to the world of ethical-communal life. The experience of transcendence is thought to bring profound knowledge, including metaphysical knowledge of the very structures of creation.

The second chapter of *The Fig Tree* tells the story of Zable's father's last years, after he has dismantled for the final time the market stall where for five decades he sold cheap clothing. In retirement, seeing his 'later life as graced by a sense of freedom' [*FT*, 17), Meier rediscovers the passion to write Yiddish poetry. Arnold reports that his father is now communing again with his 'muse'. As he 'makes his way through each successive day, his mood lifts. He moves through the streets of the neighbourhood' [23], a soul reborn. Meier is no rabbi—far from it—but his imaginative rebirth reads like a belated echo of Hasidic elation, the body moving through Carlton as if through the countryside or *shtetl* of pre-Holocaust eastern Europe. The Divine Presence here is the Imagination, bearer of cultural tradition; or perhaps more precisely, the world as seen when imaginatively re-enchanted by an imagination that fuses a charged present and a legendary past.

But now a very different usage of the verb 'to move'. Towards the end of *Jewels and Ashes*, Zable arrives at the 'kingdom of darkness' [*JA*, 181] that is Auschwitz. He writes:

> Like a shadow, I move through the camp entrance under the infamous words, '*Arbeit Macht Frei*'. The sign is smaller than I had expected, partly obscured by a background of trees. The black letters carved in steel weave and twist as if dancing in the air. Welcome. You have nothing to fear. Work liberates. [*JA*, 180]

Here 'move' suggests a state in which the body registers the most terrible feelings of enervation, a loss of human substance that somehow mirrors the stupefying enormity of what the place is and stands for. It is not possible to be fully human here: even after all these years, he or she who passes through these gates must 'move' as a 'shadow' through a landscape that calls up some of the 'many levels of silence' to which Zable refers on the same page. Yet however appalled, the self that moves here is also a self that sees: the letters that 'twist as if dancing in the air', the headquarters just beyond the gates where doctors experimented on infants, and all the rest. This self can bear a belated kind of witness which, though finally removed from the personal reality of what happened at this place, can at least see without the distortion that can be occasioned by extreme trauma.

Not so for Zofia, one of the central characters in *Scraps of Heaven*. Zofia, who is based on Zable's mother, is succumbing later in life to the trauma of losing almost her entire family in the Annihilation. She is becoming suspicious even of her husband and son. She has moved into a room at the back of the house, into a haunted, cocooned space of her own, where she awakens calling for her long-lost mother: 'Mama. Mama.'[307] When she returns home after shopping, haunted by voices:

> She rests awhile by the kitchen table, hunched within herself, then moves along her well-worn routes: from the refrigerator to the table with lamb chops for the evening meal; from the dresser back to the table with knives and chopping boards; from the sink, cooking pot in hand, to the Kooka stove. [*SH*, 173]

A few rooms away, her son Josh can often hear her 'moving in the kitchen' [157]. This 'moving' is a haunting thing. Trauma has rendered Zofia delusional—much of what she sees is not, or is no longer, there—and her moving is a kind of stupefaction of the body, a ceasing of presence in which the distraught soul's cleaving is to darkness, loss and horror. Josh can hear his mother 'moving' in ways he has come to associate with her most anguished and distracted states, but what is true for Zable and his mother is true for Josh as well: 'You cannot imagine what it was like ... You were not there.' He cannot know what it feels like to be her. In all of his Holocaust writing Zable, like Mark Baker, Susan Varga and others, is torn between the desire to respect and observe the privacy, the silence of the survivor-parent, and the 'urge to penetrate' the parent's 'inner world' [*JA*, 159]. It is a painful ethical dilemma.

It is associated also with a recurrent aesthetic dilemma. How does one write the inwardness of a person cut off from the world by trauma; a person like Bloomfield, a character who trudges through all of Zable's books? Bloomfield is a spectral presence, who walks and walks and walks the streets of Carlton, his expression that of 'a rabbit caught and distracted in the glare of lights' [*SH*, 9]. He is a pathetically diminished version of the luftmen-*schen*, the rootless 'men of air', celebrated in *Cafe Scheherazade*,[308] who roamed eastern Europe as peddlers and small speculators before the war. A creature of the most profound privacy and silence even among fellow Jews, Bloomfield is rumoured to have been on the Yiddish stage back in Poland, and to have been one of Dr Mengele's experimental victims in Auschwitz. Sometimes Bloomfield simply walks, but at others he shuffles,[309] or tramps [*JA*, 185]. Often he just 'moves' [*SH*, 80].

Bloomfield has counterparts among recent asylum-seekers. They too walk the streets of Melbourne, haunted by trauma, loss and uncertainty. Zable's performance piece, 'The Walker', dramatizes the experience of one such individual:

> I walk because I cannot sleep. I walk because I cannot stand still. I walk because I want the night to end. I walk because I hate the night.
>
> There is a half moon. A crescent moon. I think of my life in the time before. I see the faces of my loved ones. And I think of the night I ran.
>
> I ran for my life. I had no time to wake my daughters. They lay three abreast on the same bed. How could I know that I would not see them for god knows how long? It has been five years, and now I do not run. I walk.[310]

Genial host

Arnold Zable's self-appointed (but never self-important) task as a writer is an imposing one. It presents several major challenges: how to bear witness to what cannot be imagined if one was not there; how to narrate the inwardness of those whose experiences may be remote from one's own— survivors, migrants, members of Australian ethnic minorities; how to re-enchant our post-Holocaust and still xenophobic world without rein-stating a God; and how to recast narrative convention in pursuit of these various aspirations.

Because he cannot bear direct witness, since he was 'not there', Zable employs interleaved stories and frequent shifts in narrative time. *Jewels and Ashes* moves constantly between Arnold's journey through eastern Europe, the recollections of his parents (sometimes in direct, often in reported speech), the memories of those he encounters, and writings about prewar and postwar eastern European culture. *The Fig Tree* is more vignette-like in structure, closer in both verbal texture and rhetorical mode to Zable's journalism. As befits his encomium to *filoxenia*, the narrator here resembles a character in *Scraps of Heaven*: the barber Posner, who is 'the master of ceremonies, the genial host' [*SH*, 164] in his own shop, a place frequented by Jews but also by Italians, Greeks and others. The narrator as genial host is in a sense Zable's response to a post-Holocaust and multicultural world in which 'the bonds of civility had been cut asunder'. Narrative is a way of reconstructing civility, of reanimating the empathetic emotions, of welcoming the stranger whom others would force back out to sea—a fate all too familiar to Jewish asylum-seekers. *The Fig Tree* takes its title from the 'all-embracing' [*FT*, 50] tree under which Zable's mother-in-law, Lily Varvarigos, exercised her famed 'hospitality' [52]. She too was a master of ceremonies, and in Zable's work the tree's canopy represents an empathetic inclusiveness which does not annul ethnic particularity; a sense of universal moral responsibility that respects local culture, not least for its capacity to surpass its own boundaries in enriching intercultural contact.

This, of course, is crucial to Zable's project. As life-writer and novelist he must grapple with a set of problems familiar in academic writing about multiculturalism and postcoloniality. In Charles Taylor's words, how do we reconcile the just aspirations of a levelling 'politics of equal dignity',[311] and late modernity's insistence on the inherently 'differential'[312] nature of ethnic 'authenticity',[313] the profound differences among ethnic cultures? In a sense, Zable seeks the narrative equivalent of Taylor's 'presumption of equal worth',[314] an *a priori* concern with social justice which allows intercultural contact to revise understandings of moral entitlement and of unfamiliar ethnic practices. For the writer the aesthetic and moral danger, one might say, lies in passages like the following, where the narrator of *The Fig Tree* beckons us to take a loving interest in women who have spent their lives on a Greek island: 'To understand the women, we must come to know the rock-strewn terrain.' [*FT*, 87]. He continues:

> The women descended step by measured step with the rising sun. Their voices rose, as if from a trance. They walked and talked until they parted company, and moved on to their family groves. [*FT*, 89]

Here 'moved', which is but one of many verbs of perambulation in the book, seems problematic. It bespeaks a well-meaning but finally too-anxious elation in the presence of the Other; a tendency, even, to aestheticize that other, to absorb difference into a loving, universalizing act of recognition that flattens out everything into sameness.

It is an aspect of Zable's larger response to his world that people should be loved, and that the elation the Hasidim once felt in the presence of their God should now be felt in the presence of the human Other. His humanism must find holiness in a world in which the Holocaust has driven many Jews to cry out, '*Yidn*, there is no God.'[315] In *Scraps of Heaven* the paths of disparate individuals and representatives of ethnic groups cross mysteriously, fortuitously. It is as if simultaneity emerges as a principle of order in what had seemed an utterly contingent post-Holocaust world. Zable's humanistic mysticism concludes that 'the moment itself is the haven, the true sanctuary'[316]—the moment and the Other with whom one shares it. In this sense Zable is a disciple of Martin Buber, famed editor of those Hasidic tales.

Zable's characters seldom evince Freudian psychological depth. Generally their inwardness is of a more mythopoetic kind that derives from Yiddish literature. As a chronicler of people he seems most interested in affiliative and communal emotions, ranging from passionate enchantment to horror. This allows him quite wonderfully to capture the individual in context, and to convey inwardness as a function of social life, as when in *Jewels and Ashes* he visits Buklinski, one of the last remaining Jews of Bialystok:

> Buklinski has opened a second bottle of vodka. He is up on his feet, dancing around the table like a boxer between rounds. I try to break into his monologue from time to time, but Buklinski is a bulldozer who flattens me with his manic, domineering, frenzied, suspicious, yet affectionate energy. One moment he has his arms around me, and is kissing my cheeks with joy while exclaiming how good it is to have such a guest, a son of Bialystoker come half-way around the

planet, the grandson of Bishke Zabludowski, no less, whom we all knew, and who didn't know him as he stood under the town clock selling newspapers, telling us what was going on in this twisted world, and now, can you believe it, his grandson has come to us from the very ends of the earth, like manna falling from the heavens. A miracle! [*JA*, 53]

Moments later his bliss tumbles into gloom. "'Two years," he says quietly, when he catches me looking. "For two years I was in Auschwitz."' [53] But not even the tears that come as he recollects the 'twisted world' of the past can wholly eclipse the hope symbolized by the Antipodes, the cultural elsewhere at 'the very ends of the earth'.

Revisioning the *shtetl*

Meier moves through Carlton as if through the streets of a *shtetl*—one of those provincial towns of pre-Holocaust eastern Europe in which Jews lived for centuries. In a recent interview Zable says: 'It seems that I have always been in search of the *shtetl*, the intimate community, the local community, or to put it in another way, the *Gemeinschaft* as opposed to the *Gesellschaft*.'[317] That search for intimacy is reflected in his fascination with storytelling and its venues: Posner's barber shop, the Cafe Scheherazade in St Kilda, the pubs, parks and suburban fences of Carlton where talk, that great shaper and chronicler of community, happens with the spontaneous creativity of the everyday. He writes, too, of certain public institutions which help migrants to maintain a sense of ethnic identification, of intimate cultural connection, in their adoptive cultures. One of these is the Kadimah, a Yiddish-based cultural centre located in Carlton during Zable's childhood. In 'Living in Limbo' he describes Kurdish House, a gathering-place for members of the fledgling Kurdish community of contemporary Melbourne. Musing as he so often does on parallels between post-Holocaust Jewish immigrant experience in Melbourne and that of more recent non-Jewish arrivals, he writes that 'Kurdish House reminded me of the Kadimah'.[318]

To Zable the Kadimah does not represent cultural isolationism, a refusal of the new. For him as for many other Jewish immigrants, its role was to help establish a viable balance between ongoing identification with

Jewishness and its European locales, on the one hand, and the processes of integration, on the other. The implicit model was of difference within a heterogeneous but connected local community, or *Gemeinschaft*.

Unlikely though it may seem after the Holocaust, there is some warrant for seeing the *shtetl* too as embodying aspects of this model of community. In *Shtetl*, a book that offers a counter-narrative to what she sees as Daniel Goldhagen's too-sweeping account of 'ordinary' people's antisemitism, Eva Hoffman writes that

> 'shtetl' refers not only to a specifically Jewish phenomenon, but to places where Jews lived side by side with the local population ... In the shtetl, pluralism was experienced not as ideology but as ordinary life. Jews trading horses in a small market town, speaking in haphazard Polish—that was the shtetl. Poles gradually picking up a few words of Yiddish and bits of Jewish lore—that was also the shtetl.[319]

Hoffman's notion of the *shtetl* as a kind of 'multicultural experiment'[320] is controversial, and Zable, whilst welcoming her focus on positive forms of *shtetl* cohabitation between Jews and others, suspects that it overstates the degree of receptive and productive interaction that actually occurred in many of these towns.[321] The Carlton of *Scraps of Heaven* is a kind of antipodean *shtetl*: sometimes intimate, as the title would imply, the scene of transcendence and rich inter-ethnic contact, yet shadowed by various forms of ethnic intolerance and hatred. 'Kiss the ground and say "I killed Jesus"...' [*SH*, 174] a gang of boys chant after pushing Josh over in a back lane on his way home from school. Zable, the academic social scientist turned novelist writing during the Howard era, wants to study the 'interaction between older working class residents, and the newly arrived immigrants with whom they lived side by side'.[322] His hope is that this ostensibly tolerant pluralist democracy will welcome new arrivals like Amal Hassan Basry.

Scraps of Heaven is a masterly evocation of intimate communal diversity, be it groups of fans—Jewish, Italian and others—sitting on the verandahs of their semi-detached cottages, listening to the broadcast of a boxing match [*SH*, 92], or the intimacy of the scene in which the young Jewish boy Josh enters the home of the returned serviceman, Sommers. Earlier in the day Josh has seen Sommers taking part in that most iconic of white Australian rituals, the Anzac Day march. Later, Josh notices him 'back on his verandah, pipe in hand, his face immobile in the encroaching dark' [150]. He mentions having seen him in the march and for the first time is invited in. The house, identical with the one next door, humble and in poor repair, has many mementoes of the Great War—artifacts that begin to initiate the boy into an unfamiliar world. But it is the story Sommers shares with him which makes the greatest impact:

> 'Once, after a battle, I looked at the German corpses. They were scattered over a field thick with mud. In death, they were curled up like newborn babies. I realised they were kids, just like me.'
>
> Sommers sits down opposite Josh, and ponders what to say next. He seems to choose his words with care.
>
> 'In that moment I saw the bloody truth; we were all kids. And in the forty years that've gone by, I've never stopped dreaming about them. I dream of their arms reaching out. They're begging for help. Calling for water. I can still see the thirst in their faces, their cracked lips. I can still see their glazed eyes, and I wake up in a sweat.' [*SH*, 152]

Josh hears a 'bloody truth' that the jingoistic nation-building rhetoric of Anzac Day would suppress. It is particularly significant that the boy who listens is Jewish: like all those outside the cultural 'mainstream', he will continue to feel the coercive pull of nationalistic myth, demanding that he endorse hegemonic Australian values. The old soldier's narrative warns against the perils of unthinking endorsement. That it does so through a description of German soldiers is also important because Josh's consciousness will in part be formed by descriptions such as Sommers's, but descriptions in which the victims are Jews and the destroyers Germans. In showing Germans in this light Sommers provides the boy with a perspective he would be unlikely to receive from within his own ethnic environment. Such intimate contact can shape him in ways not possible under the aegis of greater cultural homogeneity.

Werner Sollors and others have argued that ethnicity is itself in some sense 'invented',[323] that it is constantly subject to change and re-storying, and that the very notion of ethnic homogeneity is unsustainable. Like any Jew who contemplates the cultural and geographic diversity of his heritage,

Zable would agree. 'Jewishness' has meant so many things down the ages, and the Holocaust shows what perils lie in the reification of race, ethnicity and the other categories that attract delusional, sadistic attention to the Other. Like much of Zable's work, *Scraps of Heaven*, written in the wake of the Holocaust, tries to imagine community in a way that respects difference and its capacity to confer identity but resists the hardening of that difference into division and discrimination—in other words, that sees culture as having two necessary levels of manifestation: the insider's intimacy of belonging, and the multicultural citizen's inclination and capacity to enter and creatively participate in other cultural worlds. Zable's 'bonds of civility' call upon us to be citizens of a global moral community—a community whose hallmark is a special receptiveness to the specificities of local culture and to their capacity for enriching connection.

The Makor Jewish Community Library 'Write Your Story' Project

MAKOR JEWISH COMMUNITY LIBRARY

invites you to

WRITE YOUR STORY

FOR YOUR CHILDREN AND GRANDCHILDREN
OR JUST FOR YOURSELF

Thus began an advertisement that appeared in the *Australian Jewish News* early in 1998.[324] The Makor Jewish Community Library, situated in suburban South Caulfield, had received a $2000 grant from the Victorian Multicultural Commission to undertake work on aspects of the migrant experience. Julie Meadows, an experienced teacher of migrants, proposed a program which would assist Jews of all ages and backgrounds to write their life-stories. And so a remarkable project was born.[325]

The advertisement continued: 'Here is your chance to join a small group under the guidance of an experienced teacher. Don't worry about spelling, grammar, etc.' And then, in bold capitals, 'IT'S YOUR STORY THAT COUNTS'.

Nearly ten years on, the project is flourishing. It is run, as it has always been, through classes of about fifteen people, under the guidance of a facilitator. Some of those enrolled have written and even published before, but the majority have not. Teaching methods are very flexible, but in general people come for two hours to write and to consult with the facilitator, who offers all manner of assistance—from grammar and punctuation to narrative selection, style, story-shaping, tone and presentation. The writing sessions rarely take the form of workshops: group members don't read to others or receive feedback from their colleagues. There is the solitude of writing, the dialogue (sometimes verging on collaboration) with the facilitator, and some casual social contact over a cup of tea or coffee. But the process is essentially a case of 'me and my memories', and of personalized, non-intrusive guidance from facilitators who have a healthy regard for the centrality of the individual voice in life-writing, and for the individuality that each voice expresses.

Some who come lack confidence in their ability to tell a story in grammatical English; others dread re-engagement with harrowing pasts. The Makor team reports that many new participants are very anxious at the outset. Anxious but also eager. Those who have been unable to share their past, even with their own family, find that they can at last tell their story in autobiography—a form that permits a blend of personal and impersonal, intimacy and distance. Some writers arrive at the library 'like Ancient Mariners',[326] eyes blazing with a strange tale they feel driven to tell.

It takes an immense amount of work to fine some of these manuscripts down, to give them the shapeliness that is a hallmark of the series. In particularly difficult cases, where English-language skills are very limited or where trauma renders the recollecting and writing process extremely painful, the facilitator will work one-on-one at the computer with the author, thereby creating a special creative environment that combines bearing witness to a Holocaust testimony with more conventional writing-workshop methods. Nowadays some writers who have already completed a manuscript draft are coming to Makor for editorial help or possible publication through the program. About 70 percent of the first fifty Makor volumes, including the pieces that appear in the three anthologies so far produced,[327] have been authored by Holocaust survivors or their children. The gender distribution among the totality of authors is roughly 50/50. The majority are in their sixties or seventies at the time of publication. A few write in their eighties; still fewer in their nineties.

Initially, the intention was for a small number of copies of each manuscript to be xeroxed and circulated among friends and family. One copy was to be held in the library. But as word spread, and as the growing team of teachers and editors involved in the project gained access to desktop publishing, it was decided to produce book-length bound volumes, replete with photographs and individual covers. An average print-run is between 100 and 200; the higher range is 300–500. Volumes generally sell for just above $20. Authors do their own distribution but net most of the proceeds; the library makes about $2 per copy. Financial arrangements for publication are variable, depending on how much—if anything—authors can afford to contribute. Each volume is formally launched in a function room adjacent to the library. The Makor project has now published well over 50 volumes, thereby substantially increasing the already large corpus of Australian Jewish autobiography.

'A good deal of our work is therapy,' explained one of the facilitators during a meeting I had with the project team. How could it be otherwise when so many of those who write have experienced such trauma? Little wonder that 'building trust' lies at the heart of the facilitator–writer relationship. One facilitator spoke of a writer who could not achieve narrative progression in her work. Again and again she would describe a room in which she was kept hidden in the Warsaw ghetto as a child. The attempts varied only insofar as each description would survey the room from a slightly different angle, reflecting a position the girl had occupied in that space. Compulsive repetition is a familiar symptom of trauma. The special power of narrative—especially of first-person life-writing—lies partly in its capacity to supplant repetition with narrative progression: moving the story of the past forward can enable the author to move ahead with life. Revisiting the past in this way can confer the luxury of a freer future. In her Foreword to *The Porcelain Doll*, Vera Schreiber writes:

> After many decades of blocked memories and assumed indifference, I am now retracing my steps some fifty years. It is an arduous and emotional task to look back through sometimes-clouded memory. In the following pages, I start the journey to my early childhood. It took great courage to return to those dark and evil times. I feel humbled that I have survived when so many others perished. Destiny spared me, for the purpose of witnessing the perpetuation of my life and that of my children and grandchildren, living in peace and safety. The present prevails. The liberating power that writing can give one was unexpectedly revealed to me. Such is my story; it comes from darkness. It leaves behind a memory combining pain and some laughter, regret and wonderment.[328]

This passage speaks for many of the Makor Holocaust volumes. The author feels summoned to bear witness; indeed her survival for that purpose bespeaks the survival of meaning and purpose in all the 'darkness'. She writes to perpetuate memory down the generations. It hurts to do it, and sometimes the pain blocks access to memory, stifles the will to narrative progression. But with the help of the Makor project she prevails, as the 'present prevails'. She is not, finally, engulfed by misery. On the contrary, there is 'laughter' and 'wonderment' along with the pain. This fine-grained emotional self-declaration suggests that it is a mistake to read these Holocaust volumes merely as 'trauma narratives' by 'victims'. Many are intensely alive, often very funny, vitally engaged with their worlds, and extraordinarily focused on the future—not just on their children and grandchildren, but on me and my children, you and yours, people in general.

A remarkable recent addition to the series is Kitia Altman's *Memories of Ordinary People*.[329] Though it does not aspire to the compactness that many of the other Makor volumes exhibit, Altman's is beautifully written and intensely reflective. A typically powerful chapter is entitled 'The Lightning'. Dedicated to Julie Meadows, the chapter is about the flashes of insight into human nature that Altman experienced in Auschwitz and elsewhere. It is also a strikingly metaphoric meditation on the nature of the writing process—a process in which, as she has discovered as a participant in the 'Write Your Story' project, a key word can strike 'like lightning'[330] as the survivor's mind confronts thoughts that 'were born at a time when I lived my death'.[331] Altman ponders various registers of thought and sensation, and their complex relations to language and narrative structure. How can she narrate the terrible past when 'My thoughts and my memories are not correct in the world of syntax', when bygone images tumble out as if from 'an overstuffed wardrobe'?[332] This is a pained but finally a deeply affirming book which seeks to revivify murdered Holocaust souls, the 'memories of ordinary people'. Typically, 'The Lightning' ends on a note of 'illuminated' human friendship in Auschwitz.

Julie Meadows and other team members report powerful and positive emotional outcomes for many of their writers: some feel relieved to have 'done their duty' to the dead; others feel transformed 'as if a heavy stone has fallen from my heart; as if I no longer have to live in the past'; some say that

'I really didn't understand until now'—that is, until they had committed their memories to narrative.[333]

Narrative characteristics

Holocaust experience tends powerfully to shape the motivation of the writer and the kind of writing that results. Where a life has not been directly touched by the Holocaust, motivations for writing will be less predictable. Relatively few of the Makor volumes are by Australian-born Jews. Two notable examples are Sydney A. B. Benjamin's, *A Full House* and Bernard Boas's *The Five Books of Boas*.[334] In each case the desire to write has been occasioned by a successful life which the apparently buoyant author is keen to share with family, friends and readers. By comparison with the inevitable sombreness of the Holocaust-touched volumes, the antipodean sun fairly pours off these pages. As Benjamin's subtitle—*The fascinating autobiography by Sydney A. B. Benjamin*—indicates, this author is largely content with himself and his life. His penultimate sentence is: 'I realise, beyond doubt, I am a lucky person living in the *Lucky Country*.'[335] As would be expected of one who has been a psychologist, Bernard Boas is more introspective than Benjamin and provides interesting insight into his own psychological development. But he too is conscious of his 'remarkably good fortune'[336]—a reference to particular aspects of his life in the Antipodes, but also, by implication, to the fact that he was born far from the scenes of the Annihilation.

'Memory guide my hand': the solicitation makes clear that the inform-ing ethos of the project is one of narrative realism, that the aim is to tell the truth—however elusive that achievement might ultimately be—and that these volumes are not offered as fictions, factions or other species of literary invention. Given that most of these authors do not see themselves as professional writers, this is not surprising. Interestingly, only one applicant has ever been turned away from the project, and this was a person whose accounts of camp life seemed to lack factual authenticity. The three anthologies published to date are all entitled *Memory Guide My Hand*: this community of writers and teachers prizes truth-to-memory above all else. That does not, however, involve a naïve belief in the infallibility of memory. Garry Fabian is typical in wanting to leave 'a record as accurate as human memory permits'.[337] The same desire motivates the volumes by Australian-born Jews, for instance Freda Searle's attractive memoir of prewar and postwar life in Carlton, *Memory's Wings and Apron Strings*.[338]

Inevitably the facilitators bring to their task certain assumptions about what constitutes good writing, and those who come are keen to learn. Most find that memory alone cannot guide their hand. The facilitator gives guidance of various kinds. An example: in my meeting with the team I noted that the Makor Holocaust authors write about life in Australia much more frequently than do non-Makor Australian Jewish Holocaust autobiographers. Was this something the facilitators encouraged? The reply was, 'Yes: we encourage them to think about writing the whole sweep of their lives. Not just the camps, but their childhoods and their lives here as well.' In a quite literal way, then, the facilitators have influenced the narrative architecture of many of these volumes. I would guess that they are partly responsible, too, for the fact that few of these authors engage in extended editorializing or speculation. The facilitators tend to favour the ethos of 'show not tell', and so likewise do those who work with them.

Few of the Makor volumes are markedly introspective. The assumption is that memory, not the force of the authorial personality, guides the writer's hand. There are several reasons for this, reasons that apply to much first-generation Australian Jewish autobiography. First, not many of these authors grew up in introspective cultural environments, if by introspection we mean highly individualized scrutiny of one's own inner states and motivations. Those from Orthodox and even some from less observant Jewish backgrounds were schooled in a tradition that understood inwardness in ethical rather than psychological terms, and selfhood in the light of a normative mode of spiritual communal life. The question was not: 'Who am I and what makes me tick?' It was: 'Am I living a good Jewish life?' Even the more secular among them, including those from major European capitals, had little or no contact with the intensely introspective ethos of Freudian-Jewish modernity which was to become iconic of Jewish intellectuality in America, and rather later in Australia.[339]

Second, many Holocaust survivors experience 'survivor guilt': feelings of shame at having lived when six million co-religionists perished. They feel moved to bear witness but would see extended introspection as obscene self-indulgence, an abuse of their privilege of survival. Something similar often applies to those not directly affected by the Holocaust.

Third, many of these writers feel it is the events that befell them, and not their status as individuals, which make their stories worth telling and reading. As Abraham Biderman, author of *The World of My Past*, a fine non-Makor Australian Holocaust narrative, asks: 'Who am I? If it weren't for the Holocaust I would never have thought myself worth writing about.'[340]

Fourth, most of these folk received limited and disrupted educations in Europe and had to work extraordinarily hard to become established and raise families when they came to Australia. Little time there for navel-gazing, or for the self-scrutinizing habits that might result in introspective life-writing later on. Even those authors now in their sixties and seventies who were educated in Australia tend to write within the ethos of diffidence, a self-effacing decency that characterized Australian culture to the 1950s.

Finally, many survivors have been so traumatized that there is a disinclination to 'dig too deep' into the damaged psyche—for fear of what might be found, or precipitated, by introspection.

The conspicuously introspective volumes are by women. Whether in Australia or other patriarchal societies from which Makor authors come, women tend to be delegated responsibility for the interior world—the world of feeling, interpersonal connection, family, romance. Men tend to be cast for the deed, the individual journey—a training which, as feminist theorists of autobiography have noted, often differentiates the structure of their life-narratives from those of women.[341] Lucy Gould's *Empty Corners*[342] gives a nuanced account of a mother–daughter relationship torn by the pressures of war. Paulette Goldberg's *Just Think It Never Happened* includes reflections on how her Holocaust experience has affected her own parenting:

> The children were growing up nicely and we were doing well financially. I wanted so much to be a normal parent and hold my babies with love, but I couldn't connect. I found it hard to feel easy love for my children and even today, for my grandchildren, although I really love being with them. Maybe, it is because nobody loved me for so many years, during and after the war. Or maybe, it is because I taught myself very young not to get too attached to any-one, in case they were taken away from me, and I can't unlearn it.[343]

Australian-born Helen Gardner's *My Mother's Child*,[344] perhaps the most introspective of all the Makor volumes, is unstinting in its courageous exploration of inner conflict and pain. In the tradition of psychoanalytic autobiography, Gardner draws upon psychological discourse and her experience of psychotherapy to chart and narrate her changing relationship to self.

> In general, Ian [her psychologist] tended to work with present day problems, but I was in the grip of feelings generated by my past; a past which I had allowed my family to define; a past full of feelings I had pushed aside and never examined. I began the long process of giving voice to my experience.[345]

Almost all of the Makor Holocaust-related volumes feature a dedication. The one from Lenke Arnstein's *Recurring Dreams*, quoted earlier in this book (see page 82), is typical. The project's inaugurating invitation to 'write your story for your children and grandchildren' has powerfully shaped the stories that have been written. No doubt this is partly a matter of self-selection: those who wanted to communicate in this way were attracted by the advertisement. But here again it is also true that the facilitators' conception of the program has had a considerable bearing on the shape and trajectory of the narratives that have been produced.

It is hard to generalize about the writing across such a large number of texts, but on the whole the prose is lucid, direct, unadorned, and does not rise to the level of what we might think of as 'literary art'. Given the backgrounds and aspirations of these authors, this is just what one would expect. Highly accomplished writers with literary ambitions will tend to publish with commercial presses. The facilitators and editors have done an excellent job in achieving a solid general standard of stylistic proficiency across the series. It cannot be stressed too highly that narratives such as these do not need to be masterly in order to have value: they are precious human documents just as they are. It takes a very special writer—a Primo Levi—to make art out of Auschwitz.

Several of the Makor volumes evince subtle stylistic changes as they move through their authors' main life-phases. The prose about the gone world of eastern European Jewry tends to be the most assured and evocative, and the most indebted to traditional modes of Jewish storytelling. Yiddish speech rhythms, character types from Hasidic tales, and various forms of moral fable can feature here:

> The summers of my childhood stretch like a necklace woven out of sunbeams with precious jewels set in it, jewels with names like Srodborow, Swider, Jozefow... The sun always shone and I can still smell the pine needles and the resin of the conifer forests in the vicinity of Warsaw.[346]

Writing about the camps is generally very matter-of-fact. There are few attempts to achieve rhetorical emphasis or poetic intensity of description, to tap deep imaginative and linguistic resources in an effort to narrate what some see as unnarratable. Most are content to let the events speak for themselves. No doubt the fact that they are often writing for children and grandchildren is conducive to a certain restraint. They want their family and others to 'know what happened' but they don't want to overwhelm them with rage, sorrow or horror. The following excerpt by Guta Goldstein, one of the most accomplished Makor writers, takes artistry about as far as most of these authors are inclined to go:

> One night, a young woman who was left alone and ill with tuberculosis, did throw herself onto the electrified fence [in Auschwitz-Birkenau]. In the morning, a burnt shrivelled body was held by the electric current, her arms and legs stretched out resembling a spider on a web. The Germans hadn't bothered to take her off. They left her there through the roll call as a deterrent.[347]

Survivor writing about life in Australia is very different again. It naturally lacks the grim immediacy of camp descriptions and the wistful freshness of European childhood recollections. Settling and getting on in Australia presented very pragmatic challenges, and the tone in which these authors recall life here tends to be just that—pragmatic, but also, and not surprisingly, lacking in intimacy with the adoptive culture: 'In the spring of 1965 we moved to our present house in Toorak Road, East Hawthorn. It was a bit of an upheaval for us. I had to let our customers know about our new address and telephone number, Jack had to change schools, and so on.'[348]

Local-born authors can of course write with greater ease about this place, though it has to be said that even they have produced relatively little distinguished prose about Australia.

There is impressive formal and creative range among the volumes. While most employ a straightforward and unadorned chronological narrative method, some draw on other media: in *There Will Be Tomorrow*, Guta Goldstein interleaves poetry and prose narrative; Helen Max's *Searching for Yesterday* is a photographic essay about her mother, a Holocaust survivor.[349] Hania Ajzner's superb *Hania's War* is one of a few narratives that disrupt chronological sequence and allow the strange vagaries of memory to guide the storytelling hand. Kitia Altman experiments with a variety of prose genres.

Writing community

To what extent might the Makor initiative be seen as a community project? Community is a shifting concept.[350] It can denote physical habitation in a particular place; the social mores and practices—the culture—of a group, whether in one place or in a state of geographical dispersion; various kinds and degrees of identification between individuals and some collective entity. It has connotations of intimacy (the town or village as against the impersonality of the big city), loyalty, stability, shared commitments to specific values, and more. Communities of the Jewish diaspora tend to have a high level of internal differentiation but also to exist in various and often overlapping dimensions. The 'Australian Jewish community' differs in subtle ways from region to region (for instance, a larger survivor population in Melbourne than in Sydney; proportionally more South African Jews in Perth than in Brisbane). There are religious stratifications (ultra-Orthodox, Orthodox, Liberal, secular), a vast range of places of origin (Ashkenazic, Sephardic, particular national cultures), differences in class, in attitudes to Israeli and Australian politics, and so on. Yet these various constituencies overlap, even coincide in important ways: most Jews now espouse some version of Zionism; virtually all have a deep consciousness of the Holocaust. Holocaust survivors comprise something of a community within a community, or rather within communities: they may be Melbourne Holocaust survivors, but they are also members of an international population of survivors. Thus any given Australian Jewish autobiography might be said to speak for a particular segment of the Australian Jewish community with respect to some issues; and only occasionally, as in the case of the Holocaust, for Australian Jews in general.

But autobiographers are more than just passive documenters of community. They are also active beings who create narrative artifacts and actively interpret the world they witness and participate in. To varying degrees they are *agents* in their own texts.[351] Autobiography does not just 'give voice' to community—it *constitutes* and continually *reconstitutes* community. Community is a moral phenomenon which depends upon shared ethical commitments and ongoing ethical debate. Holocaust memoir in particular plays an important part in constituting *moral community*—a community which debates and reasserts human rights, denouncing genocide and other abuses of those rights. Needless to say, one does not have to be a Holocaust survivor or a survivor's child in order to write morally engaged autobiography.

The Makor Jewish Community Library is located in an area that contains the densest population of Jews in Melbourne. In fact, it is more than a library. The building in which it is housed, the Beth Weizmann Community Centre, has a restaurant and function facilities as well. Makor is as much a meeting-place as a library; many who call by seem to seek company, not just reading material and information. It really is a 'community' facility and it is staffed by people with strong commitments to that community. The ethos of the place is reflected in the books it produces. In this very important sense, Makor's 'Write Your Story' is community life writ large, in a major capital city far from the lands where most of these authors were born.

After my meeting with the Makor team, an elderly lady—a survivor in her eighties who has contributed to one of the *Memory Guide My Hand* anthologies—was sitting at a table trying to write when she became very distressed. Whimpering, one hand over her mouth, she seemed completely disoriented. Leonie Fleiszig, the library's splendid senior librarian and a key figure in the 'Write Your Story' project, knew this lady well and had seen her in this condition before. It wasn't confusion, as I had thought, but an anxiety attack—the bane of many a survivor's life. Unfussy, warm, strong and good-humoured, Leonie and several other staff took her in hand. They spoke gently and respectfully to her, contacted her husband, made arrangements for her to get home.

I went back to the meeting-room to collect my briefcase and jacket. By the time I returned to the library desk the lady was calm and composed. Such is the power of community.

Part Three

Tracings: An Anthology of Short Excerpts

Full details of all the publications from which excerpts have been quoted in Part Three can be found in the Bibliography under the authors' names or, in some cases, among the anthologies (see pp. 273–84). The brief headings that follow here include page-numbers, given in square brackets.

Old World

HANIA AJZNER, *Hania's War* [32–3]

An important landmark in the country of my childhood was the tannery. The family tannery, together with some other tanneries, was situated at Okopowa Street in a precinct owned by a man called Pfeiffer. All the tanneries were grouped close together, I suppose because of the smell, which some people may have found disagreeable. I loved it. Every day at about two o'clock in the afternoon, various women, mostly maids, could be seen converging on the entrance to the tannery carrying 'menazki', stacks of enamel containers held one on top of another with metal bands. These vessels contained hot dinners for the workers. I loved going to the factory with Malvina.

My father used to eat his dinner with the ordinary workers, not in the office with Grandfather and Uncle Moniek. Sometimes, if he had time, he would take me around the factory explaining the processes as we went. I loved the acrid smells, even the ones rising out of the evil-looking vats with hides soaking in various chemicals. I was full of admiration for the most skilled workers who used to scrape the hair off the raw hides with thin, sharp knives like long razors. One slip could ruin a valuable hide. There were also large, barrel-shaped structures which were suspended horizontally. They were about twice a man's height in diameter and about as long. They had trap-doors on their sides and gantries with cat-walks between them. The hides would be placed in them through the trap-doors and they would be tumbled inside the barrels to cure them and then to dry them. It was a most impressive sight.

I was strictly forbidden to go anywhere in the tannery by myself, not that I would have dared. The ground was slippery and slimy and the vats were sunk right into the floor. There were strange-smelling vapours rising from them. I had visions of tripping and falling right into one of the vats and getting tanned, just like one of the hides, albeit a small one.

ANNA ROSNER BLAY, *Sister, Sister* [50–51]

Hela: The shop was poorly lit, with crowded shelves and a dark timber counter polished by years of use. Everything was sold not in packets but by weight—around the shop were sacks of flour, salt and cocoa. The walls were lined with tins of tea and coffee, and on the counter sat large scales with a set of weights. Beet sugar was very expensive and was sold in hard cones. As well as groceries there were fresh vegetables, and in one corner stood a dark wooden barrel of pickled cucumbers. Whenever I came into the shop in the afternoon, the pungent sour smell made me wrinkle my nose, although I soon got used to it. We also sold cheese, a hard white cottage cheese and a yellow Swiss. Mingled with the smells of pickles and coffee and cheese was the warm dusty scent of the wooden floorboards, and the stale odour of countless working people who regularly came in to provide for their families' daily needs. In another corner was a large barrel in which live fish swam, particularly carp. Jewish women bought fish for Friday night, and non-Jews also bought fish for their festivals. I watched their creased faces and clumsy fingers as they counted out their few coins and laid them carefully on the counter. As they turned to leave I saw motes of dust floating in shafts of late-afternoon sunlight, settling silently over everything as father turned back to his book.

ITZHAK CYTRYNOWSKI, *'And I Will Remember My Covenant…'* [33]

During the war years, I had already been studying with my new rebbe, the well-known scholar, Reb. Michael Yoseph. He was, so people said, well-learned. He lived in the next building to us, so I was always the first pupil to arrive at this new heder.

Reb. Yoseph had a disciplinary whip of which he made much use. People took it as a sign of his good disciplinary strategies. He used to expound his philosophy to us quite often. One of his constant pronouncements was that he used the whip for two purposes: the tail part to beat the devil out of us, and the handle, to force the teaching into us. I considered him cruel, if not sadistic, towards his pupils. He would question a student about a subject that he had previously covered and if the boy could not respond, Reb. Michael Yoseph had a simple solution: he would grab the student by the lips, and in this manner proceed to drag him out of his seat. The wretched boy would rise, and as he did so, the rebbe's free hand would appear with the whip.

How I hated Reb. Michael Yoseph! I decided to make his life as miserable as he made ours. I did not of course succeed very well, but my limited victories gave me great satisfaction. To this day I feel a sense of satisfaction that it was I who managed to steal his whip and dispose of it in the dugout pit which served as the latrine, which was a common feature in every court-yard at that time. As I never took partners in my schemes, I was never caught as the culprit.

ITZHAK CYTRYNOWSKI, *'And I Will Remember My Covenant…'* [119–20]

I was astonished at this new turn in my life. In a very short space of time I had learned that I too needed to make promises which I was not sure I could keep. I had tried once or twice to avoid dealing in such a manner but had only suffered loss of income for my efforts, and by now I realized that everything I did was solely for the purpose of generating money.

The changes stood out more sharply when I would come into contact with very religious, pious Jews. The very men who were most reliable in the prayer-house, who were most willing to come to the aid of a fellow-Jew, providing both support and money, these men changed their approach when faced with the pressures of the business world.

It was as if a whole new field of study had been laid before me. I was a good student too, even if I did not approve of the subject. I learned because I wanted to adapt to the changes in my life—otherwise there could be no justification for abandoning my studies. But from it all I noticed something which was to guide me in my future understanding of mankind. It was this: there are two major differences between the world of the student and the world of business. In the student's world, the new acquisition of knowledge no matter how minor it may be, is always a joy in itself. In the business world, learning becomes an obligation; it is a necessity. Furthermore, no matter how generous one might be, one cannot share one's wealth in business in the manner that one can share one's wealth of knowledge. One can give away everything in the business world only to be left a pauper, but in the world of the prayer-house one might gain even more understanding, so that both giver and recipient may grow rich together.

So necessity had forced Itzhak Cytrynowski to be a businessman. Yet within, I always clung to the self image of being a student of the prayer-house. For such a student has no concern for material wealth, and no matter how little he has financially, he needs even less for his purpose in life.

GUTA GOLDSTEIN, *There Will Be Tomorrow* [44–5]

On the floor below us lived three spinster sisters. They were old, wrinkled and grumpy. The three of them looked and dressed alike. They wore long skirts and lace collars. Their hair was combed up into grey buns and there was powder in their wrinkles. I was a little afraid of them and was made uncomfortable in their presence. They never used my name but glared at me unpleasantly and called me *zydoweczka* (little Jewess) which was a deroga-tory term. I had to pass their flat on the way to my home, one storey above. For some reason, they always had their front door open and one or other of the sisters was always on a chair inside the door whenever I passed. I always greeted them politely but without stopping, and quickly ran up the stairs.

When one of the sisters died, she was laid out in her coffin, dressed in her best gown, her wrinkled face powdered and rouged. As custom dictated, the coffin was open for three days. Their door was open and people were going in and out of there to pay their respects. When I passed their door on my way home, one of the sisters forcibly pulled me in, picked me up and with a smirk of malevolent joy, insisted that I kiss her sister goodbye. The more I protested, the more she insisted and did not let me go until I did. She had a satisfied smirk on her face while I was frightened and angry. I was five years old at the time. My parents were furious but there was nothing that they could do.

MARIAN PRETZEL, *Portrait of a Young Forger* [14–15]

After a short time working on diesel engines I was sent to help build a mixing machine for a chocolate factory. The sickly-sweet smell almost put me off chocolate for life, and during this time I had a real insight into how crude and hard a mechanic's life can be.

I was learning something else, too. Being born a Jew could create problems. It had never been a problem before. We lived [in Lvov] in an area which was mostly Gentile, and where the Jewish families were liberal in their religious attitudes. I was never conscious that a Jew was so very different from a Gentile; sure enough, we had our religious instructions at school and they had theirs, but apart from that there seemed to be no real distinction. Every year, my mother, orthodox as she was, would buy a Christmas tree for our Polish maid and help her to decorate it in her little room, and we always had Christmas dinner with the family of my father's first business partner and close friend, Stanislaw Nowacki, who was a strict Catholic.

I cannot remember ever being made to feel 'inferior'. If anyone pushed me I believed it was me, Marian Pretzel, they pushed, that it had nothing to do with my being Jewish. It never occurred to me to blame my religion for anything unpleasant or unfair which happened to me. My father and I had many Polish and Ukrainian friends as well as Jewish ones, and I appreciated being able to grow among people with different backgrounds.

Although we were aware that anti-semitism was alive elsewhere in the community, my family was virtually unaffected by it. Then, in 1937, when I was fifteen, anti-semitic outbursts started to become frequent and violent...

 ❧

ALEX SAGE, *For Esther* [31]

Father must have been a magician to sire so many children, particularly the last three children, in the circumstances we lived in. There were two beds in the room that served as bedroom, living-room, kitchen and bathroom, though no-one ever bathed there. In one bed slept Mum with her two daughters, while Father and I slept in the other. How he managed it, without disturbing me or the two girls who slept in Mother's single bed, will remain a mystery.

One night, not long before I left home, I woke up hearing my parents whispering. Father was trying to talk Mother into something, and she was saying, 'No, Moshe, let me be. I cannot feed those already here. I have had enough. More than enough!'

'But Dvorah,' whispered my father insistently, 'the Torah commands us specifically to "*proo orvoo*", to be fruitful and multiply.'

'I have done my share, bearing eleven children,' my mother replied. 'I have no more energy left.'

Father continued: 'Dvorah, you know that every daughter of Israel who bears twelve children gets a golden chair near the shkhinah. Wouldn't you like to sit there among those others in a glorious golden chair?'

'I'll make do with what I get for eleven. Now let me sleep. I am very tired.'

 ❧

MARK VERSTANDIG, *I Rest My Case* [26]

In the shtetl we didn't enjoy the kind of childhood now taken for granted in western society. Our early education and upbringing were dictated by the Mishna's instruction to initiate boys in reading the Torah, that is the

Pentateuch, at the age of five. To that end, boys were taught the alphabet at three and 'Ivri' at four, 'Ivri' being the Yiddish word for the mechanics of reading, as distinct from understanding, the Hebrew of the Bible.

The school or cheder we attended was similar to the one more romantically described in Yakir Warszawsky's Yiddish song *Ofn Pripetchik* (*By the Fireplace*). Our teacher also taught the children 'kometz-alef, oh' (the first vowel in the Hebrew alphabet); but, instead of promising his industrious pupils a little flag, he used to beat the lazy and backward ones with his stick. The room exhibited the filth and wretchedness of extreme poverty. The children in the cheder didn't need Sholem Aleichem's song, *If I were a Rothschild*, to explain the meaning of the rabbi's sighs. If he had been Rothschild his wife would have ceased tormenting him for a bit of money to prepare the Shabbes.

The cheder was conducted in the kitchen where the rabbi ate and the rebbetsin baked bread. No grass ever grew in the small yard behind his cottage which was snow-covered in winter, and muddy in spring and autumn when it rained. In summer, when the ground was dry, we played football. There was never any risk of breaking the rabbi's windows, because the ball was made of old rags stuffed into a long black cloth bag, tightly bound and sewn up. Naturally, it never rose above ground level, but it was enough for us to have something to kick.

The Holocaust

HANIA AJZNER, *Hania's War* [256–7]

To one side of the sorting sheds there is a curious structure. It is white and in the shape of a truncated step-pyramid with a white dome which seems to float above it. As we walk closer, we see that the dome-like roof is supported by a thick pillar at each corner of the platform. We walk up the steps to the platform. There is a waist-high wall in the middle of the platform, enclosing an area of about three square metres. I walk up to the wall, look down, and I am struck speechless. The low wall encloses a pit which contains a mound of white ashes. Among the ashes there are bones, pieces of skulls, and teeth. This is the final resting place of eighteen thousand people, inmates of this charnel-house, who were shot, buried, and then disinterred and cremated here on the 3rd and 4th of November 1943, during the 'Erntefest' 'Harvest Feast' massacre. My father was most probably amongst them. I am actually looking down on my father's ashes. He had been stripped naked, had walked to a previously dug ditch, was ordered to climb down among the corpses already lying there, to lie on top of them, and he was then shot. This mound, and my memories of him, are all that remains of him today.

Slowly, I walk to the crematorium, which is situated beyond the sorting sheds. I place my last memorial candle inside one of the ovens, and I light it, recollecting my father lighting the memorial light on the second anniversary of his own father's death. He said then, 'I am glad that he did not live long enough to see all that is happening now.'

Slowly, I walk back through the camp. Suddenly, I hear my father's voice, almost as if he is walking alongside me:

'Przeciez wiesz ze one byly zupelnie bezradne!'—'But you know that they were completely helpless!' as though answering my wordless cry: 'Why did you desert me?' which I realise has been reverberating in my mind, drowning out the memory of his voice. I realise, and accept at last, that the reason why he'd left us was because he'd been compelled to look for his sisters, to try and bribe their way out of the Umschlagplatz, to do for them what he had done for his younger brother, that he was still looking for them, hoping against hope to be able to save them, when he got to Majdanek.

Suddenly, something cold and sharp as a dagger seems to melt deep inside me, a veil lifts in my mind, and, for the first time in fifty years, I can see his dear face in my mind's eye, smiling gently at me. The warmth of his love seems to permeate the very air around me. I have my father back.

I turn to my husband and smile at him through the tears in my eyes, and I tell him:

'I can go home now.'

ABRAHAM BIDERMAN, *The World of My Past* [57–8]

An ancient Jewish proverb teaches us that it is better to be a living dog than a dead lion. Those still alive in the ghetto persuaded themselves that somehow they would survive; but the misery and gloom deepened from day to day. The ghetto was covered by a heavy blanket of snow, with an angry frost biting mercilessly at the exhausted inhabitants, penetrating every bone, every joint of the skeletons wrapped in rags. The frost burst the pipes, causing water to leak over the staircases and down the walls.

Inside our apartment, the thick frost covering our walls froze into beautiful designs, inspiring my daydreaming as I floated away to a fantasy land on a distant continent, rich with fruit, flowers and palm trees. The tropics with their lush vegetation became a constant dream.

When not at work, people mostly stayed in bed, fully dressed, to keep warm. I would stare endlessly at the landscapes painted by the frost on the windows. In my dreams I sailed off to the Great Barrier Reef, following the journey of *The Children of Captain Grand* by Jules Verne, and explored the Australian continent. At the time, Australia was only a dream for me. My mother used to say to Lipek and me, 'One day, when you finish your education, we will go to live in Australia.' Only one of us ever made it.

ABRAHAM BIDERMAN, *The World of My Past* [61–3]

But Dr Szykier is not the only reason that No. 11 Zgierska Street is so deeply engraved in my memory. It was also because of Mr Rothschild, a Viennese Jew in his mid-sixties, who was brought into the ghetto with other western European Jews at the end of 1941. He was a man of medium stature, cultured and softly spoken; a good-natured, gentle person. When I saw him for the first time, he was immaculately dressed and cleanly shaven, the image of an upper class, western European gentleman. It was painful to watch the aristocrat become a beggar. He wandered the streets, begging for a bit of hot soup. The Jewish policeman on duty at the kitchen window urged him to go home, not to make a nuisance of himself.

'But dear sir,' Rothschild answered with tears in his eyes, 'I have no home. Please, officer, just a little bit of soup, just a few spoons. You will save my life.'

The policeman, helpless, repeated: 'Sir, please go home! I have no soup for you. You get yours like everybody else.'

But Rothschild would not listen, insisting that the policeman let him pass. He wanted to see the manager of the kitchen, ignoring the fact that begging in the ghetto was useless.

When I saw Rothschild in December 1941, the frost burned with ferocity, and the courtyard was covered with a heavy snow. He was moving the weight of his body from one foot to the other, trying to keep warm. I could hear the voice of the kitchen manager reprimanding him for behaving like a beggar, but the policeman on duty came to Rothschild's defence, telling the manager not to be hard on him.

'Give him a bit of soup. Don't you know who he is?'

The manager answered curtly. 'Who cares who he is—or who he was!'

But Rothschild persisted until the manager took the rusty pot out of his hand and brought back a bit of hot liquid, handing it to the old man. He praised the manager for having been his saviour, promising him that he would give him his signature and, after the war, the Rothschild family would reward him.

I saw his tears and heard him mumble: 'I am a respectable gentleman. I am not a beggar. I am a man with a name.' Thanking the manager and the policeman, he walked away slowly; but, day after day, he would return.

As time passed, his appearance deteriorated. He stopped shaving and washing. His shirt and tie became grubby, and his shoes fell apart. They had not been made for ghetto winters. His once beautiful grey-and-white herringbone overcoat became filthy, with its right patch-pocket half-torn, hanging down. His pants became too long, falling off his body as he shrank from rapid loss of weight. The cuffs of his trousers became frayed, wet and dirty from being constantly dragged in the mud and wet snow. His elegant hat became dirty and squashed, sitting askew on his head.

Mr Rothschild's smooth gentle face turned into a mask of misery. His voice became weaker as he stood in front of the kitchen window begging for soup day after day. At times, the manager lost his temper, shouting at him: 'Go somewhere else. I can't give you any more soup. I have no right to do that.' Yet the policemen never insulted him nor did they mishandle him. The workers from the hat factory queuing for their soup watched Mr Rothschild in silence.

One day, as I passed the courtyard at 11 Zgierska Street, I saw a body lying face down in the mud of the melting snow near the kitchen window.

The policeman on duty was bending over the body, trying to revive him by rubbing his hands and face with snow.

Someone remarked bitterly: 'What are you doing? Why are you trying to revive him? Let him be! Let him die! He's better off dead.'

On that day in the Lodz ghetto, Mr Rothschild from Vienna became just one of the many cadavers waiting to be collected by the large horse-drawn, platform carriage with a big black box mounted on top of it. It cruised the streets, collecting the dead and taking them to the cemetery to dispose of them without a funeral. No gravestone, no marking.

ALEX COLMAN, *After Forty Years Silence* [33–4]

However, remembering the way I had shared my food parcel with them they took pity on me, and returned most of my possessions to me; some of them even arranged to have me placed on a work detail, where the food was better. In the meantime, we were all surprised when a Gestapo officer came to our cell and asked me to follow him to the office, where he showed me large photo albums of SS and Gestapo officers.

'See!' he said. 'That's what you can look like. We'll give you a pistol, and a passport, and you can drive around wherever you like. All you have to do is search for your fellow believers.'

The shock of what he expected me to do hit me like a physical blow. I felt myself trembling all over; I could scarcely speak, but managed to whisper that I thought I was not suited to such a job. The Gestapo man seemed annoyed.

'Then you'll stay in Mokotow until Doomsday,' he snarled.

'It can't be helped,' I said, shaking my head. There were some prices too high to pay, I believed, and to betray my own race was one of them. I could not do it.

'It might pay you to change your mind,' he said as he escorted me back to my cell. 'We'll give you a little more time to think about it.'

According to my cellmates, I looked so white and shaken that they thought I must have been tortured.

'What happened? What happened?' they demanded as soon as the

Gestapo man had left—but I couldn't talk about it; it was some days before I could calm myself, and I was in constant terror that any moment he might reappear to take me away again. What would happen when I refused again? I tried to close my mind to the possibility of torture. How strong was I? Would I be able to bear such ill-treatment with fortitude? I knew that many of the poor wretches who had been tortured would have preferred death to further agony. So I waited.

ITZHAK CYTRYNOWSKI, *'And I Will Remember My Covenant…'* [65–6]

In moments of despair I asked of the same God of Abraham, Isaac, and Jacob, why he abandoned us to our fate in the ghettos and later again in Auschwitz. I can't help but feel cheated. I remember my reaction as a child when I learned about the patriarch, Abraham, and of his readiness to sacrifice his only son Isaac for the glory of God. I recall that the rebbe noticed my distress at the story. I asked:

'What would have happened if the angel who saved Isaac from being slaughtered would have come too late?'

My rebbe assured me that God's angel cannot come too late. And I believed him—with all my childish honesty—I believed him—I believed too, that the God of Abraham, of Isaac and of Jacob, would listen to my mother's plea—but I was cheated. I can't say by whom I was cheated, but nevertheless, the feeling remains. The angel came too late. He came too late for not only one Isaac but for one third of the Jewish population of the time. God's angel came too late for some six million Jews—one million sacrificed for each day of God's creation. Oh, God of Abraham!

JANINA DAVID, *A Touch of Earth* [207–8]

I closed my eyes, pressed my back into the earth and repeated aloud: 'My parents are dead. They died in concentration camps or, betrayed by their fellow citizens, on a city street. I shall never know how, or when, or exactly where it happened and where they were buried. There will be no tomb sheltering their remains. This whole country is a tomb, the whole earth a vast grave and, somewhere, they are a part of it. I can go away now, but as long as I can touch the earth I will be in touch with them.'

Through half-closed eyes the brilliant sky glittered. There was a shimmering pattern of leaves dancing against its hard blue background. I woke up after a long sleep in which the scent of apples and pears ripening in the sun had miraculously returned and even now was filling the air around me. The earth was soft. I lay on my back, feeling the ground yielding under me, like a warm cradle. Grass grew between my fingers, and over my body; ants crawled on my legs. I watched them calmly, without a shiver of fear. They and I, all of us, we belonged to the earth. She was the only indestructible, fundamental basis of all life. She gave us life and to her we shall all one day return. This was the sole certainty, the only consolation.

From the orchards, dreaming in the autumn sun, the warm wind brought a scent of ripening fruit. A scent of life returning. A scent of peace.

MATYLDA ENGELMAN, *The End of the Journey* [20–21]

In a bed in a corner was a young woman. She lay there, motionless, crying, staring at the ceiling. We had easy access to Mrs Moritz' house down a few stairs, from the attic. The doctor came next morning on his regular visit. He was surprised to see me:

'You too?' he asked.

'No, I was lucky. I was hidden in our cellar for two weeks. I think I might have my old trouble starting again, perhaps from the dampness of the cellar. Would you mind having a look at me and my little girl too?'

'You have a temperature all right, not very high. All I can give you now is some codliver oil for you and Wanda. That's as much as I can do for the moment. When peace comes, I'll send you to the hospital to have an X-ray. Even if you have a bit of a temperature, you are still better off than Gisela is.' He nodded towards the young woman on the bed in the corner.

'Fourteen men ... Fourteen,' he repeated.

I was speechless. I thought of all the animals in the world and I could not think of one who would do that.

Before the doctor left, he whispered:

'Try to give her some comfort, speak to her, she is badly injured and shaken.'

After a while I moved nearer to the other bed. I dried the young woman's tears:

'Don't worry, the nightmare is over. It'll heal up. Everything passes ...'

I stroked her forehead and after a while she started to speak to me, with great effort:

'I was forced at pistol point to lie down on the floor. There was a queue of men in front of me. I couldn't escape. After four or five times, I screamed and begged them to stop, to let me go but nothing helped. I was told later that an officer found me unconscious and carried me away. I will never live through it.'

GARRY FABIAN, *A Look Back over My Shoulder* [36–7]

Early in 1944, something very strange indeed happened at Theresienstadt. An official beautification program was started. Buildings were cleaned up on the outside, shops appeared and fancy street signs went up. The large huts in the town square used for war-related production of one sort or another were demolished and a garden planted. The wildest rumours circulated throughout the ghetto. It turned out in the end that a Red Cross delegation was to visit and inspect the ghetto to make a report to the International Red Cross. The whole project took on the look of a film set. Orchestras practised in a specially constructed bandstand and outdoor cafes were set up. And the place began to look like a popular spa. It was all a hollow sham. Lewis Carroll in writing *Alice in Wonderland* only had ten per cent of the imagination the Germans displayed in setting up this sham facade, specially designed to fool the Red Cross delegation ...

Apparently the beautification effort worked beyond their wildest dreams. The delegation, carefully chaperoned by the Germans, spent five hours in the ghetto. They saw what they were supposed to see and left to write a glowing report on the conditions in which Jews lived under the protection of 'the kindly masters of the Third Reich'. There was another sidelight, which we only discovered some years after the war. The Germans also made a propaganda film, *The Führer Gives a Town to the Jews*, which came to my attention decades later.

There were some rather macabre sidelights to the clean up operation. Over the years to 1944 many thousands had died in the ghetto, some of natural causes, many of disease or starvation. They had been cremated and their ashes were stored in small cardboard boxes. The Germans decided the ashes were potentially embarrassing to their claims of providing the ideal settlement at Theresienstadt. So, to avoid suspicion during the inspection, the ashes were taken down to the river and dumped. Children were used to carry out this task. While I was not personally involved in this macabre exercise, I heard about it later. With German 'thoroughness' each box was carefully labelled with a name, and when children discovered the ashes of a relative, they would exchange them saying, 'I found your grandfather! When you find my grandmother, we will swap.'

ZOSIA GETTLER, 'Luck—A Survivor's Tale', in *Memory Guide My Hand*, vol. 3 [107]

In the east, there was no food. I survived on whatever I could find: a scrap of carrot, some potato peel, grass boiled into a soup and grapes. I would also kill turtles and eat them. They tasted like chicken. But whatever food I found, it was not enough: I had no more milk to give my baby and like everyone else, I also had malaria. Tania had it too. On the night of 21 November 1941, I was lying in my bunk holding Tania. She was making little sounds, tiny little moans at regular intervals. Suddenly they stopped. My baby was dead. She was just eleven months old. The next morning I wrapped her in a sheet and took her to a nearby cemetery. I dug a small grave, placed her in the ground and covered it over. I took a piece of wood, inscribed her name on it, and put it there as a tombstone, but by the next morning the piece of wood had vanished, perhaps foraged by someone looking for firewood.

OTTO GUNSBERGER, *Choice of Profession* [98–9]

There were about fifty of us there, all seriously ill except myself, waiting for admittance. This was handled not by doctors, but by two roughneck hospital orderlies. They asked who had high temperature, who vomited blood or suffered from dysentery. I had to make a quick decision, saw that those with high fever and who vomit blood were to be taken further inside the building with another orderly. That did not look promising, so I stayed put. The orderly put me down with twenty others suffering from dysentery, led us into an adjacent room where white porcelain bedpans were lined up, one for each of us on the floor alongside the wall. We had to empty our bowels into our respective pans while the door of the room was left open and the two orderlies waited for the result in the next room. The others in the room were seriously ill with that frightful disease. I was the only one free of any sign of diarrhoea. The nature of the disease is such that those who are affected pass stools very frequently in short intervals. Within no time at all my fellow inmates filled up their bedpans and were waiting. I was the only one still squatting on an empty pan. It was a serious situation. The orderly could come in the room any minute and without any excretum produced I could be beaten up by the two roughnecks. In great desperation I begged the others next to me to share some of their product with me as they had more than plenty. They all tried to help. I just poured a quarter of my four squatting neighbours' almost liquid, blood-stained faeces in my pan. I had to do it quickly, without much noise in order not to draw the attention of the orderlies from the other room. The pans were checked and the quality and quantity of their contents satisfied admittance requirements.

LUSIA HABERFELD, *Lauferin: The Runner of Birkenau* [30]

The 'cleansing' started. So did the Warsaw Ghetto Uprising. Young Jewish people started the uprising and fought the Germans for three weeks. All they had was their tremendous courage, a very few guns and Molotov cocktails. The German Army and their tanks rolled in.

We then went into hiding in a cellar of Leszno 76, with about a hundred other people. We heard the shooting. A newly born baby was with us and the baby cried constantly, which was putting us all in danger should the Germans hear. The people in the bunker killed the baby. It was one little life against a hundred others. Poor little baby, to be born in such times... but desperation has no limits.

One day, the manhole of the cellar opened up, and people, with guns pointed, were coming down the steps. We all said our last prayers, believing that the Germans had discovered our hiding place. Imagine our surprise and relief when we realised that it was the young heroes of the uprising who came down to tell us what was happening. We shook their hands and kissed them, and wished them long life. They went on their way. I feel privileged forever for having met some of them. To me, they represent the beginning of our freedom and our homeland, Israel.

LUSIA HABERFELD, *Lauferin: The Runner of Birkenau* [56]

Then, one day, they called for volunteers to go to Auschwitz *Muster Lager,* meaning a Show Camp, four kilometers from Birkenau. Every time a Red Cross Commission came for an inspection, they were taken there as the conditions were more humane. I persuaded my mother to volunteer, it could only be better. She agreed, and we enrolled, and I no longer worked for Schmitka. But it took them a long time to send us there. In the meantime something very bad happened that could have had disastrous consequences for me. One day, they came to take our blood to send to the German army. They must have been very short of blood! We, the despised Jews, the despised, inferior race, to provide blood for the Pure Aryan race. Marriages between Jews and Aryans, or, indeed, any other contact, had been forbidden long ago. Now they needed our blood. It was unbelievable.

OLGA HORAK, *Auschwitz to Australia* [73–4]

However, I was now a 'survivor'. I was no longer a prisoner, but not yet free. There was much that had to be done before we could consider the journey home. For a start, we were so weak that we were not yet able to live without immediate medical attention. The British wanted to register us all on the first day of Liberation. A makeshift tent was set up in the grounds of the camp. At the table was an officer with two or three uniformed officers behind him. I went with my mother to the tent 'office' and we stood patiently in a line waiting for our turn. We arrived at the tent and walked in facing the officer behind the table. My mother went first. She gave her full name and other details and told the officer that she wanted to be repatriated home to Bratislava. I followed and did the same. Each of us were then issued with a small white Displaced Persons card which we had to sign. My mother was so weak she could not hold the card firmly in her hands. I had to hold the card for her. We then made our way out of the tent. Then what I dreaded most happened. My mother collapsed. I tried to get her up but nurses came and gently pushed me aside. They brought a stretcher and lifted mother onto it. She lay there ashen coloured and made no response to me. I placed my hands over her short dark stubs of hair and tried to speak to her, softly, but she did not respond. I begged her to say something to me, and kept saying over and over: 'Mama, please do not leave me now. We are free. We are going home. Please do not leave me alone!' It was in vain. My mother had survived Auschwitz, a death march from Kurzbach to Dresden, the journey to Belsen and four months in that cesspool, only to die moments after being registered as a survivor.

I was completely alone. I had lost my mother forever.

BERNARD INGRAM, *Unfinished Symphony* [77]

Late one night as I was returning from a visit with Kichka, I was stopped by the guard at the entry to the ghetto. He focused his torch on my wallet in which I was searching for my pass. He seemed to ignore the pass and continued illuminating my wallet. 'What is that?' he asked, pointing to a little photograph. It was the photograph of our beloved family cat … It happened that he had left behind a cat which he loved very much. We exchanged stories about our favourite pet. What a refreshing coincidence. In the midst of this nightmarish war, in the middle of the night, two people representing the two extremes of the human spectrum, the Gestapo man of the Master Race and the pariah Jew, having something in common, sharing something precious.

ELENA JONAITIS, *Elena's Journey* [115–16]

The hut where they queued stood on higher foundations than the rest. A long ramp led to the window through which the milk was ladled out into bowls, jugs or jars. The line was orderly, perhaps because of the guards who stood at each end with rifles over their shoulders.

Elena was halfway up the ramp when she saw below her, at the side of the ramp, a few women with children in their arms. Their faces were haggard and their clothes were rags. They seemed to be ghosts from a world much more horrible than this one. They were begging, raising their free hands with a mug or a container, beseeching with their eyes. They were begging for milk. They were ignored. The luckier women, having received their share of the precious liquid, carefully carried it past them, not seeing, or already hardened to the sight. The beggars persisted with their out-stretched hands, their imploring black eyes.

'They must be Jewish,' thought Elena. 'Don't their children get any milk? And they don't cry. Oh, like my poor baby, who cannot cry any more.'

One of the women below must have read her thoughts, for she came still closer to the ramp and without a word but fixing Elena with her eyes, uncovered the rags from the baby on her breast. It was a horrifying sight of bones covered with grey, wrinkled skin, a face so fleshless and distorted that it did not seem human. It could have been dead, but it wasn't, for the face grimaced painfully, the hands moved. The sight lasted only a moment, for the woman covered the child again with her rags and continued plead-ing with her eyes and her extended hand.

Elena went up the ramp. The woman followed below, waited for the milk to be ladled out, then continued to hold out her mug. As she descended, Elena stopped and started to pour a little milk from her jug into the beggar's mug. At that moment from one side came a blow to the jug that sent it flying from Elena's hand onto the ground.

'*Verflucht noch einmal!*' swore the young soldier who had delivered the blow with the butt of his rifle. He uttered a whole string of furious words which she did not understand and hardly heard, for her glance and her thoughts were fixed upon the jug on the ground, where precious milk was soaking uselessly into the gravel. The beggar had disappeared.

Elena was dazed and did not attempt to comfort Arunas, who was weeping softly, like an adult. Rasa stopped crying altogether, and was still. Only the warmth of her little body showed that she was alive.

EUGENE KAMENKA, 'A Childhood in the 1930s and 1940s', in *Australian Journal of Politics and History* [8]

In 1945, I became, consciously, a Jew. I could do that only by becoming a Zionist—if Jewishness was to have any meaning for me, it would have to be given secular meaning and content—something to which the nationalist manifesto and anthology of Hebrew literature that we call the Bible lends itself admirably. Of course, by 1945, the central fact in any European Jew's life and in the lives of many other Jews was the fact that 6 million Jews had died and that he, undeservedly, was not one of them. Many of us felt and many of us still feel, as I do, the constant presence of those 6 million, guilt that we were not among them and an obligation to Jews throughout the world, and especially in Israel, as a memorial to them. Like most people, and especially like people reared in a number of cultures and attached to others since then, I am a man of many loyalties. They do not always conflict and I believe I can hold them together by a coherent understanding of the human situation as a whole. But the 6 million dead mean that there is no loyalty higher than the one to their memory and to those who have survived.

TERI KORDA, *My Dear Andrea and Andris* [70–71]

Walking home from seeing Misi, Tibor and I saw a man coming towards us in the street. He seemed about sixty years old, very emaciated and sick. His face was drawn and his body, hunched over. He stared at us strangely, and, as we were about to pass him, he stopped us with, 'Tibor Korda, don't you recognise me?'

Tibor thought that he was perhaps a beggar, but asked politely, 'Do I know you?'

He cried out, 'I am Fuermann from Bustyahaza.'

I was so utterly shocked and horrified at what had happened to this tall, strong, handsome man, that I put both hands on my stomach, fearful for my baby. He couldn't have been much more than forty!

Tibor asked him with terror, 'What happened to the family... your wife, the ten children?'

This skeletal figure beat his chest with both his fists and could not stop. 'I burned them, I burned them, my wife and the children. They perished and it was my job to put their bodies in the ovens.'

We begged him to come with us and to stay with us, or whatever else we could do for him. His answer was, 'Nothing, nothing,' and he shuffled away from us.

DAVID J. LANDAU, *Caged* [1]

In the late evening hours, I sometimes catch myself contemplating the past. In such moments I also plan for the future. But at my age I have to admit that much more has accumulated in my past than will ever accumulate in my remaining years. My memories have begun to outweigh my plans, and there is nothing abnormal in that. What is out of the norm is the cage I find myself locked in. A cage made out of the past. A cage in which I am locked for the rest of my life. This cage has no physical presence, but it is as real to me as if it were made of steel rods set in concrete and fenced with barbed wire.

I am not the only one trapped in such a cage. I belong to a breed of people unknown before my generation, a breed that will be extinct within the next ten to twenty years. Our entire breed suffers from the same aberration. We survived. We cheated the sprawling German killing machine of death camps and ghettos, and came out alive from places we were not meant to survive. We live in a time warp from which only death will release us, and each of us carries within their mind a mental cage which dominates their life.

EVA MARKS, *A Patchwork Life* [62–3]

On one occasion when it was getting dark, and the guard was shouting for us to hurry up, I saw something in the distance and ran towards it. I didn't notice the cesspool pit, covered in earth, and fell right in. I was sinking fast and screamed out loud, 'Help, help!' My friend Elfie came and tried to pull me out, but she couldn't. I was nearly up to my neck in the excrement and was pulling her in with me. She started to scream, and another girl, Edith, came, and between them, after much effort, lying full-length on the ground and pulling and tugging, they pulled me out. It was touch and go.

The guard saw all this happening and offered no help. What a sight I was, covered from head to toe in excrement. And I had lost my precious sack with all the food I had collected. Nobody would walk next to me, because I stunk horribly. The guard couldn't stop laughing. When we got back to the camp and Mutti saw me, she nearly collapsed. She asked the commandant for some clean clothes for me and he refused. I took my things off and washed myself in some cold water with no soap. Mutti washed the clothes the same way. While these were drying, I sat wrapped in my grey blanket, and felt so dirty, smelly and angry, especially because, after so much effort, I had lost all the food I had collected. After the clothes dried, they still smelled disgustingly, but I had to wear them till the next lot of clothes came in from a dead German POW, which was months away. Even now, before I put something on, I smell it, just in case. I still sometimes have nightmares of drowning in that cesspool and not being saved.

EVA MARKS, *A Patchwork Life* [75]

Mutti slept next to the wall. I was beside her, and Omi was next to me. During the night, Mutti's very short hair would freeze to the wall of the train and in the morning, she couldn't sit up. If she had tried to sit up, she would have scalped herself. Every morning, I cupped my hands over my mouth and blew my warm breath onto her frozen hair again and again until I was able to loosen it from the wall.

BETTY MIDALIA, 'A Larino Kid', in *Without Regret* [249–50]

Once the war started we realised our parents were never coming out. We knew there would be no travelling and I realised the seriousness of the situation much more. We sent Red Cross messages by this stage and they did receive them for a while in Germany. Red Cross messages didn't mean that you could write big letters, you had twenty-five words on a sheet of paper and you were allowed to write in twenty-five words all your news. So they wrote to me. I remember them writing that my brother had his *barmitzvah*. It was very basic but at least I did know they were still alive and well. The funny thing is after the war I just knew my parents were dead even before it was confirmed. I knew Zvi, my brother, was alive. It was just a feeling I had. It was quite amazing. I sort of sat around waiting to hear from him. The Red Cross collected all the names. Zvi wrote this in his letter and explained it all. My parents were taken to Auschwitz on 27 February 1943 and I didn't hear from them again, ever.

ELFIE ROSENBERG, *Serry and Me* [45–6]

My greatest need was to fit in. I remember as if it were yesterday how very small and lost I felt. I hated my name, Elfrieda, which was so foreign. I had the wrong clothes, the wrong language and no parents to love and support me. Everything weighed heavily on my small eight-year-old shoulders and

I had to endure it silently. I had to remember my mother's firm instructions to be good. I was ever so conscious of the need to be polite and to follow instructions. The unconditional love that I had experienced so fully from my parents had been taken away from me and now I had to conform or risk disapproval. If someone showed disapproval, it hit me right in the pit of my stomach. I could not shout out: 'I want to go back.' I could not vent my anger at having been abandoned or cry openly with the loss and loneliness I felt. I retreated into a protective shell, to a safe place within myself to escape the pain that I was feeling. I took a step back and became an observer rather than an active participant in the many changes and adaptations that had to be made in my life. My comfort at night was Peter and Ruth, my two dolls. They were my treasures, representing my entire childhood, my security, the love of my parents and the world which I had previously known.

FELA and FELIX ROSENBLOOM, *Miracles Do Happen* [14]

In the spring of 1942 they sent us to Lohof, near Munich, where we did the same work as in Underdiessen. Later in 1942 our whole group of sixty-eight was sent to an ammunition factory in Augsburg. There we were employed in the production of very small weapons' parts. They taught us to operate machines and to use magnifying glasses and tweezers. They called us by our proper names—'Fraulein this' or 'Fraulein that'—instead of by the first names we had been called in other camps. The German supervising engineers were the first people in Germany to treat us like human beings.

Although it was strictly forbidden to have any contact with us, one incident is worth noting. A German worker quietly approached us and told us that he, his wife, and son would like to help us. He suggested that he and his young son could mend our worn shoes and his wife would try to get for us articles of hygiene, which we needed very much. Every day we left a parcel of a few pairs of worn shoes at an arranged spot and he picked it up, mended the shoes at night, and delivered them to the same spot the next day. We also got from him the articles of hygiene, which his wife bought for us. All of us were very grateful to those noble Germans. They kept helping us until we left Augsburg. As a token of gratitude, we gave them a signed picture of our whole group, taken in a previous camp. To my great surprise that picture appeared in a book of war memoirs in the 1950s, with a caption: 'A group of 68 Jewish girls, sent away from Augsburg in 1943, to an unknown destination.' The picture could only have been obtained from that German family.

ANDOR SCHWARTZ, *Living Memory* [219–20]

I walked on the frozen bodies, I thought I really didn't hurt them. They had already been dead for months. On the top of a mound, I could see an old Jew with a white beard. His body was covered in ice. I could see only his face and his hands. He was lying on his back. His eyes were open, his mouth was also open showing his teeth, grimacing, he had probably had a very painful death. Both hands were holding on to a tefillin in a nice red holder. I thought, as I had lost my tefillin, maybe that one would be good for me. I was trying to take it out of his hands, but he held onto it very firmly as he was frozen. I still managed to take it away from him.

ALEX SKOVRON, 'The Courtyard', in *Children of the Shadows* [38–9]

They hung a sign with a skull next to the doorway, to warn people away, and it scared me. But I was curious too, part of me wanted to climb the stairs and look inside the flat of the old person who died.

The skull reminds me of a book which is kept in the living room, high up in the bookshelf section of the *kredens*. It's a big book with a stiff cover and lots of black-and-white pictures, from the time of the war. I'm not really supposed to look at this book yet, but I've looked at it a few times with my father, and sometimes I climb up along the *kredens,* slide open the glass panel, bring the book down and sit at the round table to leaf through the pages by myself. It's the same spot at the table where my father shows me his stamp albums and teaches me about countries, and where I study the illustrated book called *Warszawa*. My favourite stamps in his albums are the ones from Hungary and Russia and Israel, and my favourite building in the book about Warsaw is the Palace of Culture, the highest building in the city. Anyway, that other book I'm talking about has lots of photographs, and one of them shows naked ladies. It embarrasses me a bit to look at this picture, but I always do. The ladies are walking in a line, they look very uncomfortable, they look sad, and some of them are trying to cover up between their legs. But you can still see the black hair there, and you can see their breasts, and they look so strange and clumsy walking naked in a long line. I've been told that they are going to the showers, and I think that after the showers they are going to die. There are Germans in black uniforms in many of the pictures. They wear swastikas on their arms. A while ago I got into trouble in kindergarten for drawing a plane with a swastika on it.

HETTY E. VEROLME, *The Children's House of Belsen* [120–21]

The truck drove fast. We had no idea where we were going. The night was jet black, the moon had disappeared behind the clouds. It was midnight. Nobody spoke, even the crying had stopped. I noticed that we left the camp through the main gate and that we were on the road towards Celle, but then the truck turned left and it seemed like we were driving aimlessly around in circles through the heather. For hours we drove like this. What evil plans did they have for us? The moon had come from behind the clouds and through the open rear end of the truck I could see the vast expanse of the Lüneburg Heath. There was no one in sight and no sound to be heard, only the engines of the trucks breaking the deathly silence. Then the trucks stopped. The female guard left the back of our truck and the driver from the second truck came over to our driver. We could hear them discussing something. Our driver seemed very upset as we could hear him say, 'Nein, nein,' a few times but we could not follow the conversation. What were they talking about? Were they going to kill us? We were silent, feeling the danger around us. After about ten minutes of arguing, the female guard climbed back in our truck and we started to drive again. I realised that we were driving back in the direction of the camp, and as we entered Belsen again I saw that we were going towards the Sternlager, but the truck continued along the road and then near the end made a left turn. After about two minutes it stopped and we were told to alight. We were pulled out of the truck by the female guard before two tall, strong women prisoners arrived to take over from her. They were dressed in prison clothes with scarves around their heads. On seeing those scary skinny women, the children started to cry again.

The little ones were scared out of their minds and screamed in panic. Some of them clamped onto me, preventing me from moving. I told them not to be afraid, that I was with them. It took a few minutes to calm them down. Still holding tightly onto my coat, they allowed me some movement. The second truck arrived and its lights lit up the area. When our truck started to move away, one of the women prisoners went up to the driver and asked what they should do with the children. 'I don't care,' he said. 'They can burn in hell.'

The trucks drove away and we were left standing close together in the darkness. The children were terrified and began wailing again. After my eyes became accustomed to the darkness I could see the vague outline of a barrack in front of us. A woman prisoner told us to enter the building, which looked ominous in the dark. Slowly we moved forward. When we came to the door, another woman prisoner with a scarf around her head to hide its baldness told us something in a language we could not understand and pointed in the direction we had to go. I felt very scared, but did not dare show it for the little ones' sakes. When we entered the building my heart skipped a beat. There was what appeared to be a very long corridor. It was pitch-dark, and at the end of it stood an old woman holding up a kerosene lamp.

Departures, Journeys, Arrivals

MAX FREILICH, *Zion in Our Time* [24–5]

After a long lapse of time it is difficult to recapture and describe adequately the emotions and the internal excitement we experienced on stepping down for the first time on the soil of Palestine, the land of the Bible and of our forefathers. For several days I walked the streets of Tel Aviv and the surrounding countryside in a dazed state of mind. The image of a 100 per cent Jewish city was both intriguing and challenging. The image of the Jew as a middleman, the Jew as a merchant and broker dissipated at the sight of the Jewish policeman, the Jewish factory labourer and tiller of the soil. It was the first time that we faced the reality of Jewish nationhood and the possibility of a normal national existence. Furthermore we were deeply moved by the warmth and friendliness of the Tel Avivians of that time. It was exhilarating to sit down at one long table at breakfast with other guests speaking a Babel of languages and converse with our neighbours to the right and to the left as intimately as if we had known each other for a long time. Sasha and I felt at home on our very first day in the country.

MARTIN SPITZER, *Storm over Tatra* [19]

In 1984 I revisited Žilina. The once thriving and vibrant community of three thousand Jews had shrunk to a mere hundred or so; most of them past their middle years. In their bent bodies and furtive glances one could sense their past miseries and present hopelessness. They were merely waiting for death.

By mere chance I met these lost souls at a civic memorial service to commemorate the date of Deportations. The service was held in the funeral parlour of the Jewish cemetery—a small building with its inside walls lined with marble plaques carrying the names of some two thousand nine hundred Jews who had perished. The names of my parents, my brother and twenty close relatives were among them.

Not a single gentile attended the service. No feeling of guilt, no remorse, not even an attempt to understand the pain. That is Žilina today.

GEORGE SZEGO, *Two Prayers to One God* [31–2]

In September 1938, when I was ten years old, grey clouds appeared on my horizon. They gathered slowly and insidiously, until the happiness and security of my Mezobereny childhood receded behind menacing shadows.

I have no doubt that separation anxiety influences a person's psychological development. I also strongly believe that this pathological condition gripped me with stunning force that September, and has been with me ever since.

I'm sure my parents had long discussions about my secondary schooling. I'm sure they wanted to make the right decision about my future, taking all of Hungary's contemporary sociopolitical realities into account.

However, I judge their actions harshly. I think they were motivated more by their own interests, by their own need to conform, than by a desire to spare me the earthquake of separation. But maybe it's the pain that resulted from their decision that compels me to apportion blame.

ROSE ZWI, *Last Walk in Naryshkin Park* [192–3]

A rectangular road sign straddles a ditch: *Zagare*. Alias Zhager, *der heim*. We have arrived. I photograph the sign, first from a distance, then close up. *Zagare*. Black letters on white. All around us are bleak fields smudged with green, with clumps of leafless trees in the misty background. I record everything on camera. You can't rely on memory.

'This isn't Zhager,' Leah announces. 'When you come into Zhager, you go through the *vald*, the forest. And where is Naryshkin Park?'

'Perhaps we're still coming to the Park,' Freda says.

There is nothing park-like in this desolate scene, only yellow winter grass and bedraggled pines and firs, weary from the weight of snow.

Fifty metres on, Misha pulls up at a blue rectangular sign on the right side of the road. Its arrowed end points towards trees on the far side of the field. *Fasizmo auku kapai, 0.2.* 'Memorial to the victims of fascism,' Freda translates. 'You see these signs all over the country. Usually on the edge of forests where the massacres took place.'

'This can't be Zhager,' Leah insists. 'The mass grave is in Naryshkin Park. Does this look like a park to you?'

No one contradicts her.

Misha turns the car onto a long narrow path, and we bump along the sodden field towards the memorial.

We come to a large area surrounded by trees, enclosed by a low wire fence. Three metal plaques soldered onto two iron posts stand near the gate. The top plate is in Lithuanian, the second in Yiddish, the third in Hebrew.

In this place on 2 October 1941 the Hitlerist murderers and their local helpers massacred about 3000 Jewish men women and children from the Shavel District.

Jews from Kurshan, Krok, Popilan, Yaneshok, Zaimol, Radvilishkis, Linkovo and other places had been slaughtered here, together with the Jews of Zhager. Local Lithuanians, former neighbours, had helped with the shooting. This is Naryshkin Park.

Leah shakes her head. Where are the beautiful shrubs and trees the Naryshkins had planted so many years ago? As a young girl she had strolled along its shaded paths, her heart breaking as Leib walked by with a girl on his arm. When the war is over, he had written from the eastern front in 1943, you and I will walk through Naryshkin Park. Three weeks later he was dead.

Before my parents had married, my father had walked here with his Russian teacher, and my mother had kept trysts with her faithless lover who sailed away to Africa. Young friends had posed against the dark foliage for a photograph by Shabselban, looking the camera straight in the eye, as though defying the fate that would make the Park their burial place.

Leah is silent, confused, as we get out of the car and walk down a paved path beside a very long garden bed. It takes a while to register that this is no garden bed; it is the mass grave.

Australia

LENKE ARNSTEIN, *Recurring Dreams* [73–4]

It was a hot summer day. Not a cloud in the sky, not a breeze in the air. The leaves in the trees were motionless; they seemed to be having a nap. This was the most sensible thing to do in the hot weather. My husband and I both had similar ideas but it wasn't meant to be.

Suddenly our four lively grandchildren burst into the house excitedly, 'Please Omi and Poppa, can we go somewhere?'

You can't just say 'No,' but where would we go on such a hot day? We decided that the Botanic Gardens were the best choice. It would be much cooler there; we could feed the swans and ducks.

So that's what happened. We packed a picnic basket full of goodies for the children, some bread for the ducks, and off we went. We were pleased with the decision because whenever we visited these gardens, we never ceased to admire the century-old majestic trees, surrounded by colourful bushes and flower-beds.

While my husband and the children went to feed the birds, I went for a walk myself, revelling in the solitude. Suddenly, I came across a flaming red bush, situated near a pond. By then it was late afternoon, with the sun just starting to set. The reflection of the magnificent bush danced on the surface of the water. It looked absolutely magnificent. I stood there hypnotised and could not move. I just gazed at the scene before me.

A great inner peace came over me, accompanied by total happiness. After all we had been though in our younger years, the gift of this moment and the day shared with our grandchildren, was overwhelming. The Garden of Eden could not have been more beautiful.

FLORA FORBES, 'Growing Up in a Land in Turmoil: Indonesia', in *Memory Guide My Hand*, vol. 3 [81]

I came to Australia in 1956 and felt I had arrived in Paradise. At first I was under enormous tension as deserted streets and quiet had usually signalled coming danger. I waited for something terrible to happen. It took a while to interpret this as peace. Instead of hatred, I encountered friendliness. The ultimate came when I ran for a tram that had already started. Firstly, the tram stopped for me; secondly, I tripped and hands reached out to help me. I looked up at faces and there were smiles, no hatred.

A lovely country!

JACOB FRANKEL, 'The Life of Jacob Frankel', in *Australian Jewish Historical Society Journal* [410]

We were thus standing all night, rained upon all the time, until ten o'clock the next morning, when we sighted Sydney. We actually came to the wharf about twelve. Hundreds of people were standing there to inquire the reason for our not coming in as usual the night before. The Captain said 'you may thank yourselves that you see her at all, and the passengers also, as I never experienced such a gale in my life, and I am off and on this coast for the last sixteen years.' All the time it rained in torrents, and all our luggage that had been saved was thrown on the wharf. We were as stiff as a poker, numbed in such a deplorable degree that some of the bystanders were paid to lead us along. We were all but dead, having nothing to eat nor to drink for twenty-four hours, standing in one position. I believe that was one of the shortest and one of the worst passages I ever had, and believe me, I never wish for another such like.

LOLO HOUBEIN, *Wrong Face in the Mirror* [31]

What the Chinaman and the Gypsies had started to awaken in me now rose powerfully to my lips. Why, oh why, was I so pale, if I could have been, should have been, otherwise... different? I had discovered the diversity of the human race and with it came the knowledge that I was born into the wrong tribe. My shape was alright, the form of my eyes too, my hands and narrow long feet did not disturb me, but the colour of my hair, my eyes, my skin were wrong! My hair should have been raven black, my skin mahogany and my eyes two pools of brown liquid.

I looked in the mirror and faced a stranger. From that day dates my alienation from my outer appearance, which does not match who I am inside. I resolved to change the stranger by every means within my power.

The most ready means was my Inner Life. That evening, before going to sleep, I transformed into a sleek brown girl with oiled and coiled hair. Hitching my sarong over my bare feet, I climbed a sandy path to a grove of palm trees where my friend was waiting. His name was Kunan, it turned out. I'd made it up. I liked the sound. And he answered to it.

Loneliness was banished once more. Kunan took me by the hand and we walked to the village where the tribe lived. We went out to have adventures every night and did many good deeds to help people and animals in distress. Kunan was a hero and as I shared his deeds I quietly, almost without being aware of it myself, became a heroine.

LOLO HOUBEIN, *Wrong Face in the Mirror* [94–6]

One hot summer's day, Ronald and I were driving back to Adelaide in our little open Mini Moke, having spent the weekend in the Flinders Ranges, the fabulous wild land on the way to the west.

As we came over a rise, we saw a woman standing on the road, waving us down. We stopped and saw their family car parked by the side of the road with a flat tyre. An elderly man and a young one were changing the wheel. A grey-haired woman, two young ones and a boy sat waiting on the brown grass.

The woman asked whether I had a jack. I did and gave it to the man. Then I tried to start a conversation with the woman. They were an Aboriginal family on their way to Port Augusta to bring a son back to his place of work. They lived not far from us in an Adelaide suburb. These details emerged with much prying on my part, as she was reluctant to talk. To fill in the time, I decided we should have drinks all round, since the heat was stifling.

Getting out the container of cordial and two plastic cups, I instructed Ronald to bring drinks first to the men, who were sweating in the dust under the car. The grey-haired auntie had walked off with one of the girls. Next, Ronald brought drinks to the young woman and boy and then filled up for me and the woman who had stopped us. I'd invited her to sit in the car with me, out of the sun, but she had refused. But when she realised that we were all drinking out of the same two cups, she seemed suddenly to change her mind about sharing such close proximity with me and accepted. So we sat in the car, talking as two women do when they don't know each other.

Suddenly she turned and said: 'We were just lucky it was you who came past.'

'Why?' I asked surprised. 'Anyone would lend you a jack if they carried one.'

'The others didn't even stop,' she said grimly.

Then I realised that in the five or so minutes before we reached this spot, at least three cars had come from the opposite direction. None had stopped. This has been the life of Aboriginal people for most of the two hundred years since white people came here. They've been left standing in the dust of their own land, with a hand raised to draw attention, while the intruders flash past in their cars on the roads they built for themselves, too callous to stop, or too frightened.

KALMAN KATZ, *Memories of War* [67]

After we settled in Australia we found that it was not easy to adjust again to living a normal life. We had lost almost all of our loved ones and all of our possessions, and we wondered whether it was worthwhile to continue living, to start again from the beginning. On the other hand, we had survived, and wanted to have a family again and to continue life.

I would not call it 'normal' life. To me it was living a 'double' life. I have tried to have a happy, normal life and enjoy my family; yet today, when I look at my granddaughter, she reminds me of my younger sister who was about the same age when she and the rest of my family were hacked to death by vicious Ukrainian murderers, and left lying in puddles of their own blood. Later they were covered with leaves that fell from the trees. Dogs or wild animals then scattered their mutilated bodies around the bushes. Not one day has passed since the war ended when I have not thought about the past. I do not believe that anyone can switch off the past and live normally again, not unless they did not suffer during the entire period of the war.

Out of the thousands of Jewish families who lived in Przemyslany pre-war, today there is not one Jewish soul left living there.

STAN MARKS, 'The Dinner Guest', in *Memory Guide My Hand*, vol. 3
[260–62]

By a bizarre set of circumstance Eva and her mother, grandmother and stepfather ended up in the infamous Soviet Gulag, remaining there for six years until 1947, not aware for some time that the war was over. Sixty-three members of her family perished in Nazi concentration camps, including an uncle who was a renowned Austrian member of parliament. Unlike now, it wasn't a time to talk about Nazism, Hitler and his henchmen. Few of our friends knew Eva's story. It wasn't something people wanted to hear anyway—Jewish or non-Jewish.

Eva asked George about his wartime experiences. Where had he been? What had he done? George became remarkably quiet. His willingness to talk on all and any matters had ceased. He seemed a different George. He kept refilling his wine glass and refused to be drawn into our discussion. It was clear that Eva was feeling uneasy and the mood became a little tense.

Being by nature a direct person, she asked straight out, 'George, were you in the German army? Isn't yours a German-American accent?'

He nodded, 'Yes,' explaining, 'I was an infantryman in the German army.'

'Where?' persisted Eva.

'On the Russian front,' mentioning a number of places in the Soviet. He seemed rattled and poured himself another glass of wine.

Eva looked George straight in the eyes. 'Where were you, really? Come on, George, don't lie to us. Tell us what you really did. Were you an SS man?'

She was really worked up and determined to discover the truth. 'I'll bet you were. Which camp? How many did you kill? One, a hundred, a thousand?'

The others present were too stunned to say anything. For some reason, maybe it was the wine, George came right out with it.

'I was an SS man. Want to see the insignia tattooed under my arm?' He began to unbutton his shirt. Even these many years later, Eva and I can't understand why George volunteered, in such a manner, to show us his insignia. He could have tried to lie. It would have been plausible for him to claim that he had migrated to the United States before the war. Maybe it was his large consumption of wine, arrogance, a spur of the moment action, or some other reason a psychiatrist might fathom. The others sat, silent, frozen.

A highly-distressed Eva excused herself and went into the kitchen. I followed. She insisted that George go. She didn't know what she might do if he stayed.

'I don't want to hear his excuses. He is sure to be full of them. They all are. He must go. I don't want him in my house. Get him out—now!'

JULIE MEADOWS, 'Pesach in My Parents' Home', in *Memory Guide My Hand*, vol. 1 [44]

So, did we ever have this semi-secular *Pesach* event? The answer is never. Man proposes and woman disposes! Mum said, 'Are you *meshugeh*? We've come to *Sholtach Ti* (the Yiddish version of Woop-Woop). Do you want the children to know nothing of our customs? In Zelechow, your precious *chaverim* ate *chazer* in the streets on Yom Kippur. To spit on our beliefs and traditions!' When she got scornful to that degree, her voice would scorch our ears. 'I know why you didn't follow their example. It's because you knew it would kill your parents. Are you going to start now, just because they can't see what you're up to?'

'Who is talking about eating pig, *loi alenu*?' pleaded Dad. He tried to remind her of that time in their courtship when she had shared his views of a different future, free from the shackles of the past. She answered him with a soliloquy, her favourite form of reply, since it didn't allow for interruption. 'This is Oistralia. Our future here is different enough, already. We left our past in *der Alter Heim*, which we have forsaken along with our families. Who knows how they'll manage.' It was just before the war. She was reminded how worried she was and became tearful. 'What we knew there and what we did there, came with our mothers' milk. We're at the absolute end of the earth. What will our children become here if we don't stay with what we've always done?' 'Kangaroos?' muttered Dad under his breath.

This was in the early days when Dad hadn't yet learnt that he could never, under any circumstance, win an argument with Mum and he would try to win her over with facts. 'We aren't alone here. Carlton is full of Jews, the Kadimah is round the corner. There's Yiddish theatre with some of the best actors from Warsaw, a Yiddish school, a secular Hebrew school, *shules*, *cheders*. There are Communists and Zionists of all political shades fighting each other and here we can finally be full Bundists, without upsetting your parents or mine.'

But Mum was adamant, something she was very good at being. She also had her facts and would deliver them with such high emotion and force they constituted 'Truth' itself, which it seemed, she would die defending.

MIRKA MORA, *Wicked but Virtuous* [71]

Saturday mornings were always kept for breakfast with the Percevals. The café was a kind of home on these mornings—more facilities for cooking than in the studio and more food. All our cups and saucers were made by John Perceval and many were stolen, as they were works of art. So we kept giving more orders for more cups and saucers.

Cupid with his arrow went upstairs and downstairs and many romances started at the Mirka Café, and great dramas. Frank Werther was very worried about my attachment to one of the painters. Suffice to say that it was at the Mirka Café that Georges and I gave each other back our wedding rings. John Reed's prophecy?

Great excitement when we decided to have a show at the café of Joy Hester's great work. I can still feel the atmosphere of the café; all her works were black and white and some people called the Mirka Café a funeral parlour while the show was on. Yet the work was so vibrant and tumultuous, like Joy's mind. Just like a song of Edith Piaf's. The work tore you to pieces if you dared to look at it, particularly the little love drawings of Joy and Gray as lovers in bed. Only two works sold, one to Georges Mora and one to me.

YETTA ROTHBERG, *Thousands of Years through the Eyes of a Child* [4]

The time is about the 1920s. The setting is Carlton. The broad wide main streets criss-crossed narrow lanes or side streets which cocooned people in their box-like, one-sided passaged houses. Rathdowne Street swept up majestically to the Exhibition Gardens, topped by the imperial dome of the Exhibition Building. The gardens, often a long way from home, yet became a centre for young and old. The old folk fed their meagre crumbs to galleon-like swans. Lovers retreated and twisted in the shadows of the grand oaks. Children played wildly or were sick from the smell of the tan of the play area. It was the era of the juggernauting cable tram, the horse and buggy, and the big open Buicks, Studebakers, and the silver stick!

Into this area came a particular type of migrant, from Russia, Poland, often via England, picking up a little of the language *en route*. They came unheralded, unwelcomed. Often their boldness and motivation were unknown. One heard fragments of their background, childhood dreams, poetry read under a remote tree, stories of village weddings. Unheralded they came, their boldness and optimism often unrecorded.

They brought their families here, they augmented their families in the new environment. Slogged away at their work, maintaining their dignity and love of their religion. They picked up the crumbs of friendship and were accustomed to the barbs of persecution. They carried a strange, noble optimism and dignity in their work, dress, and dedication to their own group and to the new land around them. Many of their ideas and dreams they projected on to their children. An extension of themselves, often the latter suffered from the ambivalence of their own personalities, the expectations demanded of them, and the guilt of failure.

The first image then of this area, the first stepping stone in this promising free country, was Drummond Street, bounded by Elgin and Faraday Streets. It held many areas of wonder, excitement and terror, especially for the children who lived nearby.

❧

NATHAN F. SPIELVOGEL, 'How My Life Was Spent', in *Australian Jewish Historical Society Journal* [13]

In May, I went down to Ballarat for my sister's wedding. It was a wonderful change from the sordid life I was living at Dimboola with its boozing and gambling and dirt and discomfort to come back to the homely and cleanly surroundings of my dear mother's home. She, good soul, knew nothing of the licentious life I was living. Attired in frock suit and top hat, I helped in the joyous ceremony. I mixed with respectable and decent people at dances and parties for a week, and then went back to my pig-sty of a place at Lochiel.

Only one man in Dimboola, a bookseller named Lehman, put out a hand to save me. He got me to come in and play chess and talk. All the others seemed to want to push me over the precipice.

So the months went by. Rarely was I in bed before 4 a.m. My house got filthier and filthier. I never thought to scrub it out and never thought to clean out the fireplaces. It was a relief to get away into the pubs of Dimboola, and I drank and gambled and wasted the days away. Sad, sinful Dimboola!

Generations

AGI L. BAUER, *'Black' Becomes a Rainbow* [10]

This process of alienation has many shades, many moods. There is the always pressing guilt in the mother of a *Baalat Teshuvah* (henceforth, for the sake of brevity, B.T.); she will keep on asking herself: 'Where did I go wrong?' With each passing day our child distanced herself farther from us, and we asked ourselves this same question over and over again, without ever finding the real answer. The hurt, shock and humiliation of losing our child to the 'black' world of Orthodox Judaism was hard to bear.

JOSIANE BEHMOIRAS, *Dora B* [204]

At the end of our last visit, my mother stands next to me as I open the car door to put my daughter in the baby-capsule. She says to me, 'I will behave well. I will sit behind you on the plane, not next to you. Behind you I will sit and I'll be quiet. Take me with you.' She is kneeling on the ground and I have to say to her, 'Please, *maman*, get up. You know I can't take you.'

I leave her standing on the footpath. She is wearing the dress she made for herself from my old pleated cream-coloured skirt. Her arms hang loose at her sides. She is smaller than me. Smaller than my baby. Just a dot in the rear-vision mirror.

JUNE EPSTEIN, *Woman with Two Hats* [xiii]

Giving up my child was the worst thing that ever happened to me. I could not see any meaning in this most unnatural act; only now do I believe I am beginning to understand. In my turbulent adolescent years when I was preparing to become a concert pianist or a writer (or both), I had a friend, an old lady called Kitty Lander. Never having known her parents and having lost, one after the other, her husband and all her children, three beautiful gifted daughters, she could still take delight in music, poetry and laughter. She taught me that every life has its pattern—it is only when you look back that you can see where the threads come from and perceive the design. Sometimes a motif that seemed secondary leaps to the eyes as the most significant, and *vice versa*. Thus the central point of my own pattern appears not in my professional career as a musician or writer, but on that day of renunciation. Everything seemed to lead towards it and afterwards developed from it, and it gave meaning to the whole fabric of my life. Not that mine is a tragic story. It holds more light than darkness, and more, much more laughter than tears.

RICHARD FREADMAN, *Shadow of Doubt* [25–6]

The Paul Freadman I came to know later in life was a painfully, finally a tragically, diminished man. Beholden as we are to Freud, we assume that sons desire conquest over the father. No doubt this is often true. But it's also true that many sons want the father to prosper and to prevail. It's reassuring, makes one feel less mortal; and even the angry and competitive son can want the world to be fundamentally well for a father he esteems and cares about. So I think that cricket shot keeps coming back for another reason. It's not all about fear, awe, enervation, envy; it's also about retrieving that father who was very good at many things, even masterful, in his prime. The man he was before he became the person he was to become.

A few months ago that man appeared in a dream of mine. I don't remember the context in any detail, but I was going somewhere with some friends. We were experiencing some sort of difficulty. There was something odd about the sensation of 'me-ness' in the dream: I was at once my current adult self, and myself as child. My feelings seemed to zigzag between then and now, as if trying to connect various incarnations of myself, and to accommodate these to what I was seeing. What I saw was Paul Freadman circa 1942—nine years before I was born. He was lean, wiry, upright, his wavy, thick hair and thin moustache jet black; he had on a green army anorak, his blue eyes were clear. He walked quickly and confidently and seemed to exude assurance. I know this figure. It's the Paul Freadman I've seen in photos from his days as a navigator in the Australian air force. Indeed I have one such picture, recently given to me by my mother in a tasteful light wood frame, in my study at home. Perhaps I know him too from early in my own life, from the era of that leg glance, when he did indeed stand upright and move with a kind of brisk, wiry assurance, when I was too young to register the deep hesitations and inner doubts that he was to pay so dearly for. Oddly, I don't remember what he *did* in the dream. My impression now is just of his having done *something*, something efficacious, and of a feeling of relief on my part. Relief because he'd helped avert some problem. But more than this: relief because he'd appeared in the guise he had. He was returned to a kind of flourishing; and the two me's in the dream seemed almost to be comparing notes, checking to see whether it could actually be that Paul (as I called him from an early age) really was this okay, that I really was the son of such a man.

᪥

HELEN GARDNER, *My Mother's Child* [84–5]

I had been told to forget Nursie and I more or less did. Or at least, what I did was to disconnect from my feelings for her. It has always seemed to me that at this time I 'killed' the child Helen and replaced her with a façade: someone who would be more acceptable in her new surroundings. In later years it seemed to me that my life began when I was eleven. It was not just that I had few memories of the time before then, or even that the occasional memory that I had was like a black and white still photograph: no colour, no sound, no movement, no emotional content. It was much more that I felt that I didn't exist until I was eleven: that there was a frozen, black void where my childhood should have been.

It was at this time, too, that my 'black moods' began. I never knew what triggered these moods or what made them go away. They came without warning, they lasted about a week, and they disappeared as inexplicably as they had come. They were regular occurrences throughout my entire adolescence, and I simply endured them. I was often suicidal at these times. Suicide seemed the only means of escape. Its attraction lay in the nothing-ness, which promised a blessed relief from the overwhelming intensity which threatened to tear me apart.

᪥

GEORGE HALASZ, 'Beyond the Wall of Silence', in *Children of the Shadows* [62–3]

We knew that 'double pain'. Survivors' children learnt, as if by instinct, that in order to survive we, like our parents, also needed to split our awareness and experiences. Our first pain was to learn that lesson; the second, either to relive the lesson or to remember it. I found myself contemplating the image of a baby feeding, attempting to engage its mother's gaze while suckling at her breast.

The baby feels itself securely held, and nourished, and the two are gazing into each other's eyes: 'in love', as it were. Suddenly, mother's mind disconnects—the infant is 'dropped'. No warning. Mother's empathy, her unique emotional knowing of her baby, vanishes temporarily. But for the infant that moment lasts an eternity. In that critical moment, the mother and her baby have been cast adrift, their anchorage in each other lost.

How did this happen?

The mother is a survivor. She had a sudden flashback. Her baby's feeding triggered her memories of near-starvation—her own, or her sister's, or maybe her mother's. The flashback in turn triggered the state of panic of the starved: the 'every-crumb-is-precious' state.

The baby has become anxious, refuses the breast, regurgitates the precious milk. Mother and baby are in a whirlpool of anxiety: the past is alive in the present. Chaos. The vulnerable feeding moment, and no secure anchorage. The infant experiences a catastrophe.

This scene is repeated. The infant can no longer tolerate it—cannot tolerate the repeated episodes of chaos. To cope, it must split itself in two. It must develop an alternative self.

NANCY KEESING, *Riding the Elephant* [2–3]

Also on board was Wirths Circus returning to Australia from its annual tour of New Zealand. In the dining saloon my parents shared a table with the tall man and the dwarf who were great friends and excellent company, they reported. Children ate at an earlier sitting so we did not meet the fabulous pair directly, though we saw them from a distance promenading the deck reserved for grownups, and very incongruous they were, for the tall man was strikingly thin and the dwarf a roly-poly.

The circus animals travelled in holds below deck. The decking above the elephants' quarters had several largeish holes cut in it for, I suppose, light and air but also for the delight of children who, carrying apples and bits of bread, were taken to feed the jumbos. Through each hole elephant trunks, three or four I think, sprouted like strange prehistoric growths. Each tough, leathery, sinuous sprout ended in a gaping aperture, pink and red and runny with mucus—and into this mysterious mouth, that according to my father was not a mouth, but a sort of nose, we thrust our offerings. Holding food the trunks withdrew briefly, to where? To what? I'd never seen and could scarcely imagine, Elephant.

How fortunate the elder daughter of table companions of the tall man and the dwarf. One morning I was escorted (by father? by whom?) to the elephants' hold where monstrous shapes loomed in brown gloom and pachyderm legs rose like vast but flabby tree trunks, supporting flanks like the shapes of old coats that slowly move in a cupboard when an opened door admits a draught. High above me their ear-flaps, and their great docile heads from which trunks uprose to the pinholes of light far away, down which peered the eyes of ordinary children holding bread and apples in ordinary sunlight.

And one trunk snaked down. 'Hold your apple out. See, she's putting her trunk down to your hand. Now place the apple in her trunk and see how she gets it to her mouth.' Her mouth was a smiling cavern, her yellow, sawn-off tusks... There is a smell, warm and foetid rather than rank, and of bodies rather than manure. The hold becomes more visible as eyes adjust to its darkness. It is very clean. The elephant keeper and the trainer, with scraping brooms and buckets of water and mops, swab living leather and moist flooring.

The trainer, a saturnine man, calls something to the hugest elephant and oh! horror! her trunk is around my waist. I had never then seen a snake but atavistically I sensed, and invented, boa constrictor. I was too shocked to make a sound. I was twisted away from the floor sideways; nearly upside down. I was near the roof. I was on her back and somehow—ladder? rungs in the wall?—the keeper had perched on her rough, rock rump and held me securely. I rode the elephant.

The face of a child I knew in another life appeared close by through one of the holes in the deck. I returned its stare seriously. This was no moment for poking grimaces. For I am supreme. I am the lord, I am the lord, I am the lord of everything.

The trainer utters another call. His hands guide me back to the trunk. Head upright I am enclosed; lowered; reduced...

Against injustice, failure, sheer laziness. For ever after, for evermore, I say to myself: '*Once* I rode an elephant. *When* I rode *the* elephant...'

❧

SERGE LIBERMAN, 'A Mother's Bequest', in *Forever Eve* [37–8]

That love underlay it all could not be discounted, though when it came to Mother, my mother, there was more, much more—the selflessness, the disregard of her own welfare when that of her family was as much as touched, the dedication to work and provision that rose above mere ethic to reach the realm of commandment, and courtesy, hospitality, charitableness in word as in deed, and the readiness to tolerate, accept, forgive and give the benefit of any doubt. If any legacy there was that she could pass on, it lay in this—in the example of her nature, in the rightness of her priorities and values, and in the conduct of her very life that rendered her more than mere mother, more than mere Jewish mother, but most honour-meriting among unstinting, dutiful, concerned, giving and unsung human beings: in the words of *Proverbs*, a woman of worth whose price was above rubies, one whom it had taken her son, to his shame, forty years and more to fully acknowledge and appreciate.

And now in her twilight—in the twilight of years as also of mind when forgetfulness expands as awareness recedes—she lives in one long sustained aloneness not mitigated by visits either by myself or the dwindled few who still remain of a coterie that have vanished one by one variously to a garden cemetery, or to homes for the aged, or becoming themselves too ill or staggery to visit, or too deaf for contact by phone. All of this leading to an attrition of companionship that would once have seen her, as if by sleight-of-hand, produce biscuits, chocolates, fruit and cups of tea out of the ether, an attrition that has increasingly left her with long disoriented unvisited days of physical, mental, emotional, spiritual and world weariness where her pacemaker virtually alone thwarts the consummation of her wish, repeated to all who will listen, to be with Father again, himself now six years gone.

And so it goes on, each day etched from the same invariable template, for long periods confining herself to the living-room couch, quieting as well as she can with assorted anodynes the debilitating sometimes relentless pains in a badly deteriorated neck, holding on to chair, table and wall at every aberration of her capricious blood pressure, and repeating as one would an entrenched mantra, 'I have had enough. Enough already. Why am I being so punished with years I don't want?'

To this point has Mother, my mother, come.

❧

SERGE LIBERMAN, 'Pebbles for a Father', in *Voices from the Corner* [230–31]

'So, Doctor, you are obviously an important man if we don't see you from Sunday to Sunday. I'm surprised you still remember where your parents live.'

'So, Writer, you write for the newspapers, you edit this journal and that, you have a few books to your name, you peddle culture about town. So? What does it all get you? Aren't you neglecting your patients, maybe? Or your family, hmm, your wife, your children?'

Distant as at times he seemed, he missed little. When it came to aiming his barbs, an archer could not have had a deadlier eye.

This was but one volatile ingredient, fifty years multiplied, that could with the most unguarded remark precipitate a torrid boiling over. Suffice it to say, without elaboration, that the roof beneath which that cauldron seethed was so wanting for peace, for harmony, for a kindly and recipro- cated word (whether matters between the son's parents had to do with the choice of Sunday school or the cost of curtains, the size of a gift or the introduction of sandwiches into their delicatessen) that there were evenings when he fled his study, when he *had* to flee for the quieter, gentler tidal and arboreal hushes of St Kilda Beach, where, as an adolescent writer-in-the- making and his mother's son far more than his father's, he would forge in his mind's-eye a drama of Shakespearian mould in which a key line was, 'Bind these hands lest they do harm, do foul, shed blood!'

Questions arise here:

Where did the son lose the father he might have had?

Conversely, where did the father begin to lose his son?

And what kind of son did the father want?

And what kind of father could have held the son's affection?

And was the father truly a difficult man?

Or the son a particularly difficult child?

Such questions are seldom asked. So the son never learned, and even now he does not wholly know. Perhaps he can still make some sense of it all, however late (even if too late) the learning comes.

◦ॐ

MORITZ MICHAELIS, *Chapters from the Story of My Life* [154–5]

Ere I close I desire to say that one of the pleasantest recollections of my childhood is that of the Friday evenings, every preparation being made to render them festive and happy. My father, accompanied by we boys, went to the evening service as usual, special solemnity being added by the songs and hymns introducing the Sabbath. On our return home we found my mother and sisters awaiting us in the dining-room, which was lighted by the seven-branched Sabbath lamp suspended over the table. We received our parents' blessings, my father recited a hymn and then Solomon's song in praise of a good wife, which you always hear me say. After my father had solemnly pronounced the blessing over the wine and bread of which the whole household then partook, we sat down to dinner. The table was beautifully laid only our finest linen being used. After saying grace we spent the evening in happy and pleasant converse, visitors to the town being often present. Your mother and I have considered it our duty to gather you around us on the Sabbath eve in the same manner and I do not think I am wrong in saying that it has been of great benefit and pleasure to us all. I hope that you in your turn will act in this as your grandparents and we have done, so that your children may know and appreciate the blessedness and happiness of the Sabbath.

Should God in His great goodness grant me a few more years of life, and anything noteworthy take place, I will if possible add it to these reminiscences. I trust you will feel and evince towards one another the same brotherly love as heretofore, and that as your dear mother and I brought you up, so will you bring up your children to become good men and women.

I have told you before that I have been from my twenty-eighth year a Jew by conviction as well as by birth, and I can but hope and trust that you will try to be so likewise and bring up your children to learn and appreciate the great truths which Moses our law-giver has taught us.

Should I, as is most probable die before your dear mother, I rely upon you and your children continuing to treat her with that love and respect which you have always shown to both of us. I hope further that no one of you will ever attempt to alter the smallest item in my will, in which I have tried to treat your dear mother and all concerned in accordance with what I deem to be both just and right.

RITA NASH, 'The Last Barrier', in *Children of the Shadows* [72–3]

My mother told me about cold which was so bitter that her urine would freeze on her inner thigh, causing a lifelong rash. This particular story haunts me so much that even today, when I walk into my tastefully renovated bathroom with all its accoutrements for bodily hygiene, I am often assaulted by two images: my mother using a communal outdoor toilet in a Russian winter, and the filthy mass latrines of the camps.

My parents weren't aware of the devastating effect such stories had on me. Even though I really was too young and too impressionable to be told these few anecdotes, I somehow understood that my parents' need to unburden was so strong that I would have to endure the stories without complaint, squirm though I might. Sadly they were never relieved by any joyous, warm-hearted accounts of good times or loving family experiences. Perhaps such experiences or good times had never happened. If not, what an indelibly sad existence my parents must have led, and what a depressing legacy they had bequeathed to me and to my brother. It was possible too that their psychological makeup prevented them from experiencing much joy and thus they were unable to pass it on to their children.

All the stories, together with my own imaginings, created an urgent need for safety, for warmth and light.

GEORGES RICH, 'The Candidate', in *Children of the Shadows* [200–201]

Forty years later, Mamie, my eldest daughter and I are on Bondi Beach for a morning canter. At seventy-five she is super-fit and makes her bodily health a case of survival. None of her friends come anywhere near her stature as a 'working' human. We keep up with her pace as we discuss the passers-by, sometimes stopping to talk to them. Then Mamie casually points to a skin-and-bone man she knows, slowly treading the waves, his feet submerged, so frail-looking that at any moment a gust of wind could sweep him away. She nods in his direction and says, 'Auschwitz. That's how they looked, walking skeletons.'

I focus on the figure, a wiry, back-lit silhouette, contrasting perversely with the playful sparkle of sun and sea, and in one instant a giant shadow is cast. *Shoah*, a deformed monster, dormant, is called to life. By the slightest breach in the fabric of 'normality', by the merest interplay of words and events, the monster has risen to remind us of its presence. For me, the Shoah's existence is a matter of imagination and empathy; while for Mamie and her fellow survivors, such insights open up all the reality of pain, anguish and stolen lives. Here, imagination cannot cross the bridge to reality.

The walk continues, our delight at nature's gifts singed by the experience of reliving, if only by the tiniest of fractions, the horror of the past.

EVELYN ROTHFIELD, *The Future Is Past* [19]

He wrote the most beautiful letters. And claimed that I did too. Then the letters stopped and I heard from a friend that he had been arrested. As a Jew and a socialist he was an obvious candidate for concentration camps but fortunately his friends were able to get him out and the last I heard was that he had managed to get to Palestine.

Life goes on,

And death too.

My darling mother became ill and had to have an operation.

It was cancer—cancer of the ovary.

The stupid surgeon took out only one ovary—the other he said, was healthy.

The following year he had to remove the other ovary. But the cancer continued to spread. And she never recovered.

I was seized with a terrible feeling of guilt. My mother had not been happy about the affair with Carli—she had worried a lot about it. And I was sure that it was worry on my account that led to her illness. For years after her death I dreamt about my mother every night—it was as though she was reproaching me for my folly. It took me many years to live down that guilt feeling. And I wept inwardly for never would I be able to tell her that I loved her, that I hadn't meant to be wilful and cause her pain. I wept in the knowledge that I would never feel forgiven for being 'naughty'.

RICHARD SELIGMAN, *Very Convenient Everywhere* [210–12]

Prague, February 1, 1945.

My dear, good son,

[...]

I turned out as I was and still am: a reliable, sober worker but not a doer, a craftsman rather than a fighter, a rationalist, who demands his rights but does not expect any miracles. Generally such a fellow is called a pedant or a pessimist; it all depends which way you prefer to look at him. You ask why I tell you all this? Because it may explain to you a few things that you couldn't have understood as a child but you must have felt. It may perhaps also explain something about your own character. A child grows up both accepting much and consciously rejecting much of its parents.

In the case of such rejection right next to you, it may require all your wisdom, good-heartedness and love not to deny the child its rights. Don't forget that, you and Lise, when you have children. That grandparents are usually more affectionate to their grandchildren seems to me due to their instinctive gratefulness for being able to correct some of the things they failed in with their own children. I suppose we shall never have the joy of seeing our grandchildren grow up and receiving through them the blessing of a second childhood before death. I have one request to you and Lise, which involves them: Keep the enclosed Star of David and show it to them when they are old enough to understand; tell them that in order to expose them to any conceivable injustice and humiliation their ancestors were forced to wear this symbol, and that they wore it with courage and dignity.

❧

MINA SHAFER, 'Bitter Herbs Dipped in Salt', in *Children of the Shadows*
[44-7]

The *Haggadah* guides the *Seder* and it opens with the Four Questions,
which are the theme for the night. My niece Karen, the youngest in the
family, asks the main question, and each of its four parts in turn; the family
sings the answer to each part in chorus.

> *How is this night different from all other nights?*
> On all other nights we eat leavened or unleavened bread;
> > *but on this night*, only unleavened bread.
> On all other nights we eat any kind of herbs;
> > *but on this night*, only bitter herbs.
> On all other nights we do not dip herbs even once;
> > *but on this night*, we dip twice.
> On all other nights we eat either sitting upright or reclining;
> > *but on this night*, we all recline.

What strange questions, I think. The main question seems presumptu-
ous—surely every night is distinctive? Certainly all of the festivals have
their own particular flavour. The Day of Atonement is obviously different
because we fast and atone. So why is the question posed at all? What is this
formality about seeing the night as different?

[...]

'I also have questions. What kind of daughter am I? Am I the wise
daughter who asks, "What is the meaning of this ceremony, enactment and
judgment that our family engages in?" Or am I the wicked daughter saying,
"What does this ritual mean to *you*?" Or am I the simple daughter who
asks, "What's going on here?" No, I think that to you I am the young daughter, the one who is seen as too young to ask. So my questions are not
noticed—instead I am *told* what is said, and why. Don't you think a good
storyteller needs to know his listener? Don't his answers have to appeal to
all different types of people?'

Suddenly my mother pipes up, 'Why did God do this to me?'

'The four sons had their questions answered,' I jump in, 'but you don't give me answers, Mum, you don't give me stories. I have had so few stories from your past. Nothing to accept and nothing to reject. Just nothingness. Why don't you tell us something about your birth and your childhood? I want some stories from your past so that I can find myself, by finding you in the stories.'

Bruria lowers her eyes and stares into space. 'I'll give you a story,' she says, nodding sadly to herself. Then, in a tentative childlike voice, she begins. She perforates time and enters her family's pre-war past. It is many years ago, in a small village near Seirijai, in Lithuania.

'Our home was on the outskirts of the village—a small rustic cottage sitting by an unpaved road, with two barns attached, one for a carriage and the other for animals. Our fields surrounded the cottage. We had an orchard, vegetable gardens, and it was beautiful. [...]'

PETER SINGER, *Pushing Time Away* [243]

In writing it, I have felt that it is something I can do *for my grandfather*, some way of mitigating, however slightly, the wrong that the Nazis did to him. Is that a defensible thought? I don't believe in an afterlife any more than he did, so I have no illusions about him looking down from above on what I am writing. It can make no difference to him *now* if he and all his writings are left in the obscurity that has enveloped them for the past sixty years, or if *I* read them and bring them to a wider audience. So shouldn't I simply dismiss as nonsense the feeling that I am writing this book for him? Perhaps I should; yet I cannot entirely dismiss the feeling that by allowing David's writings to reach across the years to me, I am doing something for him.

Jews and Jewishness

JANINA DAVID, *A Square of Sky* [63–4]

In a little side street he found a Jewish innkeeper who, moved by our plight, allowed us to stay with his family. I was put in a huge double bed smelling of strange bodies, and immediately fell asleep.

When next I opened my eyes the picture before me made me sit up with a gasp. I was in a strange room, lit only by candles standing on a large table. Around their flickering light dark figures rocked in all directions, chanting and moaning. They were all men, in long black caftans, with flowing beards and sidelocks. They wore skullcaps, and in the uncertain light of the candles their pale faces and hands swam, mysteriously disembodied. Behind them hovered feminine figures clad in long dark dresses. Their eyes glowed as they approached the pool of light, and steaming dishes appeared on the white tablecloth.

Mother, sitting on the bed beside me, caught my hand and whispered to keep quiet. But already faces turned towards us, surprised and hostile. To this pious Orthodox family it seemed impossible that a Jewish child might be so ignorant of the Sabbath ritual. Throughout the whole evening I sat pressed to Mother's side, watching as the circle around the table swayed, wept, sang and prayed, listening to the accents of fear and resignation so clearly expressed in a foreign tongue.

At the end of this strange evening they all rose and, still chanting, marched in single file towards a large wardrobe. The door was opened and one by one they disappeared inside.

MAYER HARARI, *Second Exodus* [8–9]

One religious happening that sticks in my mind is the Bar Mitzvah of Emile, my eldest cousin. On the morning of the Bar Mitzvah the whole family gathered in front of his apartment building and we walked to Shule, lined up like soldiers. What was unusual was that we were surrounded by a brass band of Arabs playing for dear life and by a mass of Arab children attracted by the band. They escorted us to Shule. When the service was over, the same procession occurred in reverse.

This practice was discontinued for subsequent Bar Mitzvahs in the family, because by then we had moved to the CBD where such public celebrations did not take place.

One incident is etched in my memory. It was 1929. There had been massacres of Jews in Palestine, echoed by anti-Jewish demonstrations in Cairo where a number of Jews had been killed in the street. One morning my father was going to work with his brother Zaki (Isaac) in the latter's car. I happened to enter my father's bedroom where he was dressing and saw him take from his dressing table a Browning pistol that he slipped into his pocket. That was a sobering scene for a nine year old. It was only one of many happenings over the years that kept reminding us that we were a minority tolerated in the country only under sufferance.

BERNARD MARIN, *My Father, My Father* [55–6]

'It is *Hallel*,' she said. 'The story of the Exodus from Egypt.'

Urisz stopped and turned to me.

'You should have learned these things already,' he said. 'Learn your Hebrew. Learn to ask the questions. It is part of Haggadah tradition. In Torah, it says, "In time to come, when your son asks, 'What does this mean?' you shall say to him, 'With mighty hand the Lord brought us out from Egypt, the house of bondage.'" You should know all of this.'

Urisz turned back to his praying, the guttural consonants and chanting vowels of his Hebrew. Then the insistent rhythm of the prayer shook and faltered. Another loud recitation was coming from the other side of the room. It took a moment to recognise that it was my father's voice. He was sitting at the table. In a loud voice, he was reciting the winners of the daily double and the trifecta from Saturday's *Sporting Globe*. He read the winners and placegetters, the starting prices, and the totalisator payouts down to pounds, shillings, and pence. Urisz stopped praying, and I watched him, aghast at what would happen next.

My father read on and on, while Urisz simply stood in the middle of the floor with an indescribable look on his face. After a while, my father finished reading the page, and folded up the paper. He got up to go. As he walked past, Urisz said, 'You bring shame on this house.' He spat out the words like a curse. My father stopped and looked at him.

'It won't help anyone,' he said. 'It's all rubbish. We are living in Australia now. You should give it up.'

'You are a Jew,' Urisz said, excitedly, then pointed to me. 'Your son is a Jew. And he knows nothing of his people.'

My father just shrugged contemptuously.

'What is there to know?' he said. 'All this muttering and ranting? All your backward, selfish ideas? Your jealous God?' He shook his head. 'There is no God, so forget it.'

PHILIP OPAS, *Throw Away My Wig* [125–6]

The hardest choice involved religion. Religion had never meant much to me. Stella and I were married in St Kilda Synagogue by Rabbi Danglow. He was the senior chaplain and doyen of the chaplains of all denominations in the armed forces. Surprisingly, there was no Jewish chaplain in the RAAF. Rabbi Danglow had seen extensive overseas service during the first war and he was a man's man whom I very much admired.

He sent for me just before I had embarked for New Guinea. He did not beat about the bush. 'Phil, you are going away with the Air Force. We must be realistic. Not only is it possible that you might not come back but it is possible, being in the Air Force, that we might not find any trace of you.'

I realised that but did not want to dwell on it.

'In the last war we had a lot of difficulty about that sort of thing but it is nothing to what we might expect this time. It meant, in cases like that, that the wives of missing men could never marry again... at least not in a synagogue.'

I was appalled: 'Surely you can presume death?'

'I wish we could. Unfortunately when the rules were made the only way a man could be killed in battle was by a sword, a spear, a stone or a club, and then one had to find a body which could be identified and buried. The rules haven't kept up with modern war, and I can't change them.'

I argued with him: 'That's ridiculous. What sort of religion have we got if it stays in the dark ages?'

'Phil, I can't do anything about that. But why I have called you in is to ask you to do something special for Stella. If something happened and you were never found, you would not want her not to be able to marry again, would you?'

Faced with this problem, one which had never occurred to me, I was deeply shocked.

'I know you are a sensible chap who would not want to hurt Stella. I want you to give her a provisional get so that if you fail to return within twelve months of the cessation of hostilities, Stella will be free to re-marry.'

'But she will then marry as a divorcee, not a widow,' I expostulated.

'I know it is asking a great deal of you but it really is an honourable thing to do.'

A get is a religious divorce which has no recognition in the civil law courts. Even with a civil divorce, a Jew cannot marry in an Orthodox synagogue without the additional get (which only the husband can obtain).

I asked, 'Does Stella know about this?'

'No, nor should she know. I want you to keep it a secret from her. There is no need to upset her and, please God, it won't be needed. If you are spared to come back it will have no effect whatever.'

I was very much in love with my young wife. I felt as though I was facing a death sentence. Nevertheless, I agreed to do what he asked. I attended before the Beth Din, a religious court of three rabbis, two of whom were Rabbi Danglow and Rabbi Super. I was too stunned to remember the name of the third. I was given no paper to evidence the provisional divorce. Stella was not informed of it.

SAMUEL PISAR, *Of Blood and Hope* [53–4]

One evening in June 1967 when I returned home from the office, I saw an unbelievable, an unimaginable, sight on my television screen: Israeli soldiers, white prayer shawls covering the machine guns on their backs, steel helmets serving them as yarmulkes, praying at the foot of the Wailing Wall. Suddenly, I burst into uncontrollable sobs, sobs of which my children never thought their father was capable, sobs from the depth of my being and from the wells of time.

My mind, my training, my experience told me that the sight I saw was pregnant with unfathomable complications. I was aware that to follow to the comma the strictures of an ancient book about the sacredness of this or that speck of soil was an oversimplification that bordered on the fanatical. I knew that the legitimate rights and ageless passions of others were also involved. But the memory of what I had lived through, of what an entire nation had lived through for millennia, had broken the emotional dam in front of this eternal symbol of sorrow and of hope.

Yes, on that day, the trains headed for Treblinka, Maidanek, and Auschwitz had finally reached their destination.

Sexes, Sexuality, Body

DENNIS ALTMAN, *Defying Gravity* [103]

Everyone has to create their sense of identity out of a mixture of inheritance and social possibilities, but a lesbian or gay identity differs from that of, say, a Jew, a Christian Scientist or an Aborigine, in that it is very rarely passed on through the biological family, and its signposts are often hidden, even in a time when Mardi Gras has become prime-time television viewing. The growth of gay communal events has led to some rhetoric about the need to pass on 'our' history to 'our' young people, but contemporary gay identity remains particularly modern in that it is created usually against, rather than as an extension of, the teachings of family, church and school.

I have heard many coming-out stories from different parts of the world and what strikes me is their similarity, a similarity which transcends time and place, at least within those worlds where a homosexual identity can be meaningfully imagined. It is not that contemporary ways of being homosexual/lesbian/queer/gay or whatever have replaced previous ones; it is rather that they co-exist with them, so that each sixteen-year-old, even a sixteen-year-old growing up in Sydney or San Francisco, still has to negotiate the break with parental and peer norms and face often unpredictable consequences. Adolescents tend to be very unforgiving of those who don't conform, and teenagers coming to terms with being homosexual often have a very difficult time. As David Leavitt put it, 'Even in places where people tell you it's okay to be gay, you have to tell *them* you're gay first, and that's never easy.'

ALIDA BELAIR, *Out of Step* [55–6]

In the ballet world you had to suffer: bleeding toes, aching limbs and an injured soul were all an integral part of the grand myth. You had to be scourged and disciplined before you could—or was it would?—be allowed to emerge as a creature of beauty. So we were all gradually inured to pain, and smugly delighted if we could punish the feet to the point of bleeding, or whip the old body to the point of dropping. After all, as Madame so often reminded us, we were in good company. Pavlova had danced until the blood stained her satin shoes red. Maybe, I couldn't help thinking sacrilegiously, it was out of such acts of martyrdom that the inspiration for the Dying Swan was born.

ZELDA D'APRANO, *Zelda* [73]

I took a day off from work and called into the local shopping centre to buy something for tea. Ken too was there shopping and, after exchanging greetings, I explained I wasn't feeling very well and had decided to take the day off. He also had some business to attend to and was off from work. Later, during the day, there was a knock on the door and I was surprised to see Ken standing there. 'Thought I'd call around for a cup of tea,' he said. After inviting him in and making the tea, we sat at the kitchen table and talked and drank the tea. There were several tasks I wished to attend to so, when some time had lapsed, I cleared the table and proceeded to rinse the cups out at the sink. As I turned away from the sink, he grasped me in his arms.

After all these years I was now back in the same scene. As I fought, I tried to talk to him, I tried to make him understand that I wasn't interested in him and pleaded with him to release me. He was like an animal. I struggled and fought; he began to drag me towards the bedroom and I used my legs to try to prevent him dragging my body through the doorways in my attempt to escape from his grip. He was so powerful and managed to push me on to the bed. His full weight was upon me and I then began to yell, 'No, no, no, can't you see what you are doing?' I broke down and then pleaded with him, but to no avail. He was beside himself with a coldness of steel. I could no longer struggle, my heart was pounding and my energy spent. I knew I had no energy left to fight him. I lay there like stone. This was my first rape. A worker, a married man and a communist. He left immediately after.

ROBIN DALTON, *An Incidental Memoir* [255–7]

Half a century and more later, I am asked sometimes, as if I am an expert, my opinion of Australian men, in the context of the sexual gavotte: in what way I think they differ in their amatory—for want of a more apt word—approaches. Let me quote just one glorious example, my old friend George.

George was generally thought to be, in his day, one of Australia's richest men, his riches based on what was then the solid foundation of Australia's economy—wool. Good merino wool, endless acres; but all augmented by George's fertile business brain. He was never physically pleasing, and in our shallow pleasure-seeking teenage world to be avoided as he was prone to pounce. This was not always easy, as George believed in the most direct approach. Speech could be dispensed with if nubile flesh was within grabbing distance. I managed to escape being grabbed all through my Australian youth, but one day, living in London, George caught up with me. He telephoned daily and after a few weeks I realised I could not pretend a prior engagement every night, every week, every month. As he was living at the Dorchester, I thought that I would, at least, have a decent dinner. We met in his suite: my heart sank. A table was set for two, champagne in bucket, George at the ready. All through dinner (passable) I managed to get him to talk, and talk with interest, on his ruling passion—sheep. So far so good. I began to relax as I settled on the sofa for coffee. Not so George. Rubbing his palms together, hitching up his pants as at a starting post, he launched himself full length across me, pinning me to the sofa. I pushed him off, but he was not easy to shift, and determined to plead his case.

'Aw, come on—I've had my eye on you since you were seventeen. You were the most eligible virgin in town only John Spencer got there first [which of course, he hadn't] and from what I hear of that English boyfriend of yours, you could do with a good, virile Australian.' The English boyfriend was David.

Later that same week I learnt that, failing with me, George had managed to track down two other Australians living in London: his grabs were in taxis this time. To Valerie Fairfax, it was: 'Why didn't you tell me you'd gone on the sex wagon before I bought you a feed?' And to the other, upon being rebuffed, 'Don't tell me you've turned lezzo.'

George eventually married, produced a family, gave up the chase, but still, on his occasional visits to London, kept in touch. Years later he came for treatment for cancer and I visited him in the London Clinic.

'Come here,' said George, patting the bed. I came and perched on it. 'I've been trying to get a feel of your tits for thirty years. Now I'm dying do you think you could give me a feel?' I hitched open my blouse—George slipped his hand inside my brassiere and gave a contented sigh.

'I can die happy now.'

MORRIS LURIE, *Whole Life* [116–17]

When it's my sister's birthday and we've had the party, the cakes and the lemonade and the blowing out the candles and everything, and now everyone's playing in the back and I don't know how, nobody knows how, except Hymie's playing with the mattock and suddenly there's an accident, he gets my sister with it in the toe—because she's got sandals on—and straightaway there's blood and screaming and dad comes running out of the house and mum and everyone's angry and shouting and the whole party's spoilt and Hymie gets a hit and has to go straight home.

When it's my birthday and we're all playing in the street running up and down before we're allowed inside, and in between two cars someone's put wire and I trip over it and it's my birthday my own birthday and I'm bleeding and crying on mum's bed and everyone has the party because it's all ready on the table but I can't, I don't.

And one day it's a holiday and there's nothing to do and I'm miserable and I'm sitting on the floor in the passage without even any shoes on or even any socks and mum is doing the sewing machine and I'm grizzly and whiney and picking my toes and she won't even listen to me, she doesn't even care, she's busy, she's always busy, and I'm sitting there for hours and she doesn't pay attention and it's awful, and then someone calls out, it's the kids in the street, the front door's open so you can look down—*Hey, we're all goin' t' the pictures, why'ncha come?*—and I start to say, *Naah, I'm not allowed*, and suddenly mum says, *Go! Quick! Here! Here's money! Have a good time!* and I've got my shoes and socks on and all miserableness is gone and forgotten and I'm in the street laughing and running with all the other kids going to the pictures.

Sing of the flowers, the things that grow. Of pussy willow. Of snapdragons. Of pansy faces. Of buttercups. *Ja like butter? Gissa look!* Shining the flower onto the white innocence of your offered up throat where the answer was always yes.

The power of the woman!

The magic!

Careers

LOUIS KAHAN, 'A Sketch of My Life', in *Strauss to Matilda* [113–14]

Beside portraiture, most of my work is devoted to figure compositions, and the nude in particular. Although I love the bush, I found no artistic rapport with it. Maybe my first impression of the landscape, especially in Western Australia, was one of sameness of colours. Perhaps because I am essentially a city dweller, people have always been the most important part of my work. But two very Australian themes were subjects of my one-man exhibitions: 'Waltzing Matilda' and 'Sheep and Shearers'. A newcomer to a country is often better able to define characteristics of a people, and the swagman with his dislike of authority, sense of independence and love of freedom, was to me the Australian in a nutshell.

❧

NANCY KEESING, *Riding the Elephant* [90–91]

Normally the clerk would have filled in the detailed form needed to open a file. Grumpily I found one on her desk and, with none too good a grace began to complete it while the mother, tiredly, explained that they had arrived from a distant country town this morning by train, that they had not understood hospital procedures or the delay involved, that they had never been in a city before and were bewildered, that they had very little cash but Casualty had said the Almoner's Department could provide money for emergencies, and... and... a sad tale I'd heard countless times before, from countless weary mothers and worried fathers.

'Yes, yes, but first I must register the baby on this form.' Name? Date of birth? (it was a first child), parents' names, father's job and income? etc. etc. I glanced at the referral form again. Casualty had not specified the child's illness. Strange. No doubt late Saturday morning-itis prevailed there, too.

Through all this the beautiful baby slept peacefully in its mother's arms. The father shifted restlessly in his chair and looked increasingly distressed.

'Now, what is the matter with the baby?' The father gave a cry. I looked up. Never had I seen such agonised expressions on two faces. The woman stood, put the baby on my table, and without a single word unwrapped the shawl. A lovely face; a perfect body; no legs or arms.

People in professions like social work, the law, medicine, must be able to put out of mind, out of working hours, or at least as much as possible, the terrible tragedies and problems of their jobs. Perhaps saints can carry intolerable cares and not falter, but saints are rare. More common are those who become callous and cynical, or take to the bottle or drugs. That baby (perhaps an early victim of thalidomide whose dire effects were not yet recognised) scars my mind for ever. I could combine the *Bulletin* and ballad collecting with the problems of ordinarily ill children, with bashed and abused children, with even the Polio Ward, but I could not share that limbless baby with any other career.

It was, and remains, my most appalling memory. I spent a good part of the afternoon arranging for cash vouchers, and all the routine involved. The People's Palace had a room, and would, bless the Salvos, be understanding and helpful in many ways. Then I wrote up the case for whomever would tackle it on Monday, when I, of course, would not be there. I never saw the baby or its parents again. I could not continue to shilly-shally. I resigned from the hospital a few days later. I at least knew that, with the generous reference I was given, I could return to Social Work if I failed as a writer.

Endnotes

1   Serge Liberman, *Bibliography of Australian Judaica*, Mandelbaum Trust and University of Sydney Library, Sydney, 1991.

2   Robert and Roberta Kalechofsky (eds), *Jewish Writing from Down Under: Australia and New Zealand*, Micah Publications, Marblehead (MA), 1984.

3   See, for instance: Steven J. Rubin, (ed.), *Writing Our Lives: Autobiographies of American Jews, 1890–1900*, Jewish Publication Society, Philadelphia, 1991; Howard Simons (ed.), *Jewish Times: Voices of the American Jewish experience*, Houghton Mifflin, Boston, 1990; Elena Lappin (ed.), *Jewish Voices, German Words: Growing up Jewish in postwar Germany and Austria*, Catbird Press, North Haven (CT), 1994; Gerri Sinclair and Morris Wolfe (eds), *The Spice Box: An anthology of Jewish Canadian writing*, Lester and Orpen Dennys, Toronto, 1981; Robert and Roberta Kalechofsky (eds), *Echad: An anthology of Latin American Jewish writing*, Micah Publications, Marblehead (MA), 1980; Robert and Roberta Kalechofsky (eds), *The Global Anthology of Jewish Women Writers*, Micah Publications, Marblehead (MA), 1990.

4   Otto Gunsberger, *Difficulties of Remembering: Reflections about an exhibition*, Otto Gunsberger, Melbourne, 1997.

5   Otto Gunsberger, *Choice of Profession: Message from a survivor to the succeeding generations*, Nustyle, Melbourne, 1990. See also Gunsberger, *Oldman's Story*, Melbourne, 1995; and Gunsberger, *Came from Central Europe and Other Stories*, Nustyle, Melbourne, 1991.

6   Gunsberger, *Difficulties of Remembering*, p. 43.

7   Lily Brett, *In Full View: Essays by Lily Brett*, Picador, Sydney, 1997.

8   Nancy Keesing, *Riding the Elephant*, Allen & Unwin, Sydney, 1988.

9   Nancy Keesing (ed.), *Shalom: Australian Jewish stories*, Collins, Sydney, 1978.

10 Keesing, *Riding the Elephant*, p. 138.

11 See Erik H. Erikson, *Identity: Youth and crisis*, W. W. Norton, New York, 1968, pp. 159–65; and Paul John Eakin, *Fiction in Autobiography: Studies in the art of self-invention*, Princeton University Press, Princeton, 1985.

12 Judah Waten, 'My Two Literary Careers', reprinted in David Carter (ed.), *Judah Waten: Fiction, memoirs, criticism*, University of Queensland Press, Brisbane, 1998, p. 152.

13 See Sidonie Smith and Julia Watson, *Reading Autobiography: A guide for interpreting life narratives*, University of Minnesota Press, Minneapolis, 2001, Appendix A, p. 206.

14 The term 'autobiographical pact' was coined by the eminent French theorist of autobiography, Philippe Lejeune. See Lejeune, *On Autobiography*, ed. Paul John Eakin, University of Minnesota Press, Minneapolis, 1989, pp. 3–30.

15 ibid., pp. 119–37.

16 Kay Schaffer and Sidonie Smith, *Human Rights and Narrated Lives: The Ethics of recognition*, Palgrave Macmillan, New York, 2004, pp. 7–8.

17   Leigh Gilmore, *The Limits of Autobiography: Trauma and testimony*, Cornell University Press, Ithaca, 2001, p. 7.

18   Richard Freadman, review of Sidonie Smith and Julia Watson: *Reading Autobiography: A guide for interpreting life narratives*, in *Biography* 26:2, 2003, pp. 298–306.

19   The point is not that Smith and Watson ignore agency (they don't); it's that their conception of agency, as derived from the Marxist philosopher Louis Althusser and others, is itself oddly—indeed paradoxically—deterministic.

20   Richard Freadman, *Threads of Life: Autobiography and the will*, University of Chicago Press, Chicago, 2001.

21   Leona Toker, 'Toward a Poetics of Documentary Prose—from the Perspective of Gulag Testimonies', *Poetics Today*, 18:22, Summer 1997, pp. 187–222.

22   Primo Levi, *If This Is a Man* and *The Truce*, trans. Stuart Woolf, Abacus, London, 1979.

23   Theodor W. Adorno, *Prisms*, trans. Samuel and Shierry Weber, Neville Spearman, London, 1967, p. 34.

24   In fact, Adorno does not seem to have intended to repudiate aesthetic subtlety *per se* in post-Holocaust writing but rather to unsettle a certain kind of unthinking reverence for Art in a world in which one of Europe's great artistic cultures had perpetrated barbarity on an unprecedented scale. See also Susan Gubar, *Poetry after Auschwitz: Remembering what one never knew*, Indiana University Press, Bloomington, 2003.

25   The term was coined by the historian/historiographer Hayden White. See his *Tropics of Discourse: Essays in cultural criticism*, Johns Hopkins University, Baltimore, 1978, p. 66.

26   Itzhak Cytrynowski, '*And I Will Remember My Covenant…*', A. Cytrynowski, Melbourne, 1998.

27   David Martin, *My Strange Friend*, Picador, Sydney, 1991.

28   Mark Raphael Baker, *The Fiftieth Gate: A journey through memory*, Flamingo, Sydney, 1991.

29   Lolo Houbein, *Wrong Face in the Mirror: An autobiography of race and identity*, University of Queensland Press, Brisbane, 1990.

30   Diana Encel (ed.), *Jewish Country Girls: A collection of memories*, Sydney Jewish Museum, Sydney, 2005. Note that just over half of these narratives are written by Diane Encel herself.

31   Alida Belair, *Out of Step: A dancer reflects*, Melbourne University Press, Melbourne, 1993.

32   George Szego, *Two Prayers to One God: A journey towards identity and belonging*, Hardie Grant Books, Melbourne, 2001.

33   Diane Armstrong, *Mosaic: A chronicle of five generations*, Random House, Sydney, 1998.

34   Susan Varga, *Heddy and Me*, Penguin, Melbourne, 1994.

35   Anna Rosner Blay, *Sister, Sister*, Hale & Iremonger, Sydney, 1998.

36   Helen Max, *Searching for Yesterday: A photographic essay about my mother, a Holocaust survivor*, Makor Jewish Community Library, Melbourne, 2001.

37   Josiane Behmoiras, *Dora B: A memoir of my mother*, Viking, Melbourne, 2005.

38   Richard Freadman, *Shadow of Doubt: My father and myself*, Bystander Press, Melbourne, 2003.

39   Fela and Felix Rosenbloom, *Miracles Do Happen: Memoirs of Fela and Felix Rosenbloom*, Scribe, Melbourne, 1994.

40   Moshe and Stefa Robin, *Stepping into Life*, Makor Jewish Community Library, Melbourne, 2002.

41   Zoltán and Adi Schwartz, *Survivors*, Lina, Sydney, 1999.

42 James Mitchell, *Henry Krongold: Memoirs*, Allen & Unwin, Sydney, 2003.

43 Sir Zelman Cowen, *A Public Life: The memoirs of Zelman Cowen*, Melbourne University Press, Melbourne, 2006.

44 June Epstein, *Woman with Two Hats: An autobiography*, Hyland House, Melbourne, 1988.

45 Elena Jonaitis, *Elena's Journey*, Text, Melbourne, 1997.

46 Julie Meadows (ed.), *Memory Guide My Hand: An anthology of autobiographical writing by members of the Melbourne Jewish community*, Makor Jewish Community Library, Melbourne—vol. 1, 1998; vol. 2, 2000; vol. 3, 2004.

47 Karl Bittman (ed.), *Strauss to Matilda: Viennese in Australia 1938–1988*, Wenkart Foundation, Sydney, 1988; Louise Hoffman and Shush Masel (eds), *Without Regret*, Centre for Migration and Development Studies, University of Western Australia, Perth, 1994; Kathy Grinblat (ed.), *Children of the Shadows: Voices of the second generation*, University of Western Australia Press, Perth, 2002; Konrad Kwiet and John A. Moses (eds), *On Being a German-Jewish Refugee in Australia: Experiences and studies*, special issue of *Australian Journal of Politics and History*, vol. 31, no. 5, 1985.

48 Nina Stone (ed.), *Silent No More: Melbourne child survivors of the Holocaust*, Child Survivors of the Holocaust, Melbourne, 1999.

49 Suzanne D. Rutland, *The Jews in Australia*, Cambridge University Press, Cambridge, 2005, pp. 118–19. For findings based on recent focus-group interviews with Australian Jewish women, see Suzanne Rutland and Sol Encel, 'Major Issues Facing the Jewish Community: Women's perceptions', *Australian Journal of Jewish Studies*, XX, 2006, pp. 169–98.

50 See Barbara Bloch and Eva Cox, 'Mending the World from the Margins: Jewish women and Australian feminism', in Geoffrey Brahm Levey and Philip Mendes (eds), *Jews and Australian Politics*, Sussex Academic Press, Brighton (UK), 2004, pp. 145–59.

51 Doris Brett, *Eating the Underworld: A memoir in three voices*, Vintage, Sydney, 2001; Susan Varga, *Heddy and Me*; Helen Max, *Searching for Yesterday*; Kitia Altman, *Memories of Ordinary People: For those who have no one to remember them*, Makor Jewish Community Library, Melbourne, 2003.

52 Blay, *Sister, Sister*, pp. 121–2.

53 The term 'performativity' derives principally from the work of the American Jewish feminist Judith Butler. For an introduction to postmodern feminism, including Butler's work, see *The Norton Anthology of Theory and Criticism*, W. W. Norton, New York, 2001. The section on Butler is on pp. 2485–501.

54 Dennis Altman, *Defying Gravity: A political life*, Allen & Unwin, Sydney, 1997.

55 On relational and associated tendencies in women's autobiography, and proposed contrasts with male narratives, see Sidonie Smith's critique of the 'androcentric paradigm' in *A Poetics of Women's Autobiography: Marginality and the fictions of self-representation*, Indiana University Press, Bloomington, 1987; Regenia Gagnier, 'The Literary Standard, Working-class Autobiography, and Gender', in Susan Groag Bell and Marilyn Yalom (eds), *Revealing Lives: Autobiography, biography, and gender*, State University of New York Press, Albany, 1990; and also Estelle C. Jelinek (ed.), *Women's Autobiography: Essays in criticism*, Indiana University Press, Bloomington, 1980.

56 Richard Freadman, '"Heddy and I": Relational life-writing in *Heddy and Me*', *Australian Book Review*, no. 238, Jan. 2002, pp. 20–23.

57 Paul John Eakin, *How Our Lives Become Stories: Making selves*, Cornell University Press, Ithaca, 1999. See especially chapter 2.

58 Helen Gardner, *My Mother's Child*, Makor Jewish Community Library, Melbourne, 2001; Elfie Rosenberg, *Serry and Me*, Makor Jewish Community Library, Melbourne, 2001; Marilyn Schimmel with her sisters Annette and Sharon, *Pola's Story*, Makor Jewish Community Library, Melbourne, 2005; Lucy Gould, *Empty Corners*, Makor Jewish Community Library, Melbourne, 2000.

59 Vera Schreiber, *The Porcelain Doll*, Makor Jewish Community Library, Melbourne, 2000.

60 Hania Ajzner, *Hania's War*, Makor Jewish Community Library, Melbourne, 2000, p. 188.

61 Zelda D'Aprano, *Zelda*, Spinifex, Melbourne, 1995.

62 Galina Kordin, *East West and Nowhere*, Spectrum, Richmond, 1987.

63 Robin Dalton, *Aunts Up the Cross*, Viking, Melbourne, 1998.

64 Amirah Inglis, *Amirah: An un-Australian childhood*, Heinemann, Melbourne, 1983.

65 Helena Rubinstein, *My Life for Beauty*, Bodley Head, Sydney, 1964.

66 Rae Mandelbaum, *Echoes from the Past: The Rifka Norman story*, Makor Jewish Community Library, Melbourne, 1999, p. 48.

67 Maria Lewitt, *Come Spring*, Scribe, Melbourne, 2002, p.17.

68 Suzanne D. Rutland, *Edge of the Diaspora: Two centuries of Jewish settlement in Australia*, Collins, Sydney, 2000.

69 Melvin Ember, Carol R. Ember and Ian Skoggard (eds), *Encyclopedia of Diasporas: Immigrant and refugee cultures around the world*, Kluwer Academic Publishers, Dordrecht (Netherlands), 2004.

70 Robin Cohen, *Global Diasporas: An introduction*, University of Washington Press, Seattle, 1997, p. 27.

71 ibid., p. 180.

72 The distinction is proposed by Gabriel Sheffer and is cited in Nicholas van Hear, *New Diasporas: The mass exodus, dispersal and regrouping of migrant communities*, University of Washington Press, Seattle, 1998, p. 4.

73 Cohen, *Global Diasporas*, p. xi.

74 ibid.

75 Hilary L. Rubinstein, *The Jews in Australia: A thematic history*, vol. 1 (1788–1945), and William D. Rubinstein, *The Jews in Australia: A thematic history*, vol. 2 (1945 to the present), Heinemann, Melbourne, 1991.

76 Some other recommended texts are W. D. Rubinstein (ed.), *The Jews in the Sixth Continent*, Allen & Unwin, Sydney, 1987; Hilary Rubinstein, *Chosen: The Jews in Australia*, Allen & Unwin, Sydney, 1987; W. D. Rubinstein, *The Jews in Australia*, AE Press, Melbourne, 1986; J. S. Levi and G. F. J. Bergman, *Australian Genesis: Jewish convicts and settlers 1788–1850*, Rigby, Adelaide, 1974; Paul R. Bartrop, *Australia and the Holocaust 1933–45*, Australian Scholarly Publishing, Melbourne, 1994; Alan Jacobs (ed.), *Enough Already: An anthology of Australian–Jewish writing*, Allen & Unwin, Sydney, 1999; Gael Hammer (ed.), *Pomegranates: A century of Jewish Australian writing*, Millennium, Sydney, 1988; Nancy Keesing (ed.), *Shalom: Australian Jewish stories*, Collins, Sydney, 1978.

77 In constructing this sketch I have at times followed the account given by W. D. Rubinstein, one of the finest historians working in the field, in his introduction to *Jews in the Sixth Continent*.

78 For instance, the establishment in 1911 of the Kadimah, a centre of Yiddish-based culture and political activity in Melbourne, and the growth of Yiddish theatre. On the latter, see Arnold Zable, *Wanderers and Dreamers: Tales of the David Herman Theatre*, Hyland House, Melbourne, 1988.

79 Hilary Rubinstein, *The Jews in Australia*, p. 55.

80 W. D. Rubinstein, *The Jews in the Sixth Continent*, p. 5.

81 For discussion of this complex history see, in addition to the sources already listed, Colin Golvan, *The Distant Exodus: Australian Jews recall their immigrant experiences*, ABC, Sydney, 1990; and on the sometimes disingenuous intricacies of Australian government policies, Chanan Reich, *Australia and Israel: An ambiguous relationship*, Melbourne University Press, Melbourne, 2002.

82 For an interesting overview which includes Jewish and indigenous perspectives and pays careful attention to cultural literacy within multicultural settings, see David Myers (ed.), *Reinventing Literacy: The multicultural imperative*, Phaedrus, Rockhampton, 1995.

83 Rutland, *The Jews in Australia*, p. 153 ff.

84 Kathy Reisman, *More Than Nine Lives*, Makor Jewish Community Library, Melbourne, 2002.

85 Leo Cooper, *The Long Road to the Lucky Country*, Makor Jewish Community Library, Melbourne, 2005, p. 256.

86 Max Freilich, *Zion in Our Time: Memoirs of an Australian Zionist*, Morgan Publications, Sydney, 1967, p. xiii.

87 ibid., p. 24.

88 ibid., p. 126.

89 ibid., p. 206.

90 Bernard A. Boas, *The Five Books of Boas: The autobiography of Bernard A. Boas, OAM*, Makor Jewish Community Library, Melbourne, 2001, pp. 174–5.

91 Behmoiras, *Dora B*, p. 42.

92 For introductions to postcolonial studies, see Bill Ashcroft, Gareth Griffith and Helen Tiffin, *The Empire Writes Back: Theory and Practice in post-colonial literatures*, Routledge, London, 1989; and Leela Gandhi, *Postcolonial Theory: A critical introduction*, Allen & Unwin, Sydney, 1998.

93 Edward W. Said, *Orientalism*, Pantheon, New York, 1978.

94 For an introduction to Foucault's work, see *The Norton Anthology of Theory and Criticism*, pp. 1615–70.

95 Jana Evans Braziel and Anita Mannur (eds), *Theorizing Diaspora: A reader*, Blackwell, Malden (MA), 2003, p. 7.

96 ibid, p. 239. Elsewhere Hall has argued for the need to 'retheorize difference' in order to address some of the difficulties presented by the Derridean orientation. See for example Stuart Hall, 'New Ethnicities', in Donald James and Ali Rattansi (eds), *'Race', Culture & Difference*, Sage Publications, London, 1992, p. 257.

97 Rey Chow, *Writing Diaspora*, Indiana University Press, Bloomington, 1993.

98 For some specialized studies of the genre see: Sydney Stahl Weinberg, *The World of Our Mothers: The lives of Jewish immigrant women*, University of North Carolina Press, Chapel Hill, 1988; Magdalena J. Zaborowska, *How We Found America: Reading gender through East European immigrant narratives*, University of North Carolina Press, Chapel Hill, 1995.

99 In such matters mere duration is only a very rough guide: someone who has lived in Australia for ten years within an extremely insular ethnic community might be less moved and affected by the place than someone who has partaken of the broader Australian community for twelve months.

100 Mary Besemeres, *Translating One's Self: Language and selfhood in cross-cultural autobiography*, Peter Lang, Oxford, 2002, p. 9.

101   ibid., p. 30.
102   ibid., p. 60. The term 'self-translation', coined by Besemeres, is not actually used by Hoffman.
103   Sneja Gunew, *Framing Marginality: Multicultural literary studies*, Melbourne University Press, Melbourne, 1994, p. 4.
104   Sneja Gunew and Kateryna O. Longley (eds), *Striking Chords: Multicultural literary interpretations*, Allen & Unwin, Sydney, 1992, p. 45.
105   Gunew, *Framing Marginality*, p. xii.
106   David Carter, *A Career in Writing: Judah Waten and the cultural politics of a literary career*, Association for the Study of Australian Literature, Toowoomba, 1997, p. 6.
107   Kitia Altman, *Memories of Ordinary People*, p. 411.
108   Bittman, *Strauss to Matilda*, p. xi.
109   Israel Kipen, *A Life to Live ...: An autobiography*, Chandos Publishing, Melbourne, 1989, p. 180.
110   ibid., p. 188.
111   Besemeres, *Translating One's Self*, p. 21.
112   Lolo Houbein, in Gunew and Longley, *Striking Chords*, p. 83.
113   Amirah Inglis, *Amirah: An un-Australian childhood*, Heinemann, Richmond, 1983, p. 82.
114   Zyga Elton (Ealbaum), *Destination Buchara*, Dizal, Ripponlea, 1996.
115   Abraham H. Biderman, *The World of My Past*, Random House, Sydney, 1996; Mark Verstandig, *I Rest My Case*, Saga Press, Melbourne, 1995; Richard Seligman, *Very Convenient Everywhere*, Vantage Press, New York, 1991; Joseph West, *Survival, Struggle & Success*, JFW Publications, Melbourne, 1995; Max Heitlinger, *In the Nick of Time: Escape from Nazis, wars, sickness, boredom—An autobiography 1899-*, Max Heitlinger, Melbourne, 1985.
116   Paul Kraus, *A New Australian, a New Australia*, Federation Press, Sydney, 1994, p. 80.
117   ibid., p. 15.
118   ibid., p. 37.
119   ibid., p. 51.
120   ibid., p. 101.
121   Or so the book suggests. In a recent conversation Paul Kraus told me that in fact Jewishness remains a very important aspect of his identity.
122   Sabiha Abi David Jawary, *Baghdad I Remember*, Makor Jewish Community Library, Melbourne, 2001.
123   Kipen, *A Life to Live*, p. 184.
124   Andor Schwartz, *Living Memory*, Schwartz, Melbourne, 2003, p. 299.
125   Elie Wiesel, 'The Holocaust as Literary Inspiration', in Elliot Lefkovitz (ed.), *Dimensions of the Holocaust*, Northwestern University Press, Evanston, Illinois, 1990, p.9.
126   ibid., p. 8.
127   Just to repeat and elaborate: I use 'Holocaust autobiography' as an umbrella term for all retrospectively composed first-person and purportedly factual Holocaust narratives (i.e. not letters or journals written at the time of the events). This umbrella term includes works that display some of the characteristics often associated with memoir (tendencies to episodic focus and personal reticence), and also texts much given to first-person witnessing, or testimony. Of course in many narratives episodic focus and reticence will naturally accompany the bearing of witness. The umbrella term also embraces what might be called 'full-blown' autobiographical narratives—works that cover a chronological sweep from cradle to grave's edge and are deeply introspective.

I reserve the generic label 'testimony' for narratives which are narrowly focused on bearing witness to traumatic events.

128 On the contexts of 'reception' of various forms of testimony, see Schaffer and Smith, *Human Rights and Narrated Lives*, pp. 6–9.

129 Robert Eaglestone, *The Holocaust and the Postmodern*, Oxford University Press, 2004, p. 191. Eaglestone quotes Cathy Caruth's claim that postmodernism does not deny representation; it only rejects notions of representation that are modelled on those of natural science. One would need to know precisely how this differentiation is made, and whether the postmodern representation Caruth has in mind is entirely distinct from the patterns of observation and interpretation that occur, in so many different forms, in the natural sciences.

130 See for instance *The Norton Anthology of Theory and Criticism*, pp. 1815–76.

131 Richard Freadman and Seamus Miller, *Re-thinking Theory: A critique of contemporary literary theory and an alternative account*, Cambridge University Press, Cambridge, 1995, chapter 5. For a recent alternative account of 'truth' by a major non-Derridean philosopher, see Bernard Williams, *Truth and Truthfulness: An essay in Genealogy*, Princeton University Press, Princeton, 2002.

132 C. A. J. Coady, *Testimony: A philosophical study*, Oxford University Press, Oxford, 1992.

133 Maurice Blanchot, *The Writing of the Disaster*, trans. Ann Smock, University of Nebraska Press, Lincoln, 1986, pp. 20–21.

134 Derrida quoted in Eaglestone, *The Holocaust and the Postmodern*, p. 279.

135 Jacques Derrida, *Without Alibi*, ed. and trans. Peggy Kamuf, Stanford University Press, Stanford, 2002, p. 52.

136 Eaglestone, *The Holocaust and the Postmodern*, p. 2.

137 For a detailed and discerning discussion of Adorno's sometimes shifting views about the Holocaust, see Michael Rothberg, *Traumatic Realism: The demands of Holocaust representation*, University of Minnesota Press, Minneapolis, 2000, pp. 19–58.

138 Dominick LaCapra, *Writing History, Writing Trauma*, Johns Hopkins University Press, Baltimore, 2001, p. 177.

139 Since the trace is by definition beyond definition I will leave it to Robert Eaglestone, a follower of Derrida, to provide a verbal approximation of the concept. See Eaglestone, *The Holocaust and the Postmodern*, p. 287.

140 For an even-handed and recent discussion of Heidegger's relationship with Nazism, see Rüdiger Safranski's *Heidegger: Between good and evil*, trans. Ewald Osers, Harvard University Press, Cambridge, 1998.

141 Eaglestone, *The Holocaust and the Postmodern*, p. 315.

142 Yehuda Bauer, *Rethinking the Holocaust*, Yale University Press, New Haven, 2002, pp. 263–4.

143 James E. Young, 'Interpreting Literary Testimony: A preface to rereading Holocaust diaries and memoirs', *New Literary History*, vol. 18, no. 2, Winter 1987, p. 413.

144 ibid., p. 416.

145 ibid., pp. 416–17.

146 David Rousset, *L'univers concentrationnaire*, Éditions de Minuit, Paris, 1965.

147 Wiesel, 'The Holocaust as Literary Inspiration', p. 7.

148 Andrea Reiter, *Narrating the Holocaust*, trans. Patrick Camiller, Continuum, London, 2000.

149 Alex Colman, *After Forty Years Silence*, Jewish Holocaust Centre, Melbourne, 1990, p. vi.

150 ibid., p. v.

151   Abraham Wajnryb, *They Marched Us Three Nights*: A *journey into freedom*, Jewish Holocaust Centre, Melbourne, 1988, p. 83.

152   Kitia Altman, *Memories of Ordinary People*, p. 312.

153   Stephen A. Mitchell, *Relational Concepts in Psychoanalysis: An integration*, Harvard University Press, Cambridge, 1988, pp. 263–5.

154   Schmul Schwartz, *Under Red Skies: Dreams and reality*, trans. Tania Bruse (Schwartz), Makor Jewish Community Library, Melbourne, 2002, p. 9. This is one of only a few memoirs that recall Stalin's gulags.

155   Lawrence L. Langer, *Holocaust Testimonies: The ruins of memory*, Yale University Press, New Haven, 1991, p. 63.

156   Tzvetan Todorov, *Facing the Extreme: Moral life in the concentration camps*, trans. Arthur Denner and Abigail Pollack, Phoenix, London, 2000, p. 158. In fact, Todorov is best known for early scholarly work which was structuralist in character.

157   ibid., p. 40.

158   Viktor E. Frankl, *Man's Search for Meaning*, Rider, London, 2004, p. 74.

159   ibid., p. 75.

160   Shoshana Felman and Dori Laub, *Testimony: Crises of witnessing in literature, psychoanalysis, and history*, Routledge, New York, 1992, p. 72.

161   Guta Goldstein, *There Will Be Tomorrow*, Makor Jewish Community Library, Melbourne, 1999, p. 17.

162   ibid., p. 165.

163   Rothberg, *Traumatic Realism*, p. 140.

164   ibid., p. 100.

165   ibid., p. 108.

166   Saul Friedlander, *Probing the Limits of Representation: Nazism and the 'final solution'*, Harvard University Press, Cambridge, 1992.

167   His cover features a drawing by Art Spiegelman, son of a survivor and author of the famous cartoon narrative of his father's Holocaust experience, *Maus*. The drawing contains three artistic styles: in the foreground a mouse, representative of his father as Nazi victim, is drawn in a realistic manner; holding the mouse is a self-image of the artist, drawn in the semi-realistic medium of the *Maus* narrative; behind him is a pure cartoon image of Mickey Mouse. Each level represents a different register of Holocaust representation. For Rothberg the drawing is exemplary in that it invites us to both identify and limit identification, so that we're aware not just of what is being presented to us but of *how* it is being done—all the way along a spectrum of representation that runs from realism to the mass-market cartoon.

168   Eaglestone, *The Holocaust and the Postmodern*, p. 4.

169   ibid., p. 43.

170   Young, 'Interpreting Literary Testimony', p. 410.

171   Coady, *Testimony*, p. 149.

172   David George Gilbert, *The Lights and Darkness of My Being: My life story as a survivor*, Vantage, New York, 1991, pp. 52–3.

173   Alexander Nehamas, *Nietzsche: Life as literature*, Harvard University Press, Cambridge, 1985, p. 49.

174   Terrence Des Pres, *The Survivor: An anatomy of life in the death camps*, Oxford University Press, New York, 1976.

175   Bauer, *Rethinking the Holocaust*, p. 67.

176   Jacques Derrida, *Writing and Difference*, trans. Alan Bass, Routledge and Kegan Paul, London, 1978, pp. 282–3.

177   Todorov, *Facing the Extreme*, p. 39.

178   ibid., p. 40.

179   Des Pres, *The Survivor*, p. 37.

180   ibid., p. 35.

181   ibid., p. vii.

182   Eaglestone, *The Holocaust and the Postmodern*, p. 337.

183   Langer, *Holocaust Testimonies*, p. xiv.

184   ibid., p. xi.

185   See his major study, *Sources of the Self: The making of the modern identity*, Cambridge University Press, Cambridge, 1989.

186   Langer, *Holocaust Testimonies*, p. 193.

187   ibid., p. 199.

188   See LaCapra, *Writing History, Writing Trauma*, pp. 79–80. On trauma and autobiography see also Leigh Gilmore, *The Limits of Autobiography*, and Suzette A. Henke, *Shattered Subjects: Trauma and testimony in women's life-writing*, St Martin's Press, New York, 1998.

189   Cathy Caruth, *Unclaimed Experience: Trauma, narrative, and history*, Johns Hopkins University Press, Baltimore, 1996.

190   Schaffer and Smith point out that the notion of 'trauma' that dominates this field is a 'Western trope of trauma' which is not appropriate to all cultural contexts. See *Human Rights and Narrated Lives*, p. 23.

191   Felman and Laub, *Testimony*, p. 57.

192   See Freud's discussion of trauma in *Beyond the Pleasure Principle*, trans. James Strachey, Bantam, New York, 1967, pp. 28–47.

193   Wajnryb, *They Marched Us Three Nights*, p. 73.

194   Felman and Laub, *Testimony*, pp. 81–2.

195   Martin Buber, *I and Thou*, trans. Walter Kaufmann, T&T Clark, Edinburgh, 1970.

196   Felman and Laub, *Testimony*, p. 69.

197   ibid., p. 62.

198   Samuel Pisar, *Of Blood and Hope*, Cassell, London, 1980, pp. 55–7.

199   Gilbert, *The Lights and Darkness of My Being*, p. 38.

200   Jacob G. Rosenberg, *Sunrise West*, Brandl & Schlesinger, Blackheath (NSW), 2007, p. 147.

201   Lenke Arnstein, *Recurring Dreams*, Makor Jewish Community Library, Melbourne, 2002, p. iii.

202   Coady, *Testimony*, p. 30.

203   Several authors in Kathy Grinblat's *Children of the Shadows* discuss such feelings.

204   Jacob G. Rosenberg, *East of Time*, Brandl & Schlesinger, Blackheath (NSW), 2005; hereafter cited in the text as *EOT*, followed by the page-number.

205   Jacob G. Rosenberg, *Sunrise West*, Brandl & Schlesinger, Blackheath (NSW), 2007; hereafter cited as *SW*, followed by the page-number.

206   For what is still one of the best introductions to literature, and a fine anthology of Yiddish writing, see Irving Howe and Eliezer Greenberg (eds), *A Treasury of Yiddish Stories*, André Deutsch, New York, 1955. See also Irving Howe's classic study, *The World of Our Fathers: The journey of the East European Jews to America and the life they found and made*, Harcourt Brace Jovanovich, New York, 1976.

207   Jacob Rosenberg in interview with Richard Freadman, 20 Feb. 2006.

208   Solomon Maimon, *An Autobiography*, trans. J. Clark Murray, University of Illinois Press, Chicago, 2001.

209 Jacob G. Rosenberg, *Twilight Whisper*, Focus Words, Melbourne, 1997, p. 41.

210 Mary Besemeres, *Translating One's Self*. For a discussion of Besemeres's notion of translation, see pp. 9–35 in that work.

211 I've opted for the term 'vignettes' to denote the short narrative chapters that comprise both *East of Time* and *Sunrise West*.

212 This phrase seems to have been employed first by Van Wyck Brooks, 'On Creating a Usable Past,' *Dial* 64, 1918, pp. 337–41. There has been a good deal of recent debate as to whether Holocaust experience is in fact 'usable'. See for example the relatively sanguine view expressed in David G. Roskies, *The Jewish Search for a Usable Past*, Indiana University Press, Bloomington, 1999.

213 See Grinblat, *Children of the Shadows*.

214 Jacob G. Rosenberg, *Behind the Moon*, Five Islands Press, Wollongong, 2000, p. 34.

215 In conversation with the author, Sep. 2005.

216 Bruno Bettelheim, *The Uses of Enchantment: The meaning and importance of fairy tales*, Penguin, Harmondsworth, 1978.

217 Jacob G. Rosenberg, *Lives and Embers*, Brandl & Schlesinger, Blackheath (NSW), 2003, p. 75.

218 See the discussion of Koestler in my *Threads of Life: Autobiography and the will*, University of Chicago Press, Chicago, 2001, chapter 6.

219 Langer, *Holocaust Testimonies*, p. 121 ff.

220 Lipek was the brother of Abraham Biderman, whose distinguished autobiography, *The World of My Past*, includes a detailed account of Lipek's life and death.

221 Jacob G. Rosenberg, *My Father's Silence*, Focus, Melbourne, 1994, p. 40.

222 Rosenberg, *Lives and Embers*, p. 137.

223 Richard Freadman, 'Decency and its Discontents', *Philosophy and Literature*, vol. 28, no. 2, Oct. 2004, pp. 393–405. I also discuss the Australian ethos of decency in my memoir, *Shadow of Doubt: My father and myself*, Bystander Press, Melbourne, 2003.

224 David Hume, *A Treatise of Human Nature*, Oxford University Press, Oxford, 1978, p. 417.

225 On this and other aspects of decency, see John Kekes, *Moral Tradition and Individuality*, Princeton University Press, Princeton, 1989.

226 David Martin, *My Strange Friend*, Picador, Sydney, 1991, p. 98; hereafter cited in the text with page-numbers only.

227 The term is from John Barbour. See his *Versions of Deconversion: Autobiography and the loss of faith*, University of Virginia Press, Charlottesville, 1994.

228 St Augustine, *Confessions*, trans. R. S. Pine-Coffin, Penguin, Harmondsworth, 1961.

229 Jean-Jacques Rousseau, *The Confessions of Jean-Jacques Rousseau*, trans. J. M. Cohen, Penguin, Harmondsworth, 1960, p. 122.

230 ibid., p. 17.

231 ibid., p. 25.

232 Richard Crossman (ed.), *The God that Failed: Six studies in communism*, Hamish Hamilton, London, 1950.

233 Stephen Spender, *World within World: The autobiography of Stephen Spender*, St Martin's Press, New York, 1994.

234 See the discussion of this sub-genre, and of Koestler and Spender in particular, in my *Threads of Life: Autobiography and the will*.

235 Andrew Riemer, *Inside Outside*, Angus & Robertson, Sydney, 1992, p. 195; hereafter cited as *IO*.

236 For a detailed, if also at times tendentious, treatment of Koestler's relationship to

Judaism, see David Cesarani, *Arthur Koestler: The homeless mind*, Heinemann, London, 1998. The most detailed account of Koestler as an autobiographer appears in my *Threads of Life*.

237 For other discussions, see David McCooey, *Artful Histories: Modern Australian autobiography*, Cambridge University Press, Melbourne, 1996; Rosamund Dalziell, *Shameful Autobiographies: Shame in contemporary Australian autobiography and culture*, Melbourne University Press, Melbourne, 1999; and Mary Besemeres, *Translating One's Self: Language and selfhood in cross-cultural autobiography*, Peter Lang, Oxford, 2002.

238 Andrew Riemer, *The Habsburg Café*, Angus & Robertson, Sydney, 1993, p. 270; hereafter cited as *HC*.

239 Andrew Riemer, *Sandstone Gothic: Confessions of an accidental academic*, Allen & Unwin, Sydney, 1998, p. 184; hereafter cited as *SG*.

240 By 'autobiographical consciousness' I mean not only the consciousness that crafts and is revealed in a written autobiography, but also the synthesizing 'acts' of recollection and self-constitution that we all engage in, whether we write autobiography or not.

241 Andrew Riemer, *America with Subtitles*, Minerva, Melbourne, 1995, p. 319; hereafter cited as *AS*.

242 Andrew Riemer, *The Demidenko Debate*, Allen & Unwin, Sydney, 1996, pp. 104–5.

243 For a discussion of Goldberg's career and work see Richard Freadman, 'The Quest for the Classical Temper: The literary criticism of S. L. Goldberg', *Critical Review*, no. 32, 1992, pp. 46–66.

244 See for example Terry Collits, 'Sydney Revisited: Literary struggles in Australia (circa 1965 and ongoing)', *Australian Book Review*, no. 210, May 1999, pp. 23–8; and John Wiltshire, 'Fault Lines' (review of *Sandstone Gothic*), *Eureka Street*, vol. 10, no. 8, Dec. 1998, pp. 38–42. Riemer's characterizations of Goldberg are confronting indeed, given that both were Jews: Goldberg is said to have engendered an environment reminiscent in some respects of 'totalitarianism' [*SG*, 153]; to have been hell-bent on building a 'New Jerusalem' [163]; and to have brought to Sydney a Leavis-like religious 'fundamentalism in cultural matters' [118, 136]. I should make my own stake in these discussions clear. I knew Sam Goldberg during the last decade of his life. I found him to be a loyal and solicitous friend, and a remarkably sophisticated intellect—one of the finest I have known. Though I never worked in a department with him, and so did not see him under the pressures that departmental life can produce, I was aware that he was in some respects a deeply troubled man, and that his behaviour towards those he did not esteem could be disrespectful, even destructive. I do not therefore entirely discount Andrew Riemer's treatment of the Sydney split, but I am persuaded that it is unfair in certain important respects, and I would have liked to have seen it published during Goldberg's lifetime so that he could have had the opportunity to reply.

245 Riemer, *The Demidenko Debate*, p. 131.

246 Arthur Koestler, *The Invisible Writing: The second volume of an autobiography: 1932–40*, Stein and Day, New York, 1984, p. 358.

247 ibid., p. 193.

248 Riemer, *The Demidenko Debate*, p. 94.

249 Susan Varga, *Heddy and Me*, Penguin, Melbourne, 1994; hereafter cited in the text with page-numbers only. My thanks to my La Trobe colleagues Philipa Rothfield and Kay Souter for the help with attachment theory, and to Kay for reminding me of the Celan poem.

250 Riemer, *The Habsburg Café*, p. 275.

251   Arnold Zable, *Jewels and Ashes*, Scribe, Melbourne, 1991, p. 45.

252   Others that feature mother–daughter relationships include Anna Rosner Blay, *Sister, Sister*; Helen Max, *Searching for Yesterday*; and Lucy Gould, *Empty Corners*.

253   For discussions of relational life-writing see references above, and Paul John Eakin, *How Our Lives Become Stories*. For an excellent study of autobiographical narratives of Australian women's childhood, see Joy Hooton, *Stories of Herself When Young: Autobiographies of childhood by Australian women*, Oxford University Press, Melbourne, 1990. See also Stone Center, *Women's Growth in Connection: Writings from the Stone Center*, Guilford Press, New York, 1991.

254   Rita Huggins and Jackie Huggins, *Auntie Rita*, Aboriginal Studies Press, Canberra, 1994.

255   ibid., p. 4.

256   Melanie Klein, *The Selected Melanie Klein*, ed. Juliet Mitchell, Penguin, London, 1991, p. 180.

257   Paul Celan, *Selected Poems and Prose of Paul Celan*, trans. John Felstiner, W. W. Norton, New York, 2001, p. 31.

258   On attachment theory see for example John Bowlby, *Child Care and the Growth of Love*, Penguin, Harmondsworth, 1993; Daniel N. Stern, *The Interpersonal World of the Infant: A view from psychoanalysis and developmental psychology*, Basic Books, New York, 1985; Jude Cassidy and Phillip R. Shaver (eds), *Handbook of Attachment: Theory, research, and clinical applications*, Guildford, London, 1999.

259   Stern, *The Interpersonal World of the Infant*, p. 262.

260   See Frankl, *Man's Search for Meaning*, p. 74.

261   Mark Raphael Baker, *The Fiftieth Gate: A journey through memory*, Flamingo, Sydney, 1991; hereafter cited in the text with page-numbers only.

262   T. S. Eliot, *Four Quartets*, Faber & Faber, London, 1944, pp. 13–14.

263   Art Spiegelman, *Maus: A survivor's tale*, Penguin, London, 2003, p. 296.

264   LaCapra, *Writing History, Writing Trauma*, p. 23.

265   Emmanuel Levinas, *Totality and Infinity*, trans. Alphonso Lingis, Kluwer Academic Publishers, Dordrecht (Netherlands), 1991, p. 239.

266   Especially Kitia Altman, *Memories of Ordinary People*; Anna Rosner Blay, *Sister, Sister*; Morris Lurie, *Whole Life*, Penguin, Melbourne, 1987; Jacob G. Rosenberg, *East of Time* and *Sunrise West*.

267   See the splendidly long list of terrors in Diana Trilling, *The Beginning of the Journey: The marriage of Diana and Lionel Trilling*, Harcourt Brace, New York, 1993, pp. 3–4.

268   Lily Brett, *What God Wants*, University of Queensland Press, Brisbane, 1992, p. 87.

269   Doris Brett, *Eating the Underworld: A memoir in three voices*, Vintage, Sydney, 2001; hereafter cited as *ETU*.

270   Lily Brett, *In Full View: Essays by Lily Brett*, Picador, Sydney, 1997, p. 294.

271   See, for instance, the sisters' different versions of the short haircuts they were given as children (*In Full View*, p. 166; *Eating the Underworld*, p, 365).

272   Lily Brett, *The Auschwitz Poems*, Scribe, Melbourne, 1986, p. 137.

273   Lily Brett, *In Full View*, p. 347.

274   My focus here is ethical rather than psychological. For detailed psychoanalytic readings of Lily Brett's relationship to her mother, the Holocaust and other matters, see Esther Faye, 'Impossible Memories: Lily Brett as essayist', *Meridian*, 17:1, May 1978, pp. 63–73; and '"Enjoying traumatically": The Holocaust as "the second generation's other"', *British Journal of Psychotherapy*, 16:2, 1999, pp. 184–96.

275   Philippe Lejeune, *On Autobiography*, ed. Paul John Eakin, trans. Katherine Leary, University of Minnesota Press, Minneapolis, 1989, p. 22.

276 Talk of pacts, contracts and the like leads to complex philosophical territory. Do pacts lock participants into invariable conditions, or do they function more like Wittgensteinian 'games', evolving in complex contexts of use and revision? Pacts require an embedded convention governing the giving of certain sorts of undertakings, a convention independent of any particular undertaking; they also need a set of associated rules—for instance, fairness—that enable judgments about whether undertakings have been honoured. (On such rules, see John Rawles, *A Theory of Justice*, Oxford University Press, Oxford, 1973, pp. 342–50.) Importantly, the practice of pact-making has to be learnt, and this must be done principally by example. There must be individuals who are cognizant of the conventions, rules and practices associated with and intrinsic to pact-making, and who enter with some degree of deliberative freedom into pacts. (Forced compliance does not constitute committing to a pact.) Unlike promises, pacts need to be, at least implicitly, reciprocal: we can promise without expecting anything in return, but the obligations of a pact are mutually binding.

277 See pp. 10–11 in this book.

278 Coady, *Testimony*, p. i.

279 *In Full View* is described on the title-page as *Essays by Lily Brett*, but the perpendicular pronoun is extremely prominent, and the constituent chapters clearly present as autobiographical essays.

280 Details of the titles just mentioned are: *Things Could Be Worse*, Meanjin/Melbourne University Press, Melbourne, 1990; *Just Like That*, Picador, Sydney, 1995; *Too Many Men*, Picador, Sydney, 1999; *You Gotta Have Balls*, Picador, Sydney, 2005; *New York*, Picador, Sydney, 2001; *Between Mexico and Poland*, Picador, Sydney, 2002.

281 *Just Like That*, p. 171.

282 ibid., p. 315.

283 A point noted in David Bernstein's review of *In Full View*, in *Australian Jewish News*, 12 Sep. 1997.

284 *In Full View*, p. 290.

285 ibid., p. 98. Doris disputes the veracity of this memory [*ETU*, 250].

286 *New York*, p. 146.

287 *Things Could Be Worse*, p. 118.

288 *What God Wants*, p. 14.

289 *Just Like That*, p. 9.

290 *Things Could Be Worse*, p. 133.

291 *Just Like That*, p. 1.

292 Guilt, dismay or ambivalence on the part of women who feel that they have had too many men goes way back in Brett's work, as when Ella in *What God Wants* knows that her parents are ashamed of her having had 'too many husbands' (*What God Wants*, p. 101).

293 For further discussion of this ethos see my memoir, *Shadow of Doubt: My father and myself*.

294 Arnold Zable, *Jewels and Ashes*, Scribe, Melbourne, 1991, p. 163; hereafter cited as *JA*.

295 Arnold Zable, *Cafe Scheherazade*, Text, Melbourne, 2001, p. 59.

296 George Eliot, *Middlemarch*, Oxford University Press, Oxford, 1997, p. 132.

297 See for example Arnold Zable, 'In Search of Refuge: Two tales', *The Best Australian Essays 2001*, ed. Peter Craven, Black Inc., Melbourne, 2001.

298 Arnold Zable, Imagining the Immigrant Experience, PhD thesis, University of Melbourne, 2006.

299 ibid., pp. 30–31.

300 ibid., p. 28.

301 Arnold Zable, *The Fig Tree*, Text, Melbourne, 2003, p. 166; hereafter cited as *FT*.
302 Martin Buber (ed.), *Tales of the Hasidim*, Schocken, New York, 1991, Book One, p. 216.
303 ibid., p. 107.
304 ibid., p. 239.
305 ibid., p. 253.
306 Rabbi Sholom Dovber Schneersohn, *Tract on Prayer*, trans. Y. E. Danzinger, Kehot Publication Society, New York, 1992, p. 14.
307 Arnold Zable, *Scraps of Heaven*, Text, Melbourne, 2004, p. 185; hereafter cited as *SH*.
308 Zable, *Cafe Scheherazade*, p. 149.
309 Arnold Zable, *Wanderers and Dreamers: Tales of the David Herman Theatre*, Hyland House, Melbourne, 1998, p. 53.
310 Arnold Zable, 'The Walker', unpublished performance piece.
311 Charles Taylor, 'The Politics of Recognition', in Amy Gutman (ed.), *Multiculturalism: Examining the politics of recognition*, Princeton University Press, Princeton, 1994, p. 41.
312 ibid., p. 45.
313 ibid., p. 38.
314 ibid., p. 72.
315 Zable, *Cafe Scheherazade*, p. 167.
316 ibid., p. 218.
317 Unpublished interview with the author, Sep. 2004.
318 Zable, Imagining the Immigrant Experience, p. 26.
319 Eva Hoffman, *Shtetl: The life and death of a small town and the world of Polish Jews*, Secker & Warburg, London, 1998, p. 12.
320 ibid., p. 11.
321 Unpublished interview with the author, Sep. 2004.
322 Zable, Imagining the Immigrant Experience, p. 4.
323 Werner Sollors (ed.), *The Invention of Ethnicity*, Oxford University Press, Oxford, 1989, p. ix.
324 *Australian Jewish News*, 30 January 1998, p. 5.
325 A somewhat similar project has now been established in Sydney: the Sydney Jewish Museum's 'Community Stories' program.
326 This comment was made during a meeting I had with the project facilitators in July 2003. Julie Meadows could not be present but I spoke with her a few days later.
327 Julie Meadows (ed.), *Memory Guide My Hand: An anthology of autobiographical writing by members of the Melbourne Jewish Community*, Makor Jewish Community Library, Melbourne—vol. 1, 1998; vol. 2, 2000; vol. 3, 2005.
328 Vera Schreiber, *The Porcelain Doll*, Makor Jewish Community Library, Melbourne, 2000, p. 7.
329 Kitia Altman, *Memories of Ordinary People*, Makor Jewish Community Library, Melbourne, 2003.
330 ibid., p. 402.
331 ibid., p. 404.
332 ibid.
333 Julie reported these responses to me in a set of emailed notes, 13 July 2003.
334 Sydney Benjamin, *A Full House: The fascinating autobiography by Sydney A. B. Benjamin*, Makor Jewish Community Library, Melbourne, 2000; Bernard Boas, *The Five Books of Boas: The autobiography of Bernard A. Boas, OAM*, Makor Jewish Community Library, Melbourne, 2001.

335 Benjamin, *A Full House*, p. 273.

336 Boas, *The Five Books of Boas*, p. 92.

337 Garry Fabian, *A Look Back over My Shoulder*, Makor Jewish Community Library, Melbourne, 2002, p. 1.

338 Freda Searle, *Memory's Wings and Apron Strings*, Makor Jewish Community Library, Melbourne, 2000.

339 A striking recent, albeit non-Makor, exception to this pattern is Peter Singer's *Pushing Time Away: My grandfather and the tragedy of Jewish Vienna*, Granta, London, 2003. Singer's grandfather, David Oppenheim, was a Classics scholar who knew Freud.

340 Abraham Biderman, *The World of My Past*, Random House, Sydney, 1996. The quotation is from a conversation I had with Biderman in 2001.

341 One of the early and important books to highlight this distinction was Estelle Jelinek (ed.), *Women's Autobiography: Essays in criticism*, Indiana University Press, Bloomington, 1980.

342 Lucy Gould, *Empty Corners*, Makor Jewish Community Library, Melbourne, 2000.

343 Paulette Goldberg, *Just Think It Never Happened*, Makor Jewish Community Library, Melbourne, 2002, p. 104.

344 Helen Gardner, *My Mother's Child*, Makor Jewish Community Library, Melbourne, 2001.

345 ibid., p. 163.

346 Hania Ajzner, *Hania's War*, Makor Jewish Community Library, Melbourne, 2000, p. 29.

347 Guta Goldstein, *There Will Be Tomorrow*, Makor Jewish Community Library, Melbourne, 1999, p. 166.

348 Moshe and Stefa Robin, *Stepping into Life*, Makor Jewish Community Library, Melbourne, 2002, p. 147.

349 Helen Max, *Searching for Yesterday: A photographic essay about my mother, a Holocaust survivor*, Makor Jewish Community Library, Melbourne, 2001.

350 For a good survey, see David W. Minar and Scott Greer (eds), *The Concept of Community: Readings with interpretations*, Aldine, Chicago, 1969.

351 I explore this proposition at length in my *Threads of Life: Autobiography and the will*.

Bibliography

Australian Primary Texts

Works cited and/or represented in detailed statistical analyses in Part One.

Aarons, Eric, *What's Left?: Memoirs of an Australian communist*, Penguin, Melbourne, 1993.

Ajzenbud, Moshe, *The Commissar Took Care*, trans. Leah Ajzenbud, Globe Press, Melbourne, 1986.

Ajzner, Hania, *Hania's War*, Makor Jewish Community Library, Melbourne, 2000.

Alcorso, Claudio, *The Wind You Say*, Angus & Robertson, Sydney, 1993.

Altman, Dennis, *Defying Gravity: A political life*, Allen & Unwin, Sydney, 1997.

Altman, Kitia, *Memories of Ordinary People: For those who have no one to remember them*, Makor Jewish Community Library, Melbourne, 2003.

Armstrong, Diane, *Mosaic: A chronicle of five generations*, Random House, Sydney, 1998.

——, *The Voyage of Their Life: The story of the SS* Derna *and its passengers*, Flamingo, Sydney, 2001.

Arnstein, Lenke, *Recurring Dreams*, Makor Jewish Community Library, Melbourne, 2002.

Atlas, Zygfryd, *Just One Life*, Rocham, Melbourne, 1999.

Baker, Mark Raphael, *The Fiftieth Gate: A journey through memory*, Flamingo, Sydney, 1997.

Barac, Barbara, *Escape from Destiny*, Jewish Holocaust Centre, Melbourne, 1990.

Barnett, Mel, *Arnarf Good f'r a Dalston Boy*, Makor Jewish Community Library, Melbourne, 2004.

Bauer, Agi L., *'Black' Becomes a Rainbow: The mother of a Baal Teshuvah tells her story*, Feldheim Publishers, New York, 1991.

Beckwith, Doreen, *Full Circle: The story of a chained woman*, Makor Jewish Community Library, Melbourne, 2004.

Behmoiras, Josiane, *Dora B: A memoir of my mother*, Viking, Melbourne, 2005.

Belair, Alida, *Out of Step: A dancer reflects*, Melbourne University Press, Melbourne, 1993.

Benjamin, Sydney A. B., *A Full House: The fascinating autobiography by Sydney A. B. Benjamin*, Makor Jewish Community Library, Melbourne, 2000.

Bennett, Feige-Rachel, *Dos Iz Mayn Lebn* (*This Is My Life*), York, Melbourne, 1975.

Bennett, Shmuel, *Chronicles of a Life*, Shmuel Bennett, Melbourne, 1999.

Berk, Leon, *Destined to Live: Memoirs of a doctor with the Russian partisans*, Paragon Press, Melbourne, 1992.

Biderman, Abraham H., *The World of My Past*, Random House, Sydney, 1996.

Bierzynski Burnett, Ignacy, *My Life and My Struggle*, Vit Publishing, Sydney, 1996.

Blay, Anna Rosner, '*If All the Seas Were Ink…*': *Memoirs of Jozef Gross, a 'Schindler's List' survivor*, After Hours Computer Services, Melbourne, 1993.

——, *Sister, Sister*, Hale & Iremonger, Sydney, 1998.

——, *Not Paradise: Four women's journeys beyond survival*, Hybrid, Melbourne, 2004.

Boas, Bernard A., *The Five Books of Boas: The autobiography of Bernard A. Boas, OAM*, Makor Jewish Community Library, Melbourne, 2001.

Bornstein, Zelman, *A Leaf on the Diaspora Tree*, Zelman Bornstein, Melbourne, 1994.

Brasch, Rudolph, *Reminiscences of a Roving Rabbi*, Angus & Robertson, Sydney, 1998.

Braun, Emil, *Into the Light*, Emil Braun, Melbourne, 2000.

Brett, Doris, *Eating the Underworld: A memoir in three voices*, Vintage, Sydney, 2001.

Brett, Lily, *The Auschwitz Poems*, Scribe, Melbourne, 1986.

——, *Poland and Other Poems*, Scribe, Melbourne, 1987.

——, *Things Could Be Worse*, Meanjin/Melbourne University Press, Melbourne, 1990.

——, *What God Wants*, University of Queensland Press, Brisbane, 1992.

——, *Just Like That*, Picador, Sydney, 1995.

——, *In Full View: Essays by Lily Brett*, Picador, Sydney, 1997.

——, *Too Many Men*, Picador, Sydney, 2000.

——, *New York*, Picador, Sydney, 2001.

——, *Between Mexico and Poland*, Picador, Sydney, 2002.

——, *You Gotta Have Balls*, Picador, Sydney, 2005.

Bruell, Anna, *Autumn in Springtime*, Anna Bruell, Melbourne, 1995.

Buckner, Ille, *Starts and Pauses*, Makor Jewish Community Library, Melbourne, 2002.

Cargher, John, *Luck Was My Lady*, Brolga Publishing, Melbourne, 1996.

Celemenski, Jacob, *Elegy for My People: Memoirs of an underground courier of the Jewish labor Bund in Nazi-occupied Poland 1939–45*, trans. Gershon Freidlin, Jacob Celemenski Trust, Melbourne, 2000.

Censor, Maria, *Letters to My Mother*, Makor Jewish Community Library, Melbourne, 2000.

Cherny, Sylvia, *Who Is Sylvia?*, Makor Jewish Community Library, Melbourne 2004.

Cohen, Louis, *Just for the Record*, Louis Cohen, Melbourne, 2000.

Colman, Alex, *After Forty Years Silence*, Jewish Holocaust Centre, Melbourne, 1990.

Cooper, Leo, *Stakhanovites—and Others: The story of a worker in the Soviet Union 1939–1946*, Hudson, Melbourne, 1994.

——, *The Long Road to the Lucky Country*, Makor Jewish Community Library, Melbourne, 2005.

Cowen, Zelman, *A Public Life: The memoirs of Zelman Cowen*, Melbourne University Press, Melbourne, 2006.

Cukierman, Doba-Necha, *A Guardian Angel: Memories of Lublin*, Ester Csaky, Melbourne, 1997.

Cyran, Henry B., *Inside Auschwitz, written in blood: A personal memory*, Child & Henry, Sydney, 1984.

Cytrynowski, Itzhak, *'And I Will Remember My Covenant…'*, A. Cytrynowski, Melbourne, 1988.

Dalton, Robin, *An Incidental Memoir*, Viking, Melbourne, 1998.

——, *Aunts Up the Cross*, Viking, Melbourne, 1998.

D'Aprano, Zelda, *Zelda*, Spinifex, Melbourne, 1995.

David, Janina, *A Touch of Earth: A wartime childhood*, Hutchinson, London, 1966.

——, *A Square of Sky* and *A Touch of Earth: A wartime childhood in Poland*, Penguin, New York, 1981.

Dreyfus, George, *The Last Frivolous Book*, Hale & Iremonger, Sydney, 1984.

Dror, Tamar, *A Green Parrot*, Kitia Altman, Sydney, 1999.

Eidelson, Meyer, *Books, Tanks & Radios: Stories from a family of survivors*, Makor Jewish Community Library, Melbourne, 2003.

Eisfelder, Horst 'Peter', *Chinese Exile: My years in Shanghai and Nanking*, Makor Jewish Community Library, Melbourne, 2003.

Elton (Elbaum), Zyga, *Destination Buchara*, Dizal, Melbourne, 1996.

Engelman, Matylda, *The End of the Journey*, Lantana, Melbourne, 1978.

Epstein, June, *Woman with Two Hats*, Hyland House, Melbourne, 1988.

Erlanger, Arnold, *Choose Life*, Makor Jewish Community Library, Melbourne, 2003.

Exiner, Robert, 'From the Spree to the Yarra: Memories of an emigration', *Australian Jewish Historical Society Journal*, vol. XII, part 3, Nov. 1994, pp. 536–58.

Fabian, Garry, *A Look Back over My Shoulder*, Makor Jewish Community Library, Melbourne, 2002.

Falk, Barbara, *No Other Home: An Anglo-Jewish story 1833–1987*, Penguin, Melbourne, 1988.

Ferster, Stanley, *My Refugee Years: 1939–1949*, Stanley Ferster, Sydney, 1982.

Firestone, Lucyna, *Aby Dalej (Just Keep Going)*, Andrew Firestone, Melbourne, 2005.

Fisher, Mary, 'Broken Biscuits', *Melbourne Chronicle*, no. 65, 1995, pp. 19–20.

Fisher, Myra, *Cossacks, Cockneys & Colonials*, Makor Jewish Community Library, Melbourne, 2002.

Frankel, Jacob, 'The Life of Jacob Frankel', *Australian Jewish Historical Society Journal*, vol. VXIII, part 3, Nov. 1996, pp. 395–412.

Fransman, Harry, *The Devil's Greed: Twelve million eyes and trillions of tears*, Harry Fransman, Sydney, 2000.

Freadman, Richard, *Shadow of Doubt: My father and myself*, Bystander Press, Melbourne, 2003.

Freilich, Max, *Zion in Our Time: Memoirs of an Australian Zionist*, Morgan Publications, Sydney, 1967.

Frenkel, Anna, 'Two Trips in Time' (part 1), *Melbourne Chronicle*, no. 63, 1993, pp. 33–7.

——, 'Two Trips in Time' (part 2), *Melbourne Chronicle*, no. 64, 1994, pp. 11–15.

Friedmann, Jakob, *Reluctant Soldier: A Jewish partisan's story*, Makor Jewish Community Library, Melbourne, 2005.

Friend, John, *Out of Darkness*, John Friend, Melbourne, 1998.

Friesová, Jana Renée, *Fortress of My Youth: Memoir of a Terezín survivor*, trans. Elinor Morrisby and Ladislav Rosendorf, Telador, Hobart, 1996.

Frydman, Gloria, *Poles Apart*, River Seine Publications, Melbourne, 1984.

Gaida, Jack, *This Is My Story*, Jack Gaida, Melbourne, 1985.

Gardner, Helen, *My Mother's Child*, Makor Jewish Community Library, Melbourne, 2001.

Gentilli, Joseph, 'Tracks along the Way: Thoughts and views from my life', *Australian Jewish Historical Society Journal*, vol. XI, part 1, 1990, pp. 93–127.

Gilbert, David George, *The Lights and Darkness of My Being: My life story as a survivor*, Vantage Press, New York, 1991.

Ginzburg, George, *A Will to Live: A story about hope and the strength of the human spirit*, Makor Jewish Community Library, Melbourne, 2003.

Glas-Wiener, Sheva, *Children of the Ghetto*, Globe Press, Melbourne, 1983.

Gluck, Catherine, *The Girl with Long Hair*, Catherine Gluck, Sydney, 1992.

Goldberg, Luba, *A Sparkle of Hope*, Luba Goldberg, Melbourne, 1998.

Goldberg, Paulette, *Just Think It Never Happened*, Makor Jewish Community Library, Melbourne, 2002.

Goldrei, Naomi, *The Champions of My Childhood*, Makor Jewish Community Library, Melbourne, 2003.

Goldsmith, Andrea, 'Childhood Deceits', *Westerly*, vol. 34, no. 3, Sep. 1989, pp. 35–40.

Goldstein, Guta, *There Will Be Tomorrow*, Makor Jewish Community Library, Melbourne, 1999.

Goodman, Philip, *And Thereby Hangs a Tale: A general practitioner's day & Myself when young*, Philip Goodman, Melbourne, 1994.

Gould, Lucy, *Empty Corners: A memoir*, Makor Jewish Community Library, Melbourne, 2000.

Goulston, Wendy, 'Coming into One's Own: Emergence from an Australian Jewish girlhood' (part 1), *Melbourne Chronicle*, no. 62, 1992, pp. 3–10.

——, 'Coming into One's Own: Emergence from an Australian Jewish girlhood' (part 2), *Melbourne Chronicle*, no. 63, 1993, pp. 19–26.

Gryff, Felix, *Red Hell*, Felix Gryff, Sydney, 1997.

Gunsberger, Otto, *Choice of Profession: Message from a survivor to the succeeding generations*, Nustyle, Melbourne, 1990.

——, *Came from Central Europe and Other Stories*, Nustyle, Melbourne, 1991.

——, *Oldman's Story*, Otto Gunsberger, Melbourne, 1995.

——, *Difficulties of Remembering: Reflections about an exhibition*, Otto Gunsberger, Melbourne, 1997.

Haberfeld, Lusia, *Lauferin: The runner of Birkenau*, Makor Jewish Community Library, Melbourne, 2002.

Halpern, F. H., *Prisoner of the British: Diary of a suspected war spy*, F. H. Halpern, Melbourne, 1991.

——, *Journey's End: Full circle*, F. H. Halpern, Melbourne, 1994.

——, *The Final Chapter: Five minutes past mid-nite*, F. H. Halpern, Melbourne, 1997.

Harari, Mayer, *Second Exodus: An autobiography*, Makor Jewish Community Library, Melbourne, 1999.

Heitlinger, Max, *In the Nick of Time: Escape from Nazis, wars, sickness, boredom— An autobiography 1899–*, Max Heitlinger, Melbourne, 1985.

Hirschbein, Peretz, 'Australia', trans. Serge Liberman, *Melbourne Chronicle*, no. 6, 1990–91, pp. 53–7.

Hoffman, Maurie, *Keep Yelling: A survivor's testimony*, Spectrum, Melbourne, 1995.

Holkner, Jean, *Taking the Chook: And other traumas of growing up*, Puffin, Melbourne, 1987.

Honigman, Ben, *Upon God's Mercy*, Ben Honigman, Melbourne, 1997.

Horak, Olga, *Auschwitz to Australia: A Holocaust survivor's memoir*, Kangaroo Press, Sydney, 2000.

Houbein, Lolo, *Wrong Face in the Mirror: An autobiography of race and identity*, University of Queensland Press, Brisbane, 1990.

Hymans, Robert, *Treasures from the Attic*, Robert Hymans, Wodonga (Vic.), 1994.

Inglis, Amirah, *Amirah: An un-Australian childhood*, Heinemann, Melbourne, 1983.

——, *The Hammer & Sickle and the Washing Up: Memories of an Australian woman communist*, Hyland House, Melbourne, 1995.

Ingram, Bernard Hellreich, *Unfinished Symphony*, B. R. Ingram, Newcastle, 1992.

Janowski, Niusia, *A Life Apart*, trans. Kitia Altman, Daniel Lewkovitz/Jewish Holocaust Centre, Melbourne, 1993.

Jawary, Sabiha Abi David, *Baghdad I Remember*, Makor Jewish Community Library, Melbourne, 2001.

Jedwab, Lou, 'Carlton Vignettes', *Melbourne Chronicle*, no. 65, 1995, pp. 14–18.

——, 'My Dad', *Australian Jewish Historical Society Journal*, vol. VXIII, part 3, Nov. 1996, pp. 477–85.

Jonaitis, Elena, *Elena's Journey*, Text, Melbourne, 1997.

Kamenka, Eugene, 'A Childhood in the 1930s and 1940s: The making of a Russian-German-Jewish Australian', *Australian Journal of Politics and History*, vol. 31, no. 1, 1985, pp. 1–9.

Katz, Ben & Pyne, Michael, *Yiheyeh Tov, It Will Be All Right: The story of Ben Katz*, Fast Books, Sydney, 1997.

Katz, Kalman, *Memories of War*, Eskay Press, Melbourne, 1995.

Kay, David (as told to Ian Grinblat), *Tough Kid: Surviving Siberia in style*, Makor Jewish Community Library, Melbourne, 2005.

Keesing, Nancy, *Riding the Elephant*, Allen & Unwin, Sydney, 1988.

Kery, Iby, *I Have Been Chosen*, Iby Kery, Melbourne, 1985.

Kipen, Israel, *A Life to Live…: An autobiography*, Chandos Publishing, Melbourne, 1989.

Kleerkoper, Hanna, *Recollections of My Century*, Vista, Melbourne, 2004.

Kochan, Maurice, *I Survived: A testimony of a teenager's Holocaust experience*, Maurice Kochan, Sydney, 1991.

Korda, Teri, *My Dear Andrea and Andris*, Makor Jewish Community Library, Melbourne, 2002.

Kordin, Galina, *East West and Nowhere*, Spectrum, Melbourne, 1987.

Korn, Henri, *Saviours: The story of a Jewish altar boy*, Makor Jewish Community Library, Melbourne, 2004.

Kozminsky-Meyerowitz, Mena, *Keeping the Promise: Memoirs of a war bride from Israel*, Makor Jewish Community Library, Melbourne, 2003.

Kraus, Paul, *A New Australian, a New Australia*, Federation Press, Sydney, 1994.

Krauss, Walter, *Austria to Australia: The autobiography of an Austrian Jew from birth to emigration 1904–1938*, Melbourne Politics Monograph, University of Melbourne, Melbourne, 1982.

Kriek, Samuel, *Forty Years*, Samuel Kriek, Focus on Israel, Adelaide, 2001.

Krupinski, Jerzy, *My Four Lives*, Vista Publications, Melbourne, 2001.

Ladanyi, Helena, *Where Do You People Come From?*, Spectrum, Melbourne, 1988.

Landau, David J., *Caged: A story of Jewish resistance*, Pan Macmillan, Sydney, 2000.

Lane (Lanker), Martin, *Six Million and—One…: My experience in Poland during the Nazi occupation*, Martin Lane, Melbourne, 1974.

Lang, Moshe & Lang, Tesse, *Resilience: Stories of a family therapist*, Mandarin, Melbourne, 1996.

Leizerson, Rachel, *My Story*, Rachel Leizerson, Melbourne, 1990.

Leperere, Helen, *Memoirs and Reflections*, Makor Jewish Community Library, Melbourne, 2002.

Lewinson, Irene Alice, *Half a Life: The first forty years*, Vista Publications, Melbourne, 1996.

Lewitt, Maria, *Come Spring: An autobiographical novel*, Scribe, Melbourne, 1980, 2002.

——, *No Snow in December: An autobiographical novel*, Heinemann, Melbourne, 1985.

Liberman, Serge, *On Firmer Shores*, Globe Press, Melbourne, 1981.

——, *A Universe of Clowns*, Phoenix, Brisbane, 1983.

——, *The Life That I Have Led*, Fine-Lit, Melbourne, 1986.

——, *The Battered and the Redeemed*, Fine-Lit, Melbourne, 1990.

——, *Voices from the Corner*, Fine-Lit, Melbourne, 1999.

Liebmann, Henriette, *Death Wore a Nazi Uniform: Memoirs of a survivor of Lodz-Ghetto, Auschwitz, Bergen-Belsen and Salzwedel*, Henriette Liebmann, Melbourne, 1988.

Ligocka, Roma, *The Girl in the Red Coat: Surviving survival*, Hodder Headline, Sydney, 2002.

Lippman, Gert, *A Link in the Chain*, Gert Lippman, Sydney, 1990.

Lippmann, Henry, 'Shipboard Diary of Henry Lippmann en route to Australia, 1857', trans. Kurt Lippmann, *Australian Jewish Historical Society Journal*, vol. VXIII, part 3, Nov. 1996, pp. 413–15.

Lissing, Betty, *God Cried at Auschwitz*, Betty Lissing, LMN Systems, Adelaide, 2003.

Lurie, Morris, *Whole Life*, Penguin, Melbourne, 1987.

Lurje, Izak, *Nothing Special: The story of my life*, Izak Lurje, Melbourne, 1999.

Mandelbaum, Rae, *Echoes from the Past: The Rifka Norman story*, Makor Jewish Community Library, Melbourne, 1999.

Marin, Bernard (with Ian Coller), *My Father, My Father*, Scribe, Melbourne, 2002.

Marks, Eva, *A Patchwork Life*, Makor Jewish Community Library, Melbourne, 2003.

Martin, David, *My Strange Friend*, Picador, Sydney, 1991.

Max, Helen, *Searching for Yesterday: A photographic essay about my mother, a Holocaust survivor*, Makor Jewish Community Library, Melbourne, 2001.

Michaelis, Moritz, *Chapters from the Story of My Life*, Norman Bros., Melbourne, 1899; reprinted Griffin Press, Adelaide, 1965.

Mitchell, James, *Henry Krongold: Memoirs*, Allen & Unwin, Sydney, 2003.

Mittelberg, David, *Between Two Worlds: The testimony and the testament*, Devora Publishing, Jerusalem, 2004.

Mora, Mirka, *Wicked but Virtuous: My life*, Viking, Melbourne, 2000.

Nadel, Lita, *From 2 Hells*, Fast Books, Glebe, 1995.

Nathan, Rick, *Memoirs of a Nonentity*, Nathan Family Trust, Southport (Qld), 1996.

Opas, Philip, *Throw Away My Wig: An autobiography of a long journey with few sign posts*, Philip Opas, Melbourne, 1997.

Pisar, Samuel, *Of Blood and Hope*, Cassell, London, 1980.

Pretzel, Marian, *Portrait of a Young Forger: A true story of adventure and survival in wartime Europe*, Arrow Books, London, 1990.

——, *There Was No Farewell*, Sydney Jewish Museum and Marian Pretzel, Sydney, 1995.

Prow, George, *Unforgettable Heroine*, George Prow, Sydney, 1996.

Quittner, Eva, *Pebbles of Remembrance*, Kerr Publishing, Sydney, 1993.

Rack, Ruth, *Book of Ruth: Memoirs of a child survivor*, Southern Highlands, Sydney, 2002.

Reinisch, George, *Shanghai Haven*, George Reinisch, Melbourne, 1984.

——, *Echoes of Youth (1962–63)*, George Reinisch, Melbourne, 1997.

Reisman, Kathy, *More Than Nine Lives*, Makor Jewish Community Library, Melbourne, 2002.

Reiss, Henry, *January 1944: A saga of survival*, Reiss family, Sydney, 1991.

Rene, Roy, *Mo's Memoirs*, Reed & Harris, Melbourne, 1945.

Riemer, Andrew, *Inside Outside: Life between two worlds*, Angus & Robertson, Sydney, 1992.

——, *The Habsburg Café*, Angus & Robertson, Sydney, 1993.

——, *America with Subtitles*, Minerva, Melbourne, 1995.

——, *The Demidenko Debate*, Allen & Unwin, Sydney, 1996.

——, *Sandstone Gothic: Confessions of an accidental academic*, Allen & Unwin, Sydney, 1998.

——, *Between the Fish and the Mudcake: Writers, dinners, cities and other diversions*, Allen & Unwin, Sydney, 1999.

Robe, Stanley, 'My Migrations', *Australian Jewish Historical Society Journal*, vol. X, part 7, 1989, pp. 569–82.

Robin, Moshe & Robin, Stefa, *Stepping into Life*, Makor Jewish Community Library, Melbourne, 2002.

Rogozinski, Szymon, *My Fortunate Life*, Szymon Rogozinski, Melbourne, 2001.

Rosenberg, Elfie, *Serry and Me: A story of the Kindertransport and beyond*, Makor Jewish Community Library, Melbourne, 2001.

Rosenberg, Jacob G., *My Father's Silence*, Focus, Melbourne, 1994.

——, *Twilight Whisper*, Focus Words, Melbourne, 1997.

——, *Behind the Moon*, Five Islands Press, Wollongong, 2000.

——, *Lives and Embers*, Brandl & Schlesinger, Blackheath (NSW), 2003.

——, *East of Time*, Brandl & Schlesinger, Blackheath (NSW), 2005.

——, *Sunrise West*, Brandl & Schlesinger, Blackheath (NSW), 2007.

Rosenbloom, Fela & Rosenbloom, Felix, *Miracles Do Happen: Memoirs of Fela and Felix Rosenbloom*, Scribe, Melbourne, 1994.

Roth, Rena, *Gizela*, Endeavour Publishing, Melbourne, 1988.

Roth, Marianne, *An Intricate Collage*, Makor Jewish Community Library, Melbourne, 2000.

Rothberg, Yetta, *Thousands of Years through the Eyes of a Child* (and *The Great Wall, or Waiting for Hank!*), Foundation for Australian Literary Studies, James Cook University of North Queensland, Townsville, 1980.

——, *A Tale to Tell*, Spectrum, Melbourne, 1987.

Rothfield, Evelyn, *The Future Is Past*, Evelyn Rothfield, Melbourne, 1992.

Rothfield, Norman, *Many Paths to Peace: The political memoirs of Norman Rothfield*, Yarraford Publications, Melbourne, 1997.

Rubin, Wolf, *Wolf: Surviving by art*, Makor Jewish Community Library, Melbourne, 2003.

Rubenstein, Bill, 'From Brooklyn to Melbourne', *Melbourne Chronicle Yearbook*, 1990–91, no. 60, pp. 77–8.

Rubinstein, Helena, *My Life for Beauty*, Bodley Head, Sydney, 1965.

Saaroni, Sarah, *Life Goes On Regardless,* Hudson, Hawthorn, 1989.

Sage, Alex, *For Esther*, Flamingo, Sydney, 2000.

Sattler, Stanislaw, *Prisoner of 68 Months: Buchenwald and Auschwitz*, Kelly Books, Melbourne, 1980.

Schimmel, Marilyn, with her sisters Annette and Sharon, *Pola's Story*, Makor Jewish Community Library, Melbourne, 2005.

Schreiber, Vera, *The Porcelain Doll*, Makor Jewish Community Library, Melbourne, 2000.

Schwartz, Andor, *Living Memory*, Schwartz Publishing, Melbourne, 2003.

Schwartz, Schmul, *Under Red Skies: Dreams and reality*, trans. Tania Bruce (Schwartz), Makor Jewish Community Library, Melbourne, 2002.

Schwartz, Zoltán & Schwartz, Adi, *Survivors* (comprising 2 vols: *The Army-Cap Boy* and *Ex Reffos*), Lina, Sydney, 1999.

Schwarz, Tess, *The First Forty Families: Bringing my family tree and forest to life*, Makor Jewish Community Library, Melbourne, 2001.

Searle, Freda, *Memory's Wings and Apron Strings*, Makor Jewish Community Library, Melbourne, 2000.

Seligman, Richard, *Very Convenient Everywhere*, Vantage Press, New York, 1991.

Silbert, Eric, *Dinkum Mishpochah*, Artlook Books, Perth, 1981.

Silver, Leon, 'With the Polish Army in the Middle East', *Melbourne Chronicle*, no. 65, 1995, pp. 39–41.

Simievic, Charles, *Letter to Timna and Gil from Your Saba Charles Simievic*, Charles Simievic, Melbourne, 2003.

Singer, Ivan, *My Father's Blessing: My salvation*, Singer Consulting, Sydney, 2002.

Singer, Ivan A., *Across Three Continents*, Ivan Singer, Sydney, 1994.

Singer, Peter, *Pushing Time Away: My grandfather and the tragedy of Jewish Vienna*, Granta, London, 2003.

Skall, Lily, *My Story*, Makor Jewish Community Library, Melbourne, 2000.

Spielvogel, Nathan F., 'How My Life Was Spent: The autobiography of Nathan F. Spielvogel', *Australian Jewish Historical Society Journal*, vol. VI, part 1, 1964, pp. 1–27.

Spindler, Arthur, *Outwitting Hitler, Surviving Stalin: The story of Arthur Spindler*, UNSW Press, Sydney, 1997.

Spitzer, Martin, *Storm over Tatra*, Martin Spitzer, Adelaide, 1989.

Sput-Stern, Anna, *On the Other Side of the River*, Aussie Publications, Melbourne, 1999.

Starkiewicz, Helena, *Blades of Grass between the Stones*, Helena Starkiewicz, Melbourne, 1998.

Steel, Helen Rose, *T. B. versus Nazi*, Helen Rose Steel, Melbourne, 1987.

Sten, George, *Memoirs of a Survivor*, George Sten, Sydney, 1996.

Stern, Max, *My Stamp on Life*, Makor Jewish Community Library, Melbourne, 2003.

Stone, Nina (ed.), *Silent No More: Melbourne child survivors of the Holocaust*, Child Survivors of the Holocaust, Melbourne, 1999.

Szalmuk, Mira, *From Tragedy to Triumph*, Puma Press, Melbourne, 1997.

Szego, George, *Two Prayers to One God: A journey towards identity and belonging*, Hardie Grant Books, Melbourne, 2001.

Tayar, Aline P'nina, *How Shall We Sing?: A Mediterranean journey through a Jewish family*, Picador, Sydney, 2000.

Valenta, Nick, *Destiny and Luck*, Nick Valenta, Sydney, 2002.

Van Apeldoorn, Jan, *Departure Delayed*, Robertson & Mullens, Melbourne, 1945.

Varga, Susan, *Heddy and Me*, Penguin, Melbourne, 1994.

Verolme, Hetty E., *The Children's House of Belsen*, Fremantle Arts Centre Press, Fremantle, 2000.

Verstandig, Mark, *I Rest My Case*, Saga Press, Melbourne, 1995.

Visontay, Czeizler Rose, *Boutique*, Czeizler Rose Visontay, Sydney, 1976.

Wajnryb, Abraham, *They Marched Us Three Nights: A journey into freedom*, Jewish Holocaust Centre, Melbourne, 1988.

Wargon, Alex, *The Several Lives of Alex Wargon*, Alex Wargon, Sydney, 1998.

Waten, Judah, *Alien Son*, Sun Books, Melbourne, 1965.

——, *From Odessa to Odessa: The journey of an Australian writer*, Cheshire, Melbourne, 1969.

——, *Fiction, Memoirs, Criticism*, ed. David Carter, University of Queensland Press, Brisbane, 1998.

West, Joseph, *Survival, Struggle & Success*, JFW Publications, Melbourne, 1995.

White, Maurice, *Lechaim!: To life*, Maurice White, 2003.

Widawski, Celina, *The Sun Will Shine Tomorrow*, Celina Widawski, Melbourne, 1993.

Witting, Peter, 'Exile to Shanghai and Finding a Home in Australia—1939–1947: A firsthand account of my experience as a Central European refugee in

Shanghai', *Australian Jewish Historical Society Journal*, vol. XV, part 2, June 2000, pp. 252–69.

Wroby, Godel, *My Battle for Survival from Mlyny to Melbourne*, Makor Jewish Community Library, Melbourne, 2004.

Zable, Arnold, *Jewels and Ashes*, Scribe, Melbourne, 1991.

——, *Wanderers and Dreamers: Tales of the David Herman Theatre*, Hyland House, Melbourne, 1998.

——, *Cafe Scheherazade*, Text, Melbourne, 2001.

——, 'In Search of Refuge: Two tales', in Peter Craven (ed.), *The Best Australian Essays 2001*, Black Inc., Melbourne, 2001.

——, *The Fig Tree*, Text, Melbourne, 2003.

——, *Scraps of Heaven*, Text, Melbourne, 2004.

——, Imagining the Immigrant Experience, PhD thesis, University of Melbourne, 2006.

——, 'The Walker', unpublished performance piece.

Ziskind, Chaya, *They Watched Over Us*, Puma Press, Melbourne, 1998.

Zwi, Rose, *Last Walk in Naryshkin Park*, Spinifex, Melbourne, 1997.

Zylberman, Halina, *Swimming under Water*, Makor Jewish Community Library, Melbourne, 2001.

Studies/Anthologies of Australian Jewish writing

Bittman, Karl (ed.), *Strauss to Matilda: Viennese in Australia 1938–1988*, Wenkart Foundation, Sydney, 1988.

Carter, David (ed.), *Judah Waten: Fiction, memoirs, criticism*, University of Queensland Press, Brisbane, 1998.

Encel, Diana (ed.), *Jewish Country Girls: A collection of memories*, Sydney Jewish Museum, Sydney, 2005.

Grinblat, Kathy (ed.), *Children of the Shadows: Voices of the second generation*, University of Western Australia Press, Perth, 2002.

Hammer, Gael (ed.), *Pomegranates: A century of Jewish Australian writing*, Millennium, Sydney, 1988.

Hapgood, Hutchins, *The Spirit of the Ghetto: Studies of the Jewish quarter of New York*, Schocken, New York, 1966.

Hoffman, Louise & Masel, Shush (eds), *Without Regret*, Centre for Migration and Development Studies, University of Western Australia, Perth, 1994.

Jacobs, Alan (ed.), *Enough Already: An anthology of Australian–Jewish writing*, Allen & Unwin, Sydney, 1999.

Kalechofsky, Robert & Kalechofsky, Roberta (eds), *Jewish Writing from Down Under: Australia and New Zealand*, Micah Publications, Marblehead (MA), 1984.

Keesing, Nancy (ed.), *Shalom: Australian Jewish stories*, Collins, Sydney, 1978.

Kwiet, Konrad & Moses, John A. (eds), special issue of *Australian Journal of*

Politics and History ('On Being a German-Jewish Refugee in Australia'), vol. 31, no. 1, 1985.

Liberman, Serge, *A Bibliography of Australian Judaica*, Mandelbaum Trust and University of Sydney Library, Sydney, 1991.

Meadows, Julie (ed.), *Memory Guide My Hand: An anthology of autobiographical writing by members of the Melbourne Jewish community*, vol. 1, Makor Jewish Community Library, Melbourne, 1998.

—— (ed.), *Memory Guide My Hand: An anthology of autobiographical writing by members of the Melbourne Jewish community*, vol. 2, Makor Jewish Community Library, Melbourne, 2000.

—— (ed.), *Memory Guide My Hand: An anthology of autobiographical writing by members of the Melbourne Jewish community*, vol. 3, Makor Jewish Community Library, Melbourne, 2004.

National Council of Jewish Women of Victoria, *Forever Eve: An anthology celebrating Jewish womankind*, NCJWV, Melbourne, 2002.

Shapiro, Ron (ed.), 'Shmooz Downunder: Australian/Jewish Writing', special issue of *Westerly*, vol. 41, no. 4, Summer 1996.

Jewish writing, autobiographical and other, from elsewhere

Buber, Martin (ed.), *Tales of the Hasidim*, Schocken, New York, 1991.

Celan, Paul, *Selected Poems and Prose of Paul Celan*, trans. John Felstiner, W. W. Norton, New York, 2001.

Delbo, Charlotte. *Auschwitz and After*, trans. Rosette Lamont, Yale University Press, New Haven, 1995.

Frankl, Viktor E., *Man's Search for Meaning*, Rider, London, 2004.

Hindus, Milton (ed.), *The Old East Side: An anthology*, Jewish Publication Society of America, Philadelphia, 1969.

Hoffman, Eva, *Lost in Translation: A life in a new language*, Vintage, London, 1998.

Howe, Irving & Greenberg, Eliezer (eds), *A Treasury of Yiddish Stories*, André Deutsch, New York, 1955.

Kalechofsky, Robert & Kalechofsky, Roberta (eds), *Echad: An anthology of Latin American Jewish writing*, Micah Publications, Marblehead (MA), 1980.

—— (eds), *The Global Anthology of Jewish Women Writers*, Micah Publications, Marblehead (MA), 1990.

Koestler, Arthur, *Arrow in the Blue: The first volume of an autobiography: 1905–31*, Stein and Day, New York, 1984.

——, *The Invisible Writing: The second volume of an autobiography: 1932–40*, Stein and Day, New York, 1984.

Lappin, Elena (ed.), *Jewish Voices, German Words: Growing up Jewish in postwar Germany and Austria*, Catbird Press, North Haven (CT), 1994.

Levi, Primo, *If This Is a Man* and *The Truce*, trans. Stuart Woolf, Abacus, London, 1979.

Maimon, Solomon, *An Autobiography*, trans. J. Clark Murray, University of Illinois Press, Chicago, 2001.

Ribalow, Harold U. (ed.), *Autobiographies of American Jews*, Jewish Publication Society of America, Philadelphia, 1973.

Rubin, Steven J. (ed.), *Writing Our Lives: Autobiographies of American Jews, 1890–1900*, Jewish Publication Society, Philadelphia, 1991.

Rousset, David, *L'univers concentrationnaire*, Éditions de Minuit, Paris, 1965.

Schwarz, Leo W. (ed.), *Memoirs of My People: Jewish self-portraits from the 11th to the 20th centuries*, Schocken, New York, 1963.

Simons, Howard (ed.), *Jewish Times: Voices of the American Jewish experience*, Houghton Mifflin, Boston, 1990.

Sinclair, Gerri & Wolfe, Morris (eds), *The Spice Box: An anthology of Jewish Canadian writing*, Lester and Orpen Dennys, Toronto, 1981.

Spiegelman, Art, *Maus: A survivor's tale*, Penguin, London, 2003.

Trilling, Diana, *The Beginning of the Journey: The marriage of Diana and Lionel Trilling*, Harcourt Brace, New York, 1993.

Australian Jewish history and society

Bartrop, Paul R., *Australia and the Holocaust 1933–45*, Australian Scholarly Publishing, Melbourne, 1994.

Golvan, Colin, *The Distant Exodus: Australian Jews recall their immigrant experiences*, ABC, Sydney, 1990.

Levey, Geoffrey Brahm & Mendes, Philip (eds), *Jews and Australian Politics*, Sussex Academic Press, Brighton (UK), 2004.

Levi, J. S. & Bergman, G. F. J. (eds), *Australian Genesis: Jewish convicts and settlers 1788–1850*, Rigby, Adelaide, 1974.

Reich, Chanan, *Australia and Israel: An ambiguous relationship*, Melbourne University Press, Melbourne, 2002.

Rubinstein, Hilary L., *Chosen: The Jews in Australia*, Allen & Unwin, Sydney, 1987.

——, *The Jews in Australia: A thematic history*, vol. 1 (1788–1945), Heinemann, Melbourne, 1991.

Rubinstein, W. D., *The Jews in Australia*, AE Press, Melbourne, 1986.

—— (ed.), *The Jews in the Sixth Continent*, Allen & Unwin, Sydney, 1987.

——, *The Jews in Australia: A thematic history*, vol. 2 (1945 to the present), Heinemann, Melbourne, 1991.

Rutland, Suzanne D., *Edge of the Diaspora: Two centuries of Jewish settlement in Australia*, Collins, Sydney, 2000.

——, *The Jews in Australia*, Cambridge University Press, Melbourne, 2005.

Rutland, Suzanne D. & Encel, Sol, 'Major Issues Facing the Jewish Community: Women's perceptions', *Australian Journal of Jewish Studies*, XX, 2006, pp. 169–98.

The Holocaust: Studies of history, autobiography and other issues

Bauer, Yehuda, *Rethinking the Holocaust*, Yale University Press, New Haven, 2002.

Blanchot, Maurice, *The Writing of the Disaster*, trans. Ann Smock, University of Nebraska Press, Lincoln, 1986.

Des Pres, Terrence, *The Survivor: An anatomy of life in the death camps*, Oxford University Press, New York, 1976.

Eaglestone, Robert, *The Holocaust and the Postmodern*, Oxford University Press, Oxford, 2004.

Faye, Esther, 'Impossible Memories: Lily Brett as essayist', *Meridian*, 17:1, May 1978, pp. 63–73.

——, '"Enjoying traumatically": The Holocaust as "the second generation's other"', *British Journal of Psychotherapy*, 16:2, 1999, pp. 184–96.

Felman, Shoshana & Laub, Dori, *Testimony: Crises of witnessing in literature, psychoanalysis, and history*, Routledge, New York, 1992.

Freadman, Richard, 'Generational Shifts in Post-Holocaust Australian Jewish Autobiography,' *Life Writing*, 1:1, 2004, pp. 21–44.

Friedlander, Saul (ed.), *Probing the Limits of Representation: Nazism and the 'final solution'*, Harvard University Press, Cambridge, 1992.

Gilmore, Leigh, *The Limits of Autobiography: Trauma and testimony*, Cornell University Press, Ithaca, 2001.

Goldhagen, Daniel Jonah, *Hitler's Willing Executioners: Ordinary Germans and the Holocaust*, Abacus, London, 1996.

Gubar, Susan, *Poetry after Auschwitz: Remembering what one never knew*, Indiana University Press, Bloomington, 2003.

Halasz, George, 'Three Generations After', *Centre News*, Sep. 2005.

Hoffman, Eva, *Shtetl: The life and death of a small town and the world of Polish Jews*, Secker & Warburg, London, 1998.

LaCapra, Dominick, *Writing History, Writing Trauma*, Johns Hopkins University Press, Baltimore, 2001.

Langer, Lawrence L., *Holocaust Testimonies: The ruins of memory*, Yale University Press, New Haven, 1991.

Lefkovitz, Elliot (ed.), *Dimensions of the Holocaust*, Northwestern University Press, Evanston, Illinois, 1990.

Reiter, Andrea, *Narrating the Holocaust*, trans. Patrick Camiller, Continuum, London, 2000.

Roskies, David G., *The Jewish Search for a Usable Past*, Indiana University Press, Bloomington, 1999.

Rothberg, Michael, *Traumatic Realism: The demands of Holocaust representation*, University of Minnesota Press, Minneapolis, 2000.

Schaffer, Kay & Smith, Sidonie, *Human Rights and Narrated Lives: The ethics of recognition*, Palgrave Macmillan, New York, 2004.

Todorov, Tzvetan, *Facing the Extreme: Moral life in the concentration camps*, trans. Arthur Denner & Abigail Pollack, Phoenix, London, 2000.

Young, James E., 'Interpreting Testimony: A preface to rereading Holocaust diaries and memoirs', *New Literary History*, vol. 18, no 2, Winter 1987, pp. 403–23.

Literary criticism and theory; social theory; psychological theory

Adorno, Theodor W., *Prisms*, trans. Samuel & Shierry Weber, Neville Spearman, London, 1967.

Ashcroft, Bill, Griffith, Gareth & Tiffin, Helen, *The Empire Writes Back: Theory and practice in post-colonial literatures*, Routledge, London, 1989.

Barbour, John D., *Versions of Deconversion: Autobiography and the loss of faith*, University of Virginia Press, Charlottesville, 1994.

Bartkowski, Frances, *Travelers, Immigrants, Inmates: Essays in estrangement*, University of Minnesota Press, Minneapolis, 1995.

Bell, Susan Groag & Yalom, Marilyn (eds), *Revealing Lives: Autobiography, biography, and gender*, State University of New York Press, Albany, 1990.

Bernstein, David, review of Lily Brett, *In Full View*, in *Australian Jewish News*, 12 Sep. 1997.

Besemeres, Mary, *Translating One's Self: Language and selfhood in cross-cultural autobiography*, Peter Lang, Oxford, 2002.

Boelhower, William Q. & Pallone, Rocco (eds), *Adjusting Sites: New essays in Italian American studies*, Forum Italicum, Stony Brook (NY), 1999.

Bowlby, John, *Child Care and the Growth of Love*, Penguin, Harmondsworth, 1993.

Braziel, Jana Evans & Mannur, Anita (eds), *Theorizing Diaspora: A reader*, Blackwell, Malden (MA), 2003.

Brooks, Van Wyck, 'On Creating a Usable Past,' *Dial* 64, 1918, pp. 337–41.

Carter, David, *A Career in Writing: Judah Waten and the cultural politics of a literary career*, Association for the Study of Australian Literature, Toowoomba, 1997.

Caruth, Cathy, *Unclaimed Experience: Trauma, narrative, and history*, Johns Hopkins University Press, Baltimore, 1996.

Cassidy, Jude & Shaver, Phillip R. (eds), *Handbook of Attachment: Theory, research, and clinical applications*, Guildford, London, 1999.

Chow, Rey, *Writing Diaspora*, Indiana University Press, Bloomington, 1993.

Cohen, Robin, *Global Diasporas: An introduction*, University of Washington Press, Seattle, 1997.

Collits, Terry, 'Sydney Revisited: Literary struggles in Australia (circa 1965 and ongoing)', *Australian Book Review*, no. 210, May 1999, pp. 23–8.

Dalziell, Rosamund, *Shameful Autobiographies: Shame in contemporary Australian autobiography and culture*, Melbourne University Press, Melbourne, 1999.

Derrida, Jacques, *Writing and Difference*, trans. Alan Bass, Routledge and Kegan Paul, London, 1978.

——, *Without Alibi*, ed. and trans. Peggy Kamuf, Stanford University Press, Stanford, 2002.

Eakin, Paul John, *Fiction in Autobiography: Studies in the art of self-invention*, Princeton University Press, Princeton, 1985.

——, *How Our Lives Become Stories: Making selves*, Cornell University Press, Ithaca, 1999.

Ember, Melvin, Ember, Carol R. & Skoggard, Ian (eds), *Encyclopedia of Diasporas: Immigrant and refugee cultures around the world*, Kluwer Academic Publishers, Dordrecht (Netherlands), 2004.

Erikson, Erik H., *Identity: Youth and crisis*, W. W. Norton, New York, 1968.

Ferbach, David (ed.), *Karl Marx: Political writings*, vol. 1, *The Revolutions of 1848*, Penguin, London, 1973.

Freadman, Richard, 'The Quest for the Classical Temper: The literary criticism of S. L. Goldberg', *Critical Review*, no. 32, 1992, pp. 46–66.

——, *Threads of Life: Autobiography and the will*, University of Chicago Press, Chicago, 2001.

——, '"Heddy and I": Relational life-writing in *Heddy and Me*', *Australian Book Review*, no. 238, Jan. 2002, pp. 20–23

——, review of Sidonie Smith & Julia Watson, *Reading Autobiography: A guide for interpreting life narratives*, in *Biography*, 26:2, 2003, pp. 298–306.

Freadman, Richard & Miller, Seamus, *Re-thinking Theory: A critique of contemporary literary theory and an alternative account*, Cambridge University Press, Cambridge, 1995.

Freud, Sigmund, *Beyond the Pleasure Principle*, trans. James Strachey, Bantam, New York, 1967.

Gandhi, Leela, *Postcolonial Theory: A critical introduction*, Allen & Unwin, Sydney, 1998.

Gunew, Sneja, *Framing Marginality: Multicultural literary studies*, Melbourne University Press, Melbourne, 1994.

Gunew, Sneja & Longley, Kateryna O. (eds), *Striking Chords: Multicultural literary interpretations*, Allen & Unwin, Sydney, 1992.

Henke, Suzette A., *Shattered Subjects: Trauma and testimony in women's life-writing*, St Martin's Press, New York, 1998.

Hooton, Joy, *Stories of Herself When Young: Autobiographies of childhood by Australian women*, Oxford University Press, Melbourne, 1990.

James, Donald & Rattansi, Ali (eds), *'Race', culture & difference*, Sage Publications, London, 1992.

Jelinek, Estelle C. (ed.), *Women's Autobiography: Essays in criticism*, Indiana University Press, Bloomington, 1980.

Klein, Melanie, *The Selected Melanie Klein*, ed. Juliet Mitchell, Penguin, London, 1991.

Leitch, Vincent B. (gen. ed.), *The Norton Anthology of Theory and Criticism*, W. W. Norton, New York, 2001.

Lejeune, Philippe, *On Autobiography*, ed. Paul John Eakin, trans. Katherine Leary, University of Minnesota Press, Minneapolis, 1989.

McCooey, David, *Artful Histories: Modern Australian autobiography*, Cambridge University Press, Melbourne, 1996.

Minar, David W. & Greer, Scott (eds), *The Concept of Community: Readings with interpretations*, Aldine, Chicago, 1969.

Mitchell, Stephen A., *Relational Concepts in Psychoanalysis: An integration*, Harvard University Press, Cambridge, 1988.

Myers, David (ed.), *Reinventing Literacy: The multicultural imperative*, Phaedrus, Rockhampton, 1995.

Pavlenko, Aneta & Blackledge, Adrian (eds), *Negotiation of Identities in Multilingual Contexts*, Multilingual Matters, Clevedon (UK), 2004.

Said, Edward W., *Orientalism*, Pantheon, New York, 1978.

Smith, Sidonie, *A Poetics of Women's Autobiography: Marginality and the fictions of self-representation*, Indiana University Press, Bloomington, 1987.

Smith, Sidonie & Watson, Julia, *Reading Autobiography: A guide for interpreting life narratives*, University of Minnesota Press, Minneapolis, 2001.

Sollors, Werner (ed.), *The Invention of Ethnicity*, Oxford University Press, Oxford, 1989.

Stern, Daniel N., *The Interpersonal World of the Infant: A view from psychoanalysis and developmental psychology*, Basic Books, New York, 1985.

Stone Center, *Women's Growth in Connection: Writings from the Stone Center*, Guilford Press, New York, 1991.

Taylor, Charles, 'The Politics of Recognition,' in Amy Gutman (ed.), *Multiculturalism: Examining the politics of recognition*, Princeton University Press, Princeton, 1994, pp. 25–74.

Toker, Leona, 'Toward a Poetics of Documentary Prose—from the Perspective of Gulag Testimonies', *Poetics Today*, 18:22, Summer 1997, pp. 187–222.

van Hear, Nicholas, *New Diasporas: The mass exodus, dispersal and regrouping of migrant communities*, University of Washington Press, Seattle, 1998.

White, Hayden, *Tropics of Discourse: Essays in cultural criticism*, Johns Hopkins University, Baltimore, 1978.

Wiltshire, John, '"Fault Lines"', review of Andrew Riemer, *Sandstone Gothic*, in *Eureka Street*, vol. 10, no. 8, Dec. 1998, pp. 38–42.

Yamamoto, Hisaye, Kingston, Maxine Hong & Kogawa, Joy, *Articulate Silences*, Cornell University Press, Ithaca, 1993.

Zaborowska, M. J., *How We Found America: Reading gender through East European immigrant narratives*, University of North Carolina Press, Chapel Hill, 1995.

Other

Augustine, St, *Confessions*, trans. R. S. Pine-Coffin, Penguin, Harmondsworth, 1961.

Bettelheim, Bruno, *The Uses of Enchantment: The meaning and importance of fairy tales*, Penguin, Harmondsworth, 1978.

Buber, Martin, *I and Thou*, trans. Walter Kaufmann, T&T Clark, Edinburgh, 1970.

Cesarani, David, *Arthur Koestler: The homeless mind*, Heinemann, London, 1998.

Coady, C. A. J., *Testimony: A philosophical study*, Oxford University Press, Oxford, 1992.

Critchley, Simon & Bernasconi, Robert (eds), *The Cambridge Companion to Levinas*, Cambridge University Press, Cambridge, 2002.

Crossman, Richard (ed.), *The God that Failed: Six studies in communism*, Hamish Hamilton, London, 1950.

Eliot, George, *Middlemarch*, Oxford University Press, Oxford, 1997.

Eliot, T. S., *Four Quartets*, Faber & Faber, London, 1944.

Freadman, Richard, 'Decency and its Discontents', *Philosophy and Literature*, vol. 28, no. 2, Oct. 2004, pp. 393–405.

Hand, Séan (ed.), *The Levinas Reader*, Basil Blackwell, Oxford, 1989.

Howe, Irving, *The World of Our Fathers: The journey of the East European Jews to America and the life they found and made*, Harcourt Brace Jovanovich, New York, 1976.

Huggins, Rita & Huggins, Jackie, *Auntie Rita*, Aboriginal Studies Press, Canberra, 1994.

Hume, David, *A Treatise of Human Nature*, Oxford University Press, Oxford, 1978.

Kekes, John, *Moral Tradition and Individuality*, Princeton University Press, Princeton, 1989.

Levinas, Emmanuel, *Totality and Infinity*, trans. Alphonso Lingis, Kluwer Academic Publishers, Dordrecht (Netherlands), 1991.

Nehamas, Alexander, *Nietzsche: Life as literature*, Harvard University Press, Cambridge, 1985.

Peperzak, Adriaan T., Critchley, Simon & Bernasconi, Robert (eds), *Emmanuel Levinas: Basic philosophical writings*, Indiana University Press, Bloomington, 1996.

Rawles, John, *A Theory of Justice*, Oxford University Press, Oxford, 1973.

Rousseau, Jean-Jacques, *The Confessions of Jean-Jacques Rousseau*, trans. J. M. Cohen, Penguin, Harmondsworth, 1960.

Safranski, Rüdiger, *Heidegger: Between good and evil*, trans. Ewald Osers, Harvard University Press, Cambridge, 1998.

Schneersohn, Rabbi Sholom Dovber, *Tract on Prayer*, trans. Y. E. Danzinger, Kehot Publication Society, New York, 1992.

Spender, Stephen, *World within World: The autobiography of Stephen Spender*, St Martin's Press, New York, 1994.

Taylor, Charles, *Sources of the Self: The making of the modern identity*, Cambridge University Press, Cambridge, 1989.

Weinberg, S. S., *The World of Our Mothers: The lives of Jewish immigrant women*, University of North Carolina Press, Chapel Hill, 1988.

Williams, Bernard, *Truth and Truthfulness: An essay in genealogy*, Princeton University Press, Princeton, 2002.

Index